Tulisa
HONEST
MY STORY SO FAR

Tulisa
HONEST
MY STORY SO FAR

headline

Copyright © 2012 Tulisa Contostavlos

The right of Tulisa Contostavlos to be identified as the Author of
the Work has been asserted by her in accordance with the
Copyright, Designs and Patents Act 1988.

First published in 2012
by HEADLINE PUBLISHING GROUP

1

Apart from any use permitted under UK copyright law, this publication may
only be reproduced, stored, or transmitted, in any form, or by any means,
with prior permission in writing of the publishers or, in the case of
reprographic production, in accordance with the terms of licences issued
by the Copyright Licensing Agency.

Every effort has been made to fulfil requirements with regard to
reproducing copyright material. The author and publisher will be glad to
rectify any omissions at the earliest opportunity.

Cataloguing in Publication Data is available from the British Library

Hardback ISBN 978 0 7553 6371 1
Trade paperback ISBN 978 0 7553 6372 8

Excerpt from 'Tulisa is feminism's new hero', Eva Wiseman/*Observer* ©
Guardian News & Media Ltd 2012

Typeset in Gotham Light by
Palimpsest Book Production Ltd, Falkirk, Stirlingshire

Printed and bound by CPI Group (UK) Ltd, Croydon CRO 4YY

Headline's policy is to use papers that are natural, renewable and recyclable
products and made from wood grown in sustainable forests. The logging
and manufacturing processes are expected to conform to the
environmental regulations of the country of origin.

HEADLINE PUBLISHING GROUP
An Hachette UK Company
338 Euston Road
London NW1 3BH

www.headline.co.uk
www.hachette.co.uk

Acknowledgements

Thanks to everyone at Headline, my management, family, friends and fans. With a special thank-you to Terry Ronald for making this book possible.

Lots of love,

Tulisa

Preface

If you asked everyone in my circle to describe mé, there's one thing they'd all say – 'Tulisa loves a drama!' But even though this has become a running joke among my friends, and I even occasionally describe myself that way, it's not entirely true. I don't exactly *love* a drama, but I guess drama does seem to have a strange habit of finding me wherever I go: drama *and* conflict. I don't know why, maybe it's just me! All I do know is that I've spent a fair amount of my twenty-four years on Planet Earth battling against one thing or another, or trying to dig myself out of some ridiculous or horrendous situation I've found myself in. Sometimes I feel like I've spent my whole life fighting, but do you know what? The times when I've achieved the most in life are the times I've had to fight for it. It's always been the same. So I suppose I've just learned to accept that this is just the way things are for me. You have to in the end, don't you?

When you're successful and so-called famous, everyone seems to have so much to say about you. You can't complain: it's part of the deal and that's what you sign up for. I've certainly heard and read some pretty wild and ludicrous stories about myself, ranging from the slightly inaccurate to complete and utter bollocks! Sometimes it's quite funny, but there are other times when it's hurtful, distressing even, and that's why I decided to write this book. So that anyone who might be interested in getting to know the real me, can. I think I'm quite a nice person, but I'll leave that up to you to decide.

While I was working on the book, a few of my friends suggested that I might want to mind my Ps and Qs; that I might want to tone down a few of the harsher facts about my past – but I just don't see the point in that. If you're gonna tell it, girl, tell it! I am who I am, and if somebody is going to judge me then I'd like them to judge me on the truth. I'd like them to decide whether or not they like me based on the facts, not on stories they've read in gossip magazines, or hearsay, or a watered-down version of events. I don't want to sugar-coat my story, and it would be impossible to do so. So here it is in a nutshell: real and raw. Honest.

Chapter One

L ooking back, I suppose it's no real surprise that I ended up where I am – in the music industry, I mean. Both my parents came from a strong musical background. My mum, Anne Byrne, was raised in Churchtown, a suburb on the Southside of Dublin, in a large family of seven children; three brothers and four sisters, and they were all musical. My mum's mother passed away when I was little, so I don't remember too much about her, but I've always been reasonably close to my granddad, Tom, who later remarried. He still lives quite close to my mum in London, and he's proper Irish – a real Jack-the-lad who still loves a drink and a fag. Tom has got to be one of the happiest people you could ever meet, and whenever I see him he always makes me laugh. Even now, at ninety-odd, he has an eye for the ladies, and they seem to like him right back. Tom was a boy soprano back in the 1930s, and he'd encourage his four daughters to sing together in harmony from a very young age, while the boys played musical instruments and sang. In fact, two of my uncles, Brian and Michael, had a number one hit in Ireland with their band, Emmet Spiceland, and then Brian went on to appear in musicals like *Jesus Christ Superstar* and *Joseph*.

By the time Mum was about eighteen, the family had moved from Ireland to Sheffield, and finally to London. Mum and her sisters (Louise, Moira and Paula) formed a four-piece vocal group called Jeep and sang 1940s jazz and cover versions of hits by The Andrews Sisters, like 'Chattanooga Choo Choo' and 'Boogie Woogie Bugle Boy'. The band started small in pubs and clubs, but after they appeared on a TV talent show called *Rising Stars*, better gigs started to come their way, and they were soon supporting big names of the day like Jimmy Tarbuck, Les Dennis and Russ Abbot. In fact, Les Dennis loved my mum's Judy Garland impersonation so much that she was asked to join him on a TV show called *Go For It*, where she did impressions of people like Marilyn Monroe, Dolly Parton and Mae West.

I grew up listening to my mum and her sisters singing those 1940s songs whenever they were together, and I learned them all myself too. It's influenced the way I sing to this day, and there are certain jazzy tones in my voice that I most definitely got from singing along to those old tunes.

My dad, Plato, was musical too, and he was a bit of a wild thing: a handsome rocker with highlighted blond hair, a well-toned body, bright green eyes and olive skin. He was born in Egypt – the son of a diplomat for the United Nations – and grew up in Ethiopia and the Congo until he was a teenager. Dad came from quite a wealthy Greek family, and had a brother, Byron, and a sister, Maria. When they eventually came to England they lived in a big house in West Hampstead, north London. He went to a private school and had the opportunity to go to university and have the best education money could buy, but he just wasn't interested. Like my mum, he loved music and he wanted to be a rock star and a rebel, so he took all the money his father gave him and built a recording studio in Dollis Hill with his brother Byron.

For the first year or so of my life we all lived in my nan

and granddad's luxurious Hampstead home. I was always called Tulisa (pronounced tu-litz-a) by my Greek grandparents, which means 'Tiny Tula', because both my nan and I were named Tula and she was 'Big Tula'. I always much preferred this nickname to my full name – Tula Paulina Contostavlos – which is why I changed it later on.

The Greek side of my family had a big influence on me when I was young, and until I was about five – when my nan and granddad moved back to Greece to build a house – I saw a lot of them. They had strong beliefs and opinions, and from a very young age I remember being lectured about how I should be and what I should think. I suppose I'm a bit like my dad, so as I got a bit older, I started to develop my own notions about how I wanted to be, but when I was a little girl a lot of my influences were quite traditionally Greek.

Uncle Byron and Aunt Zoe also lived at my nan and granddad's house with their two boys – my cousins, Spiros and Dino – but eventually my dad and his brother both moved into council flats with their own families. Uncle Byron and Aunt Zoe ended up on a council estate in Camden, and we were lucky enough to get a maisonette in Belsize Park, right on the border of the posher, greener area towards Hampstead and the more urban areas of Kentish Town and Camden. As we lived quite near each other, the two families would spend a lot of time together, and I became very close to my cousin Dino. In fact, by the time I was five years old, we were so close that we innocently made a pact to marry one another when we grew up, not yet understanding that we were family and couldn't do that. My mum would either take me to see Dino every day, or he would be round at our place with his mum and his brother Spiros, and like my dad and Uncle Byron, Dino and I became pretty much inseparable.

The flat we lived in was one of four in a converted Victorian house, and we were lucky to be on quite a nice road, with a mix of council properties and smart private homes. The rooms were quite spacious, with high ceilings, but the décor was pretty old-fashioned, even for the time, and most of our furniture had been donated to us by my dad's parents or other family members. The main problem was that there was only one bedroom, so I had to share with my mum and dad until I was about ten or eleven, and I never knew what it was like to have my own space with all my bits and pieces around me.

It's a sad thing to say, but most of my earliest childhood memories are not happy ones. It wasn't that my parents didn't love me, but my mum's illness – which started before I was born but got worse when I was a baby – completely overshadowed my childhood. Mum has schizoaffective disorder – a cross between schizophrenia and bipolar disorder – and the symptoms of these two conditions combined are pretty scary. They include manic depression, hallucinations, mood swings and paranoia.

Mum's illness first started when she was in her early twenties, and she was still performing with Jeep at that time. My aunts all tell me it was very upsetting and frightening to witness. There would be periods when she was unnaturally withdrawn and very thin, and then there were other times when she would be racing about manically, but at the same time she would seem completely blank and emotionless. When her medication was working, she might seem OK for a while, but at other times she would be extremely anxious and depressed, which would put a strain on the whole family. Although

HONEST

Mum appeared on *Go For It* for ITV after the band split up, she never really performed in public again once the illness took hold completely. The fact that my dad found it extremely hard to cope with her condition and was prone to furious outbursts only made a bad situation much worse. He simply couldn't get his head around the idea of his wife being mentally ill, and he had no idea how to deal with her when things got bad.

Dad had been in quite a dark place when he first met my mum. He'd been on the party scene and dabbled in drugs for a bit too long, and he was quite messed up and unstable. They met through my mum's sister, Aunt Louise, and from what I know, Dad was still partying hard at that time. Mum really helped Dad to sort his life out when they first started dating. What my dad didn't know then was that Mum wasn't well either, and she was already struggling with mental illness herself. Mum has always been a very beautiful woman, and she was a proper stunner back then: dark brown hair, bright blue eyes and a petite nose. She had quite fair skin, but in the sun she always turned a gorgeous dark brown, and it was easy to see why my dad fell for her.

Before either of them knew it, there was a baby on the way – me – and although the pregnancy was unplanned, my dad, coming from a respectable Greek family, decided to do the honourable thing and marry my mum. He loved her very much, and his family loved her too, so it was the right thing to do as far as Dad was concerned, and he was happy to do it. Once I was born, though, Mum's illness got worse and my dad just wasn't prepared for it. He was volatile in his younger years, and although he's got a heart of gold, back then his temper was short and his patience thin – it wasn't a good mix. I don't know whether it was the stress of childbirth and looking after a baby that made my mum's illness worse, but I'm sure it can't have been easy for her. What I do know is that my mum loved me more than anything else in the world, and she always told me I was the best thing that had ever happened to her.

I must have been about four or five when I first saw how Mum's illness affected her – and my dad – and I remember it quite clearly. Mum and Dad were shouting at one another in the kitchen of our house, and all of a sudden it got physical . . . I remember crawling into the space between the bin and the cooker, curling up into a little ball and rocking myself back and forth. I didn't cry. I don't even think I felt any deep sadness about what was going on in front of me. I just knew something was wrong, but I was too young to know exactly what it was. I didn't have any older brothers or sisters to help me understand it either. I was an only child, and a pretty weird one at that – I think I had a bit of a Wednesday Addams vibe going on. Even before I started school I was a bit of a loner, playing on my own or sitting in a corner, keeping myself to myself. I'd play with my dolls, inventing movie-like scenarios involving damsels in distress and heroes and villains. Nothing ever seemed to affect or faze me, and I was often a bit numb to what was going on around me, which, looking back, was probably a good thing.

On another occasion I remember a really bad fight in the house that ended with the doorbell ringing and a couple of police officers rushing through the front door. One minute I was standing in the hall and the next my mum was being restrained by the police and dragged out of the house screaming hysterically. I followed them to the front door and watched her being bundled into an ambulance, still shouting and screaming madly, and now crying out my name too. Again, I felt numb – I don't remember having any strong emotions about what was happening. I simply took it all in. My dad didn't come out of the house while all this was going on, but next to me at the door there was a female police officer. I remember her looking down at me, not quite knowing what to do for this weird, poker-faced five-year-old who was just standing there, staring at her mum being dragged off in such terrible distress. I remember the awkward half-smile she gave me, and even then I knew what that look meant. 'Sorry, I don't know what to say.'

After the ambulance and the police officers had gone, taking my poor mum with them, I walked back into the house and went to the kitchen. My dad was sitting at the table, clearly in bits. After a while he got up and made me some spaghetti hoops with alphabet potatoes, and I sat at the table, quiet as a mouse, and ate them. We didn't talk about what had just happened. He didn't tell me where Mum had gone, and I don't remember asking. I just accepted what was in front of me. A little while later my dad called Uncle Byron and asked if he could come and pick me up and look after me for a day or so until Dad could get his head together.

Of course, I now know that my mum had suffered a breakdown that day, and my dad just couldn't cope with her anymore. As I said, Dad had a lot of demons in those days. His excessive partying, and all that went with it, often led him to behave in ways he never would now, and he sometimes lost his temper. That day, when things got out of hand, Dad had called the hospital, as he felt Mum was a danger to herself. As there had been a fight, the police had been there to help restrain her.

A few days later, I remember my dad getting me ready to go out.

'We're going to see Mummy,' he said.

When we got to the hospital my mum came out from behind the curtain around her bed, dressed in a hospital gown. I wanted to shout out 'Mummy!' and run and hug her, but something was stopping me. This wasn't my mummy at all.

'Hi, lovey, are you all right?' she said softly, but she just looked so defeated and vacant, almost like a child version of the mum I was used to, and I felt no strength coming from her, or security being near her. It was as if I should be the one to comfort her instead of the other way round, as if the world had been turned upside down. I somehow knew that she wasn't able to take care of me while she was like that, and that feeling has stayed with me ever since.

Once Mum was finally better and back home from the hospital, I was convinced that she was going to be taken away from me again, and I became terrified of being left on my own. I was constantly either at my mum's hip, or my dad's. This made my first day of nursery traumatic, to say the least. I can remember everything about that day: walking towards the school building with my mum, exactly how the room looked, and then Mum turning and walking away from me. I couldn't understand why Mum was leaving me in this strange place with these people I didn't know, so I screamed hysterically, kicked, cried under the table, and basically went nuts for a full two hours. Mum said the teachers had never seen a tantrum like it. Eventually, when they finally managed to calm me down, another little girl came up to me and asked if I wanted to play a board game with her, and I settled down.

My aversion to being alone has never really gone away, however, and to this day I still have a massive phobia about sleeping on my own in the dark. If I'm sharing a bed with someone I don't mind darkness, but if I'm on my own I have to have a lamp on. As I said, I slept in the same room as my parents until I was about ten, so when Mum or Dad would put me to bed, they'd always leave the light on until they came to bed later. Consequently, I was never on my own when it was dark, and I guess that's what I got used to. These days I'm very rarely alone at all, and I certainly never sleep alone if I can help it. I spend most of my time with Gareth, my friend and PA, or one of my good friends, and I'll always share a bed rather than sleep separately. You so often hear people saying, 'I need some space', or 'I need some time alone', but that's not me at all. I like to have someone around me always, even if we're not talking or doing anything in particular. I like to know there's someone else present. I'm certain that stems from my childhood fears of being abandoned.

The only time I do want to be alone is when I'm angry or very stressed, and then I'll lock myself in the bathroom. This is another strange habit that started at a young age. I think it stems from the fact that my mum used to fuss around me nervously and hover over me quite a lot. As I got a bit older she could be quite overprotective, and she wanted to be close to me at all times. Consequently, whatever I was doing – whether it was reading a magazine or putting on some make-up – my mum would be following me around the house, watching me or just fidgeting on the spot behind me. It was all part of her illness, and she couldn't help it, but the only way I could get away from her sometimes was to lock myself away for an hour or two.

To this day, one of my pet hates is people fussing and faffing around me. Most people who know me and work with me have learned that the best thing to do is to be as honest and upfront with me as possible, and then leave me to my own devices. If somebody fusses too much I get really agitated, and that can sometimes lead to a spell in the bathroom with the door locked.

Only recently, during the video shoot for my first single in Miami, there was a big bust-up when a few of us got a bit drunk after the shoot. Everyone seemed to be yelling and arguing and I got extremely tense, so I just took myself off to the bathroom and sat on the floor for an hour and a half until I'd completely chilled out again. I think that's something I'll always do in times of stress. It helped me to feel calm when I was a kid, and it's something I've carried with me ever since.

Chapter Two

Sadly, my mum's breakdowns and subsequent hospitalisations continued throughout my childhood, and as time went on I started to notice the changes in my mum's behaviour more and more. But I think that because her illness had started when I was so young, I was able to adapt to and accept the way she was, because it was all I'd ever known. That was just the way Mum was. That didn't stop me getting frustrated and annoyed with her mood swings and outbursts, though, and they were sometimes totally unreasonable and out of the blue.

Mum was obsessive about locking our front door, and it was always locked from the inside with the keys still hanging in the door. One morning I noticed that although the key was in the lock, it hadn't been turned, and the door was actually unlocked. Knowing that my mum would freak out and feel vulnerable if she spotted it, I turned the key and locked the door myself. Within seconds my mum, hearing the jangle of the keys, came tearing out into the hall, screaming at me hysterically.

'You're trying to give me a heart attack! You're trying to kill me!'

I guess she thought I was trying to open the door and panicked, but she just went completely off the deep end, accusing me of wanting to make her ill or even kill her, and it went on and on.

Incidents like this were a regular occurrence in our

house, along with temper tantrums and mood swings –
even the smashing of plates and cups wasn't out of the
ordinary. It was all quite scary for a six-year-old, and
sometimes the only thing to do was to shut myself in the
bedroom. At other times I'd fight back. I remember my
mum screaming at me once because she thought I'd said
the word 'wanker', but I'd actually just mentioned Willy
Wonka's Chocolate Factory, and I told her so. Mum argued
that she knew what she'd heard, but I was determined to
protest my innocence. Still Mum was convinced she'd
heard me swearing and slapped me in the face for it.

This was a real dilemma for me. When you're a child
you're supposed to listen to and obey everything your
mum tells you, but what if your mum doesn't know what
she's talking about a lot of the time? What are you
supposed to do then? I never really knew what to expect
when I came home from school each afternoon. One day
I'd be greeted with a happy smile, and the next day she'd
be giving me evils.

I might say, 'Are you all right, Mum?'

And she'd snap back, 'What do you fucking think?'

It was like constantly walking on eggshells, and there
were periods when she was either shouting and screaming
like a witch or curled up in a ball on the floor, crying like a
baby. This meant that I often felt alone when I was in the
house with her, even though I loved her. I never felt like I
was part of a team or a family unit, and while other kids
could curl up on the sofa with their mums and feel safe, I
couldn't. The fact that my dad found it so hard to cope
with mum's illness didn't help matters either. It was only
Mum's sisters, my aunts, who I could sometimes talk to
about all these things, and eventually I ended up living
with Aunt Louise for months at a time while my mum was

in hospital. Mostly I just accepted Mum's illness, though. As I said, I didn't really know any different at the time.

During the periods when my mum was going through a good patch of health, things would improve. I remember Dad would take us for walks on Hampstead Heath on Sundays, and then we'd come home and have a roast dinner together. That was our family day and I have happy memories of those times. Mum would also sing a lot and play music when she was feeling well, and the difference in her was amazing. Music was a big part of our lives and we would listen to everything from The Police to Cher and all the great music from the eighties. My favourite, though, was Michael Jackson and the first album I had was *Bad*. Dad was into eighties sounds too, but he was more of a rocker, so I was also exposed to harder-edged stuff. Music was all around me all the time, and I was convinced from the age of about five that I was going to be a pop star! So much so that one day, when I was about five or six, after watching *The Little Mermaid*, I decided it was time I tried my hand at recording a song.

'Dad, I want to record in the studio,' I announced, and off we went to his and Uncle Byron's studio in Dollis Hill for my first ever recording session.

Dad had to pick me up and hold me up to the microphone because I was still so little, but I recorded 'Part of Your World' from *The Little Mermaid* and I loved every minute of it – that is, until I heard the playback.

'Let me hear it,' I said to Dad once I'd finished my masterpiece, and according to him I scrutinised every note, screwing up my face when my pitching wasn't just right.

'No, Daddy! That's not good enough,' I said once I'd finished listening. 'I need to do it all again.'

He later told me how funny it had been that day,

watching me pull faces as I tried to find the right notes and pitch everything to perfection, but as usual I was pretty blasé and unfazed by it all.

———————

By the time I was about seven, both Dad and Uncle Byron were playing in the band Mungo Jerry. Uncle B was the bass player, Dad played piano, and they toured and performed gigs all over the world. One of the things I remember causing a terrible fight between Mum and Dad was the fact that Dad was obviously earning money from the gigs, yet my mum and I never saw a penny of it. Meanwhile, we were struggling on benefits. One night I was being a typical nosy kid and looking through some of my dad's things when I found a slip of paper highlighting exactly what sort of money he'd been earning with the band. It turned out that while Mum and I had been living on pennies, Dad had been earning hundreds of pounds a week and either spending it on himself or just ploughing it all back into the studio. Mum went absolutely mental, as you can imagine, and after that things just went from bad to worse.

The fights were getting more and more frequent, and more violent, and I have a vivid memory of being in the bedroom one night, praying to the Mother Mary icon above my bed for the screaming and shouting to stop as a fight raged on in the kitchen. As I was lying there in bed, I could hear my dad getting angrier and angrier and I knew what was about to happen, so I got out of bed and then down on my knees, and I put my hands together.

'Please, Mother Mary, please make it stop. Please!'

Suddenly, without any warning, there was silence. In

fact, it went so quiet so quickly that I was convinced something terrible had happened, and I ran to the bedroom door to see what I could hear. When I eventually realised that everything was OK, I felt that my prayer must have been heard and answered. That was the first time I thought seriously about religion, despite the fact that I had a mother who was brought up as a Catholic and a dad from a strict Greek Orthodox background.

I wasn't even baptised as a baby because neither side of the family could agree on what religion I should be. Eventually, while I was on holiday visiting my dad's family in Greece, aged about six, they sneakily promised me 'a big day that will be all about you', which ended up being completely humiliating. It turned out to be a baptism, which meant being stripped butt-naked in front of a crowd of people I'd never met, and then being dipped in and out of a pot of oil by a Greek priest who was mumbling words that I couldn't understand.

After praying to the icon that night, though, I became a firm believer. It's not that I believe and follow the Bible to the letter; after all, it's been reinterpreted and changed so many times over the centuries. I don't like some of the control and restrictions that religion sometimes imposes on people, but there are elements of the Bible that I trust. My guide to living life is to go by plain old right and wrong, and if something feels wrong, then I know I shouldn't be doing it. I don't need the Bible to tell me that. My religion is strong, but it's my own, and it's based on what makes sense to me. It's seen me through a lot of dark times.

———————

The end of my parents' marriage came on my ninth birthday. There was a fight going on and Mum knew that she had to get away once and for all. It was never going to get any better. My dad refused to leave the family home, because he said he wouldn't be able to get a council flat, being a single man, whereas he was convinced that Mum would get one with a young child in tow. I remember thinking how unfair it all was at the time. It was my house! It was the house I'd grown up in, and I didn't want to leave it. Why did I have to suffer just because my parents couldn't stop fighting? I just didn't understand it. Still, Mum and I ended up moving out and living in a room in a bed and breakfast place in Swiss Cottage for about ten months while the divorce went through. Mum was determined that we would get the house back, but she also knew she was going to have to fight for it in court. It was going to be extremely tough, and we both knew that she might not have the mental strength to get through it.

I hated living in the B&B. From what I can remember, we had just one room with two single beds and a microwave. I especially hated the fact that I had to go out of our room and across the hall every time I needed to use the bathroom, which we shared with other tenants. I would have to carry all my bath stuff with me across the hall and get undressed once I was in the bathroom, all the time worrying that a stranger might start banging on the door to use the toilet or, even worse, just burst right in. It's another reason why my bathroom is a sanctuary to me now, and the place I go when I want to lock myself away from the world.

Leading up to the divorce, my mum's illness made her paranoid that my dad was going to snatch me away from her and leave the country, and at the same time Dad's family were constantly badmouthing my mum. Maybe they didn't realise that I heard so much of what was going on but it felt as if they were trying to turn me against her. I suppose that's just what happens when a family splits apart, but it was a horrible situation and unfortunately I was stuck in the middle. On Christmas Day that year, Mum went to her sister's and I went to see my dad, who now had a new girlfriend living in our house with him. That was bad enough in itself, but when I arrived at the house on Christmas morning, this woman was walking around in a coat belonging to my mum, which she'd taken out of the wardrobe.

Dad's family were there too, including my nan and granddad, Auntie Maria (Dad's sister), Uncle Byron and Auntie Zoe, plus Dino and Spiros. And when the two boys opened their Christmas presents they were over the moon to discover that they had both received tickets to Disneyland, Paris. Of course, I was so excited to open my present too: like most little girls, it was my dream to go to Disneyland, and I'd gone on and on about it forever to Mum. When I opened my present, though, it wasn't a ticket to Disneyland at all and I was duly gutted.

'We wanted to take you,' Auntie Maria said, 'but your mum said you couldn't go.'

I didn't know who to be more pissed off with: my mum for not allowing me to go to Disneyland, or my dad's family for making my mum look like the bad guy. Surely they could have given the boys their tickets while I wasn't around rather than making me feel as though I'd been left out. Dad's family may have meant well in trying to organise a Disneyland trip, but the way it was handled made me very resentful of my mum for a while. Looking back now I realise that I was just caught in the crossfire of the divorce.

During the separation, I stayed with my dad every other weekend, and sometimes I found the situation with Dad's new girlfriend quite hard. The relationship seemed to have sprung up so quickly, and now there she was, living in my house while Mum and I were staying in the grotty bedsit. What was worse was that I sensed that she didn't really want me there either. She didn't seem to like having to share Dad's attention. It wasn't always comfortable for me.

A little while after the split, Mum had another breakdown and had to go back into hospital. The divorce proceedings seemed to drag on for ages, and the illness, of course, slowed things down even more. Meanwhile, I went to stay with Aunt Louise for a while, until Mum was ready to face the world again. Whenever I was at Louise's I felt safe and very happy. My aunt would do her absolute best to make life as normal as possible for me, and she and her boyfriend Trevor took on the motherly and fatherly roles that were missing from my life at that time. We had proper family dinners together and went on fun family outings, and Louise would read books with me and generally spend lots of time with me. Even simple things like having a set bedtime made me feel like I was enjoying a normal, stable childhood. It was the closest I came to having a proper family life, and sometimes, when Mum was due to come out of hospital, I didn't want to go back home.

As the date for the divorce hearing finally approached, Mum made a huge effort to pull herself together, and I suddenly saw strength in her that I'd never seen before – proper female strength. She bought herself a beautiful new suit from a catalogue and started to work out to her step-class fitness videos. It was summer and she had a tan, and she looked healthier than I'd ever seen her.

HONEST

I have a vivid memory of her coming into school one day and I was pulled out of my classroom to go and talk to her in the playground. Mum was too excited to wait until I'd finished school: she wanted to tell me that the divorce settlement was finally done, and that we had got our house back and could go home again. She looked so strong and beautiful at that moment, with her hair done and her gorgeous clothes. She'd been through so much in the last few years, and for once in her life she'd fought and won a battle. I suddenly saw that motherly strength I'd been longing to see ever since that day at the hospital when I was tiny – it was there in her after all. I felt like I could finally look up to my mum, and I'll always be so proud of her for that.

Chapter Three

I'm not sure if it was because of all the turmoil going on at home, but at primary school I always felt awkward and a bit of an outsider. My school was just an ordinary state primary, nothing special, but for some reason I found it hard to make friends, spending a lot of time on my own. Maybe that was why I seemed to attract the attention of the various bullies at my school – I was often their target.

My first experience of being bullied was when I was just five years old and still at nursery. There was a fence in the playground that separated the primary school kids from us nursery kids, and there was an upturned gym bench poking through a hole in the fence: half of it on the big kids' side and half on the nursery side. Anyway, I liked to play hopscotch on this upside-down bench all on my own, and one day, while I was doing just that, I noticed an older boy staring at me from the other side of the fence. It wasn't a friendly stare either: he was giving me proper evils. I'd actually noticed him glaring at me before while I was playing, and though I didn't like the look of him much, he was on the other side of the divide, so I guess I thought I was safe.

As I innocently continued my game of hopscotch, though, the boy struck, jumping with full force onto his end of the bench and sending the other end smashing up between my legs. I was in agony, and was black and blue 'down below' for about two weeks as a result. I was too scared and embarrassed to tell anyone what had happened, so I just kept my mouth shut. I can't even remember what excuse I gave my mum for the bruising – probably that I'd slipped or fallen. I just knew I couldn't tell her the truth. There was something about that boy's nasty stare that stopped me. At the time I didn't really even think about why this kid had decided to pick on me, and I never did find out why he did it. All I felt was fear, because I knew that one day I was going to have to leave the nursery and go to the other side of the fence where the big kids played, and he was going to be there, waiting for me.

That wasn't the end of it either. I don't know what it was about me that made boys want to pick on me, but not long after that, while I was still on the nursery side of the fence, there was a second confrontation, although this time I was determined not to let another bully get the better of me. I was a proper little loner in the playground, and one morning while I was happily playing alone on the climbing frames, I clambered up a small ladder which led up to a raised tunnel that you could crawl through and then climb down the other side. Only I thought it would be much more fun to climb on top of the tunnel, and I was quite proud of my little self when I finally managed to achieve it. Now, on top of this tunnel was a blanket, which I was standing on. That is, until some smart-arse boy strolled over and yanked the blanket from under me, causing me to crash down onto the floor, scraping half the skin off my legs as I went. Nice!

The bully clearly thought this was hilarious, but as he strolled off, laughing, I got up off the floor in tears, gritted my teeth, and got right back on top of the tunnel again. This kid wasn't giving up, though, and he marched back over and pulled me off the top of the tunnel for a second time. A little while later, I was back up there again, but, once more, I came crashing down with this vile boy's help, and this went on and on and on. It was a battle of wills, and I wasn't going to give in: I was going to keep getting up on that tunnel whether he liked it or not.

I'm not sure if that made me stubborn or just stupid, but either way I was having none of it. Eventually I'd been scraped and bumped so many times that the teacher's special sweetie jar – reserved for children who'd fallen over or hurt themselves while playing – was completely empty. I'd drained it dry. I might have ended up wounded that day, but I also felt a definite sense of victory. And my determination not to be beaten was something I'd have to rely on quite often later on in life.

By the time I moved up to the reception class – and over to the big kids' side of the playground – when I was six, there was a brand-new bully for me to contend with, and this one was the scariest of all. His name was Joe and he was two years above me. He was such a renowned bully that even the boy who'd hurt me on the bench was petrified of him. Joe had a violent streak, and he had it in for me as soon as he first clapped eyes on me. He would push me and smack me about just for the hell of it, so whenever I saw him coming I used to run and hide, sometimes locking myself in a cubicle of the girls' toilets if I could get there fast enough. More often than not, though, Joe would simply march straight in after me, lying in wait outside the cubicle while I sat, terrified, inside. One afternoon my mum spotted the bruises I'd ended up with and she told the teachers about Joe, but for some reason the threat of punishment never deterred him, and the teachers never did much anyway. To them, it was just normal playground rough and tumble.

On another occasion, when I was about eight, I got really hurt. I'd been sitting on the playground floor with a mate of mine, playing finger football with some stones and using the holes in a drain as goals, when all of a sudden I noticed that my friend's face had completely drained of colour – she looked terrified. I suddenly realised that there was someone towering over me from behind, but before I had a chance to react, Joe was jumping on my back, stamping on me, punching me, and basically kicking the crap out of me. I went home black and blue, and my mum went storming up to the school, demanding that the teachers put a stop to it.

Meanwhile, I decided to try defeating fire with water. I asked my mum if she could get me a small box of chocolates and a flower, and the next morning I took them into school as a kind of olive branch for Joe. As I approached him, I was petrified, but I truly thought that this was the best way to put an end to my misery.

'I'm really sorry for whatever it is I've done to you,' I said, handing him my peace offering. 'Whatever it is, can you forgive me? And can we be friends?'

It worked, because for the whole of that day Joe was nice to me. It was *just* that day, though. The next morning it was business as usual, and he was back to punching me again. He didn't seem to care what anyone said to him or who he aimed his fury at. The little charmer even spat at my mum one day as the two of us walked past the estate where he lived, which was not too far from our house. My mum was furious and she picked up a nearby broom and chased Joe all the way down the street with it. He ran, yes, but he was laughing as he went. All this from a ten-year-old boy. It got so bad that eventually, when I was about nine, Mum moved me to a different school in Haverstock Hill. My new school was called The Rosary and it was a Catholic primary where you had to wear a uniform. I didn't mind; I was just happy to get away from Joe.

Quite a few years after all that, something quite strange happened. I was hanging out with some friends in my local area when Joe randomly turned up on the scene. I guess I was about fourteen by then, and I hadn't seen him since primary school. I was a little bit taken aback, but I didn't feel scared of him anymore. All that stuff seemed so long ago; we'd just been kids back then, after all.

'You all right?' I said, half smiling. 'How are ya?'

Joe looked slightly out of it.

'It was my mum's funeral today,' he said. He was clearly in bits.

How bizarre that all those years after he'd bullied me, I should meet Joe on the day of his mum's funeral and end up being a shoulder for him to cry on. That afternoon, I comforted him as best I could, and he told me he couldn't even remember how mean he'd been to me back in the day, and also how sorry he was. It turned out that his parents were drug addicts and he hadn't had the best of times when he was a kid. I suppose that helped me to understand a little bit why he behaved the way he did when we were younger. He told me that day that after everything that had happened to him, he didn't believe in God anymore. And there I was, sitting in a park aged fourteen, telling my former tormentor that he shouldn't lose faith, and that his mum was still watching over him.

It's funny how things turn out. I never saw Joe again after that day.

———————

I wasn't especially popular in primary school, even without all the bullying. In fact, by the time I was ten, I was anything *but* popular. I was different. A bit of a weirdo. A geek. You know the type of kid: the one who wants so desperately to be cool but always says the wrong thing, whatever the occasion. I never wore fashionable clothes: in fact, I was quite trampy, wearing my cousin Dino's hand-me-downs half the time. I had a wonky block fringe and pigtails, and I even had the mandatory geeky round glasses for reading. Despite all this, I did have one 'cool' friend, and that was Joanne, the most popular girl in school – I was her geeky sidekick. All the boys fancied her, and all the boys took the piss out of me, but for some reason Joanne accepted me as her best mate and one of her gang.

That being said, my friendship with Joanne tended to blow hot and cold, at least as far as she was concerned, and sometimes it turned into a scene straight out of *Mean Girls*. On what seemed like a weekly basis, one of Miss Popular's faithful lackeys would make it their business to inform me that Joanne didn't want to hang around with me anymore. Some weeks I was let in and out of the gang so often I didn't know whether I was coming or going. When nobody was speaking to me, I would just have to plod around school on my own until Joanne decided I was back in favour again.

The fact that I wasn't allowed to play out with the other kids only added to my lack of street cred. My mum was very overprotective, especially after the divorce, and she wanted to keep me close at all times. So while the other kids were knocking around the neighbourhood on their bikes and scooters, I was stuck inside with Mum. I couldn't always invite friends round either, especially if Mum wasn't feeling at her best. I understood why, but that didn't make it any easier. And even when I did have a mate over to the house and we were allowed outside, Mum would tell me exactly how far along the road I was allowed to venture, and I'd be in big trouble if I crossed the boundary she'd set me. Every movement was controlled and supervised, and the older I got, the more suffocated I felt. I think that's why I became so rebellious later on.

The only time I was given a little bit more of a free rein was when Dino came over to our place. For some reason, Mum would trust me to play outside with him – which, looking back, was probably quite unwise, given the fact that he was a little tearaway. But even then I wasn't allowed to stray too far from the house.

Almost all of my playtime back then was spent with Dino, which meant that I became something of a tomboy, as all the games we played together seemed to involve guns, fighting, or video games like Mortal Kombat. Dino was the one person during my childhood who never let me down: there was no 'I'll be your friend one day but not the next' with him. We were best mates all the time and we never left one another's side, whether we were at his house or mine.

Dino's favourite pastime was setting up booby traps. I remember once when we were six or seven he woke me up in the middle of the night to help him set a booby trap for my mum and dad. We snuck into their room and put toothpaste and shredded tissue on the sheets all around them, so when they woke up they'd be covered in it. We were also fond of putting toys or buckets of water on doorframes so that they fell down onto someone's head as they entered a room. The two of us carried on our tradition of practical joking for years, especially when we were on tour with N-Dubz. I remember once when a girl got drunk and fell asleep on the tour bus, we decided to see how many pieces of kebab meat we could balance on her face before she woke up – a bit like that game, Buckaroo! We did quite well, as it goes, and I think we even managed to get the pita bread to balance on her nose without her stirring.

Although I was a tomboy, the one feminine attribute I did long for was the ability to charm the boys. I understood from a young age that I wanted male attention, and I felt envious of those girls who got it. Why didn't the boys feel like that about me? Why was it that they didn't give me a second look? What did those other girls have that I didn't? For a long time I felt insecure and awkward, and then, when I was almost eleven, I got fed up with being the geeky, unfashionable loner. I decided it was time for drastic measures.

The first thing I had to do was to grow my fringe out: it covered my face and I hated it. As soon as it was long enough to pull back off my forehead, I did, and then I pierced my ears, got rid of the geeky glasses and the pigtails, and put on a bit of lip-gloss. Suddenly I had a face – I was pretty! Next came the clothes. I stopped wearing my skirts below my knee, I didn't button my school blouse all the way up to the neck and tied it in a little knot at the bottom, and I didn't wear my tie perfectly straight anymore.

I was proper excited about my new look. It was a huge

transformation, and when it was complete I proudly walked into school feeling like a whole new person with a whole new confidence. The impact was immediate. People were looking at me differently, I could tell, especially the boys. It was like something out of an American high school movie, where the girl goes from geek to popular overnight, and I was loving every minute of it. For the first time in my life I felt confident, and when a guy came up to me in school and asked me out, I knew for sure things had changed.

After that, one thing led to another, and the more male attention I got, the more other girls liked me and wanted to be my friend. That's the way it worked. Suddenly I was one of them, whereas before I'd stuck out like a sore thumb. Looking back, I think my situation at home and my introverted nature made me different, and I guess that was the problem. I never had very good social skills; I didn't know what clothes or music were cool. It was like I was living in my own little bubble for a while. Changing my look and becoming more like one of the crowd made a huge difference.

A little while after that there was another event that gave my self-confidence a massive boost. Our school play that year was *Bugsy Malone*, and I decided to audition. I'd only ever had one audition before and that was at the Sylvia Young Theatre School. I'd been dying to try out for a singing or acting agency from a young age, but with Mum's illness it had been tricky, to say the least. Sometimes when I'd ask her about it she'd say yes, but then she'd turn around the next day and say no, so I never got very far. Eventually, when I was nine, my dad decided to help me, but he went behind Mum's back, organising an audition for me without her knowing.

Sitting in the offices of Sylvia Young, I confidently belted out 'Chattanooga Choo Choo', and I noticed that everyone in the office stopped what they were doing to listen to me sing. It was a good feeling. At the end of the song everyone stood up and clapped. They were blown away with my audition, and told my dad that they'd love to have me at the school. I was so happy. When it was time to fill out the paperwork, though, Mum had to be told and she wasn't having any of it. She said I couldn't go, and I felt gutted and enraged. Mum was really pissed off that my dad had taken me to the audition. Her illness often made her paranoid, and she hated the thought that my dad was trying to take control of me away from her. It was as simple as that.

Nobody was going to stop me from auditioning for *Bugsy Malone*, though, and when it was my turn I sang a Backstreet Boys song in the school hall in front of all the auditioning teachers. When it was finally announced in class that I'd got the part of the glamorous gangster's moll Tallulah, I was over the moon. It was like a dream moment.

On the night of the performance I felt like I'd really nailed it. It felt natural and brilliant being up there on stage, and everyone, including my family, loved my rendition of Tallulah. After that night my family started to take me a little bit more seriously when I told them I wanted to be a singer, and I was all the more determined to become one. In just a few months I'd gone from the awkward geek with no mates who never won anything, to being a pretty, popular girl who'd won a starring role in the school musical. I felt appreciated and finally relevant in some way. I'd come out of my shell and people could now see me for who I was, and I finally felt free of the little world I'd been locked away in for most of my childhood. Mostly, I just felt like a normal eleven-year-old girl, and that was the best feeling of all.

Chapter Four

After primary school, aged eleven, I went to La Sainte Union, which was a very strict all-girls Catholic school in Highgate with a good reputation. This was *the* school to go to for a good Catholic girl, and quite a few girls from The Rosary went there. I was hard-working and in the top class for all of my subjects. I did well in tests, wore my uniform, got my homework in on time and kept myself out of trouble – I suppose I was a model student, really.

After a while, though, I started to fall out of favour with some of the other girls. It wasn't like I was being bullied or terrorised, but things definitely started to get more and more cold and bitchy. It was like I was back to being the unpopular loner again, and I didn't know why. It was then that something dawned on me. What had made me confident and popular towards the end of my time at primary school was the fact that I'd been a hit with the boys. After my image change, guys seemed to think I was pretty and fancied me, therefore other girls had wanted to be around me. In an all-girls school that science doesn't work – you don't get that chemistry. In that kind of environment it's the hard girls who become popular, not the pretty ones, and I certainly wasn't a hard girl. Sure, I had my moments and I had a temper when pushed, but I wasn't what you'd call tough, and I really didn't like getting angry. Once the boys were taken out of the equation, I was just seen for what I was all over again: awkward and unconfident. I was also separated from the girls who had become my friends at primary school, as we were put into different classes, and that didn't help matters either. I started to feel lost and lonely once more, and one day I woke up feeling like I had no friends at all.

Outside of school, my favourite person to hang out with was still Dino. I really admired and looked up to my cousin, and to me he was the coolest person on the planet. Dino never seemed to have any worries about being popular; he had a sort of cheeky charm that everyone seemed to love. All the girls fancied him, and all the guys wanted to be him. The fact that he was my cousin, and that I was more important to him than anyone else, made me feel like a million dollars. Being around Dino gave me a real feeling of self-worth, and now that I was eleven years old, I was able to get the bus to Camden on my own to visit him anytime I liked.

Unfortunately, Dino was not the ideal role model for an eleven-year-old Catholic schoolgirl, and it wasn't long before I was being led astray – not that I needed much leading! Dino regularly bunked off school, and one afternoon he suggested that I do the same. Why not? I didn't have any friends at school to worry about; Mum was in hospital so she would never find out. It sounded like an excellent plan. So the next morning, at Auntie Louise's house, I prepped my school uniform, got all my books together, and then left for school as normal. Instead of my usual bus, though, I jumped on a bus to Dino's place, which was on a council estate in Camden.

To me, this was really exciting. Dino's mum, my Aunt Zoe, had gone out for the whole day, so the plan was to just hang out in the yard of their house with a couple of the more popular girls from Dino's school.

'This is my cousin Tula,' Dino told the girls, who quite obviously doted on him. 'Make sure you take care of her.'

It felt great to be held in such high esteem for once.

It was on that day that I first met Dino's best mate, Fazer – or Richard, as he was then known. I remember he was a really small kid and his head only came up to my shoulder, and the next few times I saw him, he was always in the same smelly green jumper from GAP, which was covered in hot-rock holes from all the hash he smoked. Yep! The boys were already smoking spliff, aged twelve.

Anyway, that day Richard was sitting on the bed when I first walked into Dino's bedroom, and it was clear from the look on his face that he approved. He went out of his way to act as cool as possible in front of me.

'Tula, this is my best mate, I've told you about him,' Dino said.

My cousin had talked about Richard a fair amount, but as far as I could tell he was just a little dude in a smelly GAP jumper, so I didn't really take very much notice of him at first.

'He really fancies you,' Dino told me later that afternoon. 'Would you go out with him?'

At that age 'going out' with someone meant a quick snog and putting your arm around one another.

'No,' I said. 'I won't.'

And that was the end of that.

Meanwhile, unbeknown to us, a neighbour had spotted me going into Dino's place in my school uniform and had called Aunt Zoe, who in turn had called my dad. All of a sudden there was a knock at the door, and we all froze.

Dino peeked outside and then delivered the terrifying news.

'It's your dad.'

'NOOOOO!'

There was a sudden fear within me, and a horrible cringey feeling that went with it. I was crapping myself at the thought of Dad catching me skipping school, so I hid in Dino's wardrobe.

Once Dad was in the house, I could hear his voice.

'Where is she?' he demanded.

And suddenly the wardrobe door swung open and Dad was looking down at me, crouching down as small as I could and trying to cover myself with jackets. I think I was more embarrassed than I was frightened, to be honest. I hated confrontation.

'Come on you, get out,' Dad said, but he was actually very calm, and didn't even shout at me.

'Sorry, Dad.' I was still cringing.

He made me promise not to bunk off school again, and then he even sat down and wrote me a sick note, to make sure I didn't get into any trouble.

'Don't tell your Auntie Louise, though,' he said. 'Just don't do it again.'

I think my dad found it funny, to be honest. He saw a bit of his rebellious spirit rubbing off on me, and I think he quite liked that. Maybe if he'd been a little bit stricter with me in Mum's absence I might have stayed on the straight and narrow as far as school was concerned. Still, I wasn't completely out of the woods that day. My Aunt Louise discovered my dad's phoney sick note in my school bag that night and – knowing that I wasn't sick – put two and two together and realised that I must have bunked off school. So I got 'baited up all over the show' that day, which means I got exposed left, right and centre. As far as I was concerned, it had been worth it. It was the most fun I'd had in ages.

After that day I was determined that I wanted to move schools. I was lonely and I had no friends at La Sainte Union, and the prospect of another four or five years there made me miserable. Sitting all on my own during lunch break one day, I thought: I'm not having this, this is just bollocks! I thought about Dino and how popular he was, and how all his friends doted on me simply because I was his cousin. I was popular again when I was around him: the boys liked me, and the girls liked me. It was time to take action. I needed to be with Dino. I needed to go to Dino's school.

Once Mum was out of hospital again, I set about achieving my goal, pleading with her to hear me out.

'I can't go back there, Mum, I hate it,' I told her. 'I want to move schools.'

'Yes, but your grades are so good,' was her argument. 'Why would you want to ruin that?'

'I can't live my life being unhappy,' I said. 'I'm on my own again and I hate this feeling. I'm miserable at home when you're ill, I'm miserable at school because I'm lonely. I wanna have some friends, and I wanna have some fun.'

'Well, where do you want to go?' she said.

'Well,' I said sneakily, knowing my mum didn't know much about all the schools in the area at the time, 'let me go where Dino goes.'

As I was a top-grade student and I had a cousin at the school, Haverstock, which is a comprehensive in Chalk

Farm, offered me a place straight away, and I was as happy as Larry. I was going to a mixed school again, which meant male attention and hopefully less cliquey behaviour from the girls, plus I was going to get to hang out with Dino and his cool mates all the time. There wasn't even a uniform, so I could wear what I damn well pleased. The only problem was, what *should* I wear to school? I'd spent the last few months wearing a uniform every day, and when I wasn't wearing that I was still in Dino's hand-me-downs. There was still a definite air of geek about me, and I certainly didn't intend to embarrass myself on my first day at my new school. Once again it was Dino to the rescue. He was really excited about me joining his school, so he offered to take me to Camden Market to help me sort out my wardrobe dilemma. Dad gave me a hundred quid, which could buy quite a lot down Camden Market back then, and off I went for the day – aged eleven – shopping with my cool cousin.

That day, Dino didn't just teach me what clothes were cool and acceptable, he also taught me some highly important school etiquette – i.e. who I should and shouldn't talk to and/or hang around with once I got there.

'These people are cool: you can hang around with them, but don't hang around with those people,' he'd say. And 'You can talk to her, but not her – she's a slag!'

It was a proper education, and I took in every word.

'These are the trainers you should wear. Roll your trousers up like that. Wear your hair like this – that's how the cool girls do it.'

He even got one of his girl mates to teach me how to slick my hair up and scrape it back. Then we went to JD Sports, Foot Locker and GAP, and by the end of the day Dino had literally transformed me from this long-kilted

HONEST

Catholic schoolgirl with her hair tied in a nice ponytail into this cool urban-hood white chick.

On my first day at Haverstock school I was wearing a pink leather jacket, white hoodie, three-quarter-length jeans, a pair of fresh Nike TN trainers, and I had my hair tied to the side in a plait. I loved it. At break time I hung out with my cousin and his mates and everything seemed to fall into place. Everyone seemed to love Dino at Haverstock, and that was hopefully going to rub off on me too. The girls especially loved him. In fact, all the things girls love about Dino nowadays were already there when he was thirteen years old: his cheeky character, his loveable roguishness, his confidence, and one other thing . . . a dick like King Kong's!

It seems to be a well-documented fact these days, but I first learned about it one day in the playground when some girls came running over to me, giggling.

'Oh my God, your cousin got his willy out earlier and it's massive!'

'Err . . . come on, girls, I don't really want to know this!'

They all did, though. Dino was already sexually active at that age. A lot of the kids at Haverstock were by the time they were twelve or thirteen years old. I was actually one of the few girls in my group who wasn't having sex. Even though I was only fourteen when I lost my virginity, pretty much everyone I knew had already lost theirs a year or so before. This wouldn't really have seemed normal to me before I went to Haverstock, but it was certainly the norm once I was there. I'd suddenly gone from a strict Catholic school where everyone did as they were told, to a place where mayhem ruled. Nobody listened to a word the teachers said, no one did any work, there were police cars outside the school every other day, there were kids puffing weed all over the school grounds. It was more like some sort of crazy play centre than it was a school.

Although it was a bit of a shock, I revelled in it. Aside from having no friends at my old school, I'd been trapped in a house with my poor mum and her illness, sucking up all that bad energy like a sponge, and living day after day with Mum's mood swings and depression, and then suddenly . . . WOW! What was this new world? Well, this new world was going to take me away from everything I'd known before, that was for sure – and from then on I just didn't want to be at home.

Two days into my time at Haverstock I told Mum that I wanted to go and play on the Maitland Park Estate, down the road in Chalk Farm, with some of my new friends.

'I'm older now, Mum, I'm not a little kid anymore. Everyone at my new school hangs out together. You can't stop me from playing out anymore.'

Mum agreed, as long as I was home by a certain time, and then I was off. My whole life changed overnight. I was out and about on the street with my new friends, boys chatting me up, girls wanting to be my mate. I was running around after school every night having fun, getting up to mischief and feeling free for the very first time. Those first nine months after I started at Haverstock were the best of my entire school life.

Chapter Five

After my success in *Bugsy Malone* at primary school, I was determined that I would become a recording artist. At the time I really admired Aaliyah. Her song 'One in a Million' made a huge impression on me, and I loved the old-school R&B that all my mates' older sisters were listening to. I started singing in the school playground at break time, with all my friends crowding around me and shouting out requests. And even when I was out and about on the streets I'd be singing for anyone who cared to listen.

Before I did *Bugsy Malone* I was constantly trying to impress my Uncle B and convince him that I was a great singer, but he never really took me seriously. After all, I was just a kid, and as he said to me time and time again: 'Everyone thinks they're a singer, T!'

But after he'd seen me in the show, he came away with a whole new attitude.

'The way you strutted your stuff and owned that stage as Tallulah was amazing,' he said. 'I could see your confidence and hear how good your voice was. I totally see it now.'

It made me very happy, and a few weeks after I'd joined Haverstock I was put to the test.

Dino looked all set to become a footballer. He was a wicked player, and that's what he had his heart set on. Once he started hanging with the wrong crowd, however, bunking off school, smoking weed and generally getting into trouble, football sort of fell by the wayside. He then turned his attention to MC-ing and rapping, and his love of music took over. At thirteen, he started getting together with his best mate from school, Richard, and writing lyrics. Richard was already a great little DJ with his own decks, and he also had a talent for rapping – or 'spitting lyrics', as we call it. The two of them would 'clash' with one another, competing to come up with the best lyrics over old-school garage tunes. Then they started making mix tapes of their ideas and went out and clashed with other MCs in the area for fun. Eventually, Dino (who was now known as Dapper D, or Dappy, because of his sharp clothes) approached his dad – my Uncle B – to help them record some tracks in the studio. And that was when the band that would eventually become N-Dubz was born.

Once they got into the studio, my dad and Uncle B showed Dappy and Richard how to make beats and come up with melodies using a keyboard. Using a music software called Fruity Loops, Dad showed his nephew how to create a kick-drum sound and then build it into a beat, which he could then start layering up a musical track over. Step by step, the two boys learned how to produce music, using their instinct and raw talent to create something that would eventually become a full track, which they could then add their lyrics to. Once they had it all down there was only one more thing they needed: a female singer.

I wasn't the obvious choice, however. The boys knew a girl at school called Rachel who could sing and they arranged for her to come down and help them record a chorus. Rachel was in the year above me, and she was known for being a pretty good singer, but on the day of the recording session she failed to show up at the studio.

HONEST

When Dappy tried to phone her, she'd switched off her mobile. And so, aged thirteen, the boys had their first major studio crisis, with a great debut track but no vocalist to sing on the chorus.

So I got a call on my mobile from Dappy.

'T! Can you come down to the studio and sing on our record?'

I didn't have to think for long.

'No,' I said. 'I want to be a solo artist. I'm not really into the idea of getting into a group.'

Dappy was undeterred, and went on and on trying to convince me to get down to the studio and sing for them.

'Sorry, I'm not up for it,' I said snootily.

I wanted to sing on my own and I had no interest in sharing the limelight with my cousin and his mate. It's quite funny to think that I was still only eleven years old.

Before I knew it, my Uncle B was on the doorstep, trying to get me to change my mind.

'Come on, T, just come down to the studio and do a bit of singing, man.'

'Nah! I don't fancy it, Uncle B,' I said. 'I'm aiming to be a solo artist.'

'Come on, T, give it a go.'

'No, sorry.'

Uncle B took a twenty-pound note out of his pocket and held it up to me. I stared at it for a moment.

'Nah, I'm not havin' it,' I said.

So he then pulled out a fifty-pound note – a pinky – and I said, 'Cool! Done deal! When do I start?'

'Right now,' Uncle B said, laughing, and off we went for my first proper recording session.

Uncle B always joked that the only time he ever saw me get excited was when money came up in the conversation.

Even when N-Dubz started to become successful I remained unfazed, in true Wednesday Addams style. Uncle B used to act out a brilliant little sketch where he played both him and me. It went something like this:

'Hey, T, we're number one on the Kiss 100 playlist.'

'OK.'

'Hey, T, we're the number one video on Channel U.'

'Yeah, yeah.'

'Hey, T, we've got a meeting with a major record label.'

'Cool, whatever.'

'Hey, T, I've just put a grand in your bank account.'

'WOOOOOOOOOOOOOOOOOOOOOOOOO!'

I felt comfortable as soon as I arrived at the studio that first day, and not in the least bit pressured. After all, it was just my family, and by that time I already knew Richard pretty well too. We got straight in there and started working up some ideas together, and then I went in and put the chorus down. The song was called 'What Is This World Coming To', and as soon as the song was mixed and played back to us, we truly believed that we were going to be huge pop stars . . . Well, ghetto stars!

Although my singing wasn't too bad for an eleven-year-old, looking back, I sounded extremely young and quite nasal. I expect if people heard the track now they'd crack up laughing, but at the time it sounded like a proper song to me, and that was all I cared about. I was an eleven-year-old schoolgirl with my own song recorded – no matter how primitive it was.

I loved the experience of the studio, and so once I had the bit between my teeth, there was no stopping me. I was committed to and completely consumed with the idea of recording more and more tracks and getting better and better at singing. In fact, there was no stopping any of us.

HONEST

Even Uncle B was totally into the idea of making us stars, and he was genuinely over the moon about the songs we were coming up with. It became our collective obsession, and we had a plan: to make lots more tracks, then to have Uncle B shop them around the record companies, and then eventually to get a record deal. Dappy asked me to think of a name for our brand-new band, but my ideas were all pretty cheesy – The BOOM Crew being one example. In the end Dappy came up with The Lickle Rinsers because we were only little but we still 'rinsed the mic'. That was it, we were up and running.

Chapter Six

It was around this time that I met two of my closest school friends, both through Dappy. The first was Mercedes, who was going out with Dappy when I started at Haverstock. I first met Mercedes in McDonald's – that first day I bunked off school to hang out with Dappy – and she was very quiet, almost intimidating, at first glance. Mercedes has always been fairly reserved, to be honest, and she doesn't trust people easily, even now. Back then she had her own small group of mates and never seemed to run with the crowd. After a while, though, we really hit it off and, despite a few bumps in the road, we're still friends to this day.

After Mercedes and Dappy broke up there was another girl who had a crush on my popular cousin, Javina, and we also became close friends. Javina wasn't in with the popular crowd either. She knew everyone well enough, but she liked to keep herself to herself and had her own little clique away from everyone else. I first bumped into her in a PE lesson, and although she was in the year above me, we seemed to get on really well very quickly. You know what it's like when you're a kid: one minute you've only just met someone, and the next minute you're inseparable best friends. Well, that's what it was like with Javina and me, and pretty soon I was hanging out at her place all the time.

One weekend, when I was at Javina's, we discovered her older brother, who was fifteen, drinking alcohol with some of his friends in the living room while their mum was at work. It wasn't uncommon for kids at our school of his age to be drinking or smoking weed, but *I'd* certainly never tried alcohol before, and I'm pretty sure Javina hadn't either. We were intrigued.

'Do you want a drink?' her brother asked us. 'I'll let you have a little bit.'

'All right,' I said, 'I'll give it a whirl.'

This was at two o'clock in the afternoon, mind you. So Javina's brother poured us a small glass of red wine each. Now, for a twelve-year-old who's never tried alcohol before it doesn't take much wine to have an effect, but I decided to be cocky and necked the whole glass in a couple of gulps. It didn't taste great, to be honest, but I drank it so fast I barely noticed.

'Do you want a bit more?' he said.

'Yeah, I'll have a bit more,' I smiled, thinking I was dead cool. 'It's all right.'

Down went another little glass. After a while, Javina and I decided that it was time for a little walk around the estate, just to see who was out and about. That's pretty much all we did when we went out: we just hung out on the street with other kids. There really was nothing else to do. Anyway, I felt perfectly normal at that point, but as soon as we stepped outside the front door we were suddenly both completely off our faces, and laughing hysterically. Two twelve-year-olds.

'This is wicked, what is this buzz?' Javina shrieked.

'This is amazing!' I agreed.

I felt like I'd suddenly woken up at the age of twelve. Not only was I popular and cool and out on the streets, but now I was drunk as well. As crazy and out of control as it seems looking back on this as an adult, at the time it was an amazing feeling, and I had no concept of how dangerous the situation was. In fact, Javina and I enjoyed the feeling of being drunk so much that by the time we'd sobered up, we wanted to do it all again. We headed straight for the corner shop and then waited outside for someone over the age of eighteen to come along, someone who might buy us some alcohol if we bribed them with a fiver. We didn't have to wait long, and shortly afterwards we were the proud owners of a quarter bottle of vodka.

Once we were back at Javina's we started on the vodka shots, and pretty soon we were completely out of it again. This went on for the whole weekend, on and off. I called my mum and told her I was staying over at my new friend's house, and with Javina's mum working nights – leaving us in the care of Javina's older brothers and sisters and completely oblivious to what was going on – there was no stopping us. Neither of our poor mothers had a clue what their twelve-year-old daughters were up to. And at one point, things did get quite dangerous.

By the Sunday evening it was pretty obvious to me that one of the boys had a bit of a thing for me, and he wasn't making much of a secret of it. To be honest, it wasn't unheard of for an older boy to be going out with a younger girl, as the girls tended to mature a lot faster than the boys, but the fact remained that I was twelve and he was fifteen. At that point we'd run out of alcohol, but Javina's brother and his mates pitched up with a fresh supply and asked Javina and me if we wanted another drink.

'Yeah, come on then.'

This time it was Jamaican rum, which we poured into a large mug.

'Drink it slowly,' Javina's brother advised, but I was a cocky bitch.

'Fuck that!'

I downed the entire mug of rum, no mixer, in one go, and within seconds I was dizzy, disorientated and paralytic.

The next thing I remember was being on Javina's bed, only semi-conscious, not able to focus and feeling dreadful. I could vaguely hear, but my vision was blurred and I certainly couldn't move. Suddenly I was aware of somebody speaking to me and I realised that it was one of the boys.

'Sober up,' he was saying, but at the same time he was sliding his hands up under my top and then down into my pants, touching me everywhere. I was paralysed.

'Sober up,' he said again, 'or I'm going to do something you don't want me to.'

Before I knew it he was climbing on top of me, and I suddenly realised that this boy was about to try to have sex with me, yet I was still unable to move or speak. As he got closer to me, though, I suddenly puked all over him . . . and that was what saved me. Within seconds I was being violently sick everywhere and the danger had passed, but the fact was that my first time getting drunk had almost cost me my virginity – aged twelve. It was stupidity on my part, of course, but I try not to look back on that kind of event with regret. Being faced with that type of situation helped make me the person I am now, and even though it wasn't very nice, it was just one more thing that helped to teach me what I needed to know about life. Maybe if I'd had a bit more guidance and discipline from my parents, it wouldn't have happened in the first place.

———————

HONEST

During those first idyllic months at Haverstock I met my
first proper boyfriend, who was in the year above me. His
name was Carlos and he was a good-looking thirteen-
year-old Lebanese boy who was popular at school and
had a very similar style to Dappy – in fact, they were
often compared. It was a sweet relationship and I have
lots of lovely memories of it, because although all the
other couples around us were already having sex, Carlos
and I were just dating: kissing, cuddling and holding
hands. We discussed the issue of sex and whether we
were ready to take that step, but in the end, although
Carlos wasn't a virgin, we decided it was too soon. I just
wasn't ready, and he was a sweetheart about it. My mum
liked and trusted Carlos too, and she allowed me to stay
over at his house sometimes. I think she could see
happiness in me that she hadn't seen before, and in turn
that made her happy.

I was still drinking alcohol with my mates every
weekend, and although at the time I thought I was very
mature, most weekends we would get completely smashed
and just keep drinking until we threw up. I wasn't smoking
spliff then, but everyone else around me was. It was just
the norm round where I lived, although I can see now that
we were far too young for it all. Still, life was good as far
as I was concerned, and I was more than content with my
new-found freedom, my boyfriend, my mates and of
course being part of The Lickle Rinsers. All of this seemed
much more important than learning at the time, and my
previously good academic record suddenly took a fast
nosedive.

Just around the corner, though, there was a whole new
set of problems headed my way, and they were pretty
nasty ones at that. You had to be very careful what you

said to people at Haverstock, not to mention who you said it to, and one day I made the fatal mistake of chitchatting about someone else's business – and I paid dearly for it.

Chapter Seven

It all started when I got into an argument with a girl called Lori, who wasn't even all that tough. In fact, she was quite a sweet, pretty girl whom I'd previously been friendly with. I'd heard that she'd been badmouthing me to some other kids, so I warned her to shut up or she'd be sorry. I was just letting off steam, but what I didn't know was that Lori was already being bullied by a few of the other girls, and it turned out that my tirade was the straw that broke the camel's back, and she snapped. My dad had always drummed into me that if someone hit me then I should hit them back, only harder, but this girl caught me completely off-guard, running up to me in the playground and punching me in the mouth wearing a sovereign ring. Suddenly the scene erupted into a full-on playground fight witnessed by half the school, and although I gave as good as I got and matched her punch for punch, I came out of it with a bloodied mouth and so she was proclaimed the winner, despite the fact that I was still standing. Not good. From then on I was branded a 'pussy' and once the harder kids at Haverstock sensed weakness, I was fair game for all of them and they were on me like vultures. A few weeks after that there was another violent incident, and that was when things took a real turn for the worse.

Dappy had confided in me that he'd had sex with a girl at school called Michelle – not much of a revelation really – but the girl in question was a bit of a hard nut and most people were terrified of her. She was known for being violent – in fact, the general rule was that if you pissed her off, she took you down, and that was that. Luckily – I suppose because she fancied my cousin – I got on fine with her, that is, until I foolishly decided to gossip about her and her sexual encounter with Dappy. Then all hell broke loose.

I was out and about with Javina one afternoon, when suddenly Michelle and some of her mates caught me completely unawares. We were just walking out of a corner shop and suddenly there she was with three of her cronies, shouting her mouth off.

'Have you been saying that I shagged Dappy?'

Well, the truth was she'd done exactly that, but I was far too intimidated to remind her of that, what with her and her mates bearing down on me, so I said nothing and just backed down. This was a big mistake, of course, because as soon as a bully smells fear, they know they've won. If I had answered her back she might have left me alone, but as it was, all four girls suddenly and violently attacked me, and there wasn't a thing I could do about it.

All the while I was being punched and kicked on the pavement I could hear them saying things like 'get a bottle' and 'do her over the head'.

It was terrifying, lying on the floor, not knowing what may or may not be about to happen, and I basically got the shit kicked out of me. Eventually, Javina, who was a lot harder than I was, managed to stop the beating, but still I ended up bruised and battered, with black eyes and footprints across my face and head.

Not only was this incident bad for my health and absolutely petrifying, it was also the final nail in the coffin as far as my 'hard girl' rep at Haverstock went. It was bad enough that a couple of weeks before I'd been 'done over' by a girl who wasn't even seen as tough, but now this.

I felt too enraged, not to mention embarrassed, to even show my face at school; I just didn't feel like I could go back there and face people, such was my shame and fear. Javina laid it on the line for me after I was attacked in the street by Michelle and her mates.

'You've got to stand up for yourself, T!' she said angrily. 'You've got to go and confront her. If you don't, you're going to end up being beaten up every day by someone or other.'

I knew she was right. That was how it worked at Haverstock and on the streets around those estates – but what could I do? As far as everyone else was concerned, I was becoming a bigger pussy by the day, and I felt like it was completely out of my control. Javina had a plan, though.

'Come back to my place and we'll talk to my older sisters,' she suggested. 'We'll explain the situation to them and see what they come up with.'

Javina's older sisters were even tougher than she was and, unsurprisingly, one of them advised me to go straight round to Michelle's house and confront her, or my life wasn't going to be worth living. It was quite a scary prospect. The last thing I wanted, after getting such a beating, was to throw myself into another violent situation, but at the same time, I didn't think I had much choice. Even if I never went back to school, I'd be sure to bump into Michelle or her mates around the estates. So the next day Javina, her sister and I brazenly knocked on the door of Michelle's house. When her mother opened the door, I asked to see Michelle, and when she finally appeared she was clearly quite shocked to see me standing there. I wasn't there to fight her, but I wanted to let her know that I was standing my ground.

'Why the fuck did you do that to me?' I said. 'This ain't on, I ain't having it!'

Amazingly, Michelle seemed to agree, and so right there and then we squashed it – putting an end to the feud – and I dearly hoped that was the end of it.

I still felt uneasy, though, and whenever I saw Michelle around the estate there was a distinctly bad vibe between us. When I heard rumours that she was threatening to attack me again as soon as she got the chance, I knew that I had to act fast, but this time I was going to have to make sure she got the message loud and clear. Before I knew it, all-out war was declared and, once again, Javina recruited her older sister and some of her friends to help us out. Meanwhile, Michelle got her older brother and his mates involved, so it was now becoming a gang fight involving older kids of eighteen and nineteen. It was a volatile situation, and once it started it just took on a life of its own and there was no way to back out, as much as I'd have liked to. Eventually, a time was set for a rematch between Michelle's gang and mine, round the back of the Maitland Park estate, but still the whole thing just kept escalating, as we made phone calls and they made phone calls, both groups rounding up more and more people for the upcoming showdown.

My dad had a friend who worked with him at the studio. He was an older guy, but he'd always been cool with me and told me that if I was ever in trouble to give him a shout. A day before the fight I decided that I needed all the help I could get, so I called Dad's mate and told him the whole story, asking him if he could round up some boys to come and add some extra muscle. Can you imagine? I was thirteen years old at the time – it's crazy when I think about it now.

The night before the planned bust-up, a group of us was getting prepared for battle at Javina's sister's house. We were arming ourselves with baseball bats, bandanas to cover our faces, the whole works, when suddenly there was a loud banging at the front door. It was Dad and Uncle B, and Dad literally stormed in and dragged me out of the house by my ear. Luckily, Dad's friend at the studio had ignored my call to arms and had had the sense to phone Dad and tell him everything, knowing the danger I might be in.

When we got outside, Uncle B was quite calm, but Dad was raging at me.

'You're getting me out of bed at three o'clock in the morning for this shit! Getting into fights and Christ knows what!'

'You told me to be tough, Dad,' I screamed back. 'These people beat me up and you told me that if someone hits you, you have to hit them back harder. What do you want me to do?'

Dad lifted his hand to hit me and I flinched, but Uncle B grabbed his arm in mid-air.

'Don't you dare!' Uncle B said, glaring at Dad.

And Dad lowered his arm. I'm not certain he would have smacked me, but I was certainly glad my uncle was there. I think he might have saved me from a good hiding that night.

———————

Although that particular gang fight had been squashed, things got much worse for me after that, just as I suspected they would. I still couldn't go back to school, but every time I turned a corner there would be another bunch of girls waiting to try their luck with me. If they couldn't find a valid reason to pick a fight with me, they'd simply make something up.

'I heard you shagged my man' was a common accusation – it was often about sex.

The irony was I was still a virgin at the time – I hadn't shagged any man! – but that was actually part of the problem. While a lot of these girls were sleeping with dudes who wanted sex with them and nothing more, I was the girl that guys would take on dates to the cinema, and I guess that was what the other girls hated.

The fact that I was thought of as pretty – or fit – by the boys, the fact that I was a singer in a band, and the fact that I had a reputation for being a pushover, all added to my unpopularity with the girls around the estates – and the word spread like wildfire. Even girls I didn't know were giving me grief. As far as they were concerned, Tulisa was a slag to be bitched about and beaten up at every opportunity. My life went back to being miserable again overnight. Haverstock School clearly wasn't the dream world I'd hoped it would be, and so I decided that I wasn't going back, no matter what my parents said.

When I think about it now, I still don't regret leaving La Sainte Union and going to Haverstock. Yes, at the time I felt like I was going through hell, but if I hadn't gone through that I don't think I'd have ended up where I am today. I believe that things happen for a reason, and all the crap that I went through ultimately gave me strength and made me strive even harder to achieve my ambitions. I'm certain that I wouldn't be the person I am now if I hadn't had that experience.

HONEST

Once I'd stopped going to school, though, things ended up going from bad to worse. Even Mercedes, who had been one of my best mates, suddenly turned on me, believing a rumour that I was badmouthing her to other people. As if! I needed all the friends I could get, but that didn't matter. Now Mercedes, who lived very close to me on the next street, was baying for my blood as well. I couldn't even visit my boyfriend Carlos because I was too terrified to walk past Maitland Park, and when I went to see Javina in Kentish Town I took all the back roads I could, just to avoid any of the local kids. Sometimes I was too scared to even do that, so Javina's mum would come and pick me up. One night when I was ducking and diving through Euston, some girls who weren't from the area randomly attacked me – probably friends of friends of someone who hated me – and I ended up having a bottle smashed over my head. All I can say is, I must have a really hard head, because although the bottle shattered, my head wasn't cut in the slightest. I was, however, knocked senseless on the floor for a few minutes, and not surprisingly, I ended up with a massive lump on my head. From then on I started carrying a piece of wooden curtain rail with me when I was out. I know it's hard to believe, a girl of barely fourteen walking around with a weapon, but that was how scary the world I was living in had become. It was a world fuelled by alcohol, drugs, sex and violence – a dangerous urban youth culture – and I seemed to be so far into it that I couldn't get back out again. Some of you might have seen the movie *Kidulthood* – well, that's got nothing on the real deal.

The only place I felt safe was at home with my mum, and that had been the very place that I'd been trying to run away from. Now it was my only refuge, and I started to sink into a very deep depression.

Chapter Eight

Although I refused to go back to Haverstock, I couldn't get into any of the schools I did want to go to either. Eventually, I'd been absent for so long that the authorities suggested that I get some temporary home schooling, but that never really panned out. I just wasn't bothered about school, so for a year or so I simply didn't go at all.

Spending more and more time alone at home, I started to ask questions of myself. It seemed to me that my whole life had been completely abnormal: from my mum's illness and my parents' bad marriage, to school and beyond. Apart from a relatively short blast of contentment when I first went to Dappy's school, I realised that I had never been happy and that nothing had ever gone my way for very long. To make matters worse, that little bit of happiness I'd felt at the start of Haverstock now just seemed to highlight how crap the rest of it all was. And, not being able to see any light at the end of the tunnel, I went into a downward spiral, fast. I seemed to have so much going on inside me, but nobody to talk to about it. And eventually, when Carlos broke up with me because we weren't seeing enough of one another, I was left completely devastated. That was my first taste of rejection by a boy, and it ended up having a huge effect on the way I lived my life.

Although I knew I was safe when I was at home, I didn't feel like I could confide in my mum about all my troubles out on the street, so she had no idea what was going on. I knew that she was fragile and she wouldn't have been able to cope with the thought of me being attacked. So every time I came home with cuts and bruises which couldn't be covered up, I simply told her that I'd got into a scrap while I was out, and that was all there was to it. Yes, she would get upset about it, but I wouldn't have let her get involved even if she'd wanted to. With my dad, it was a lot easier to hide the truth. I only really saw him when I wanted to, and on the rare occasion when he did catch me with a battle scar, my story was the same: I just got into a fight, that's all.

'Yeah, as long as you smacked 'em back,' my dad would say.

That was his main concern: that I'd fought back. I'd never have told my dad that someone had beaten the shit out of me. No way! I didn't want either of them to know. There was always the chance that they might get the police involved if they thought I was in real danger, and I certainly didn't need that. That wasn't what street reputation was about, and I would have been labelled a snitch. It's hard to imagine for some people, I suppose, but they were the only rules I had to live by: the rules of the street.

Dappy and Richard knew what was going on, though, and they were very protective of me. There were a few times when I turned up at the studio looking like I'd been in a boxing match, and both of the boys were enraged. Dappy would sometimes confront various girls that had it in for me, and even Richard would drum up help and support from his older female cousin, who was a hard girl who nobody messed with.

Eventually, Dappy and Richard actually started training

me up, and we'd have sparring matches. They tried to
toughen me up by fighting with me, and they didn't pull
any punches either. Dappy and I would have full-on fights,
punching the shit out of one another, just to make me
stronger. I came away with black eyes and busted lips
courtesy of Dappy and Richard, but at the same time they
taught me to fight like a man, which is what I needed. It
got to the stage when I'd be sparring with all Dappy's
mates, one by one, and although I'd often end up on the
floor, I could give as good as I got if it was a fair match,
one on one. It was the only choice I had at the time. I
didn't feel like I could go running to my parents because
that would have made me look weak. It was ingrained in
me that I had to be tough to survive, because that was
the environment I was living in. Even if I had gone running
to my dad, he would have just told me to fight back and
hit them harder than they hit me.

The only good thing I had back then was Lickle Rinsers
and making music – it was the one bright spot in my life,
and when I was with the boys I felt like I was part of a
team. By that time Uncle B was fully managing us as a
band, and he was actively going out and getting us gigs
and spots on local pirate radio stations. On the radio
shows, we would be invited to clash with other crews and
urban acts. The boys would spit their lyrics and I would
sing choruses and sometimes MC a little bit myself. A
clash was like a battle between two different urban crews
to find out who could come up with the best rhymes and
songs. It was all quite aggressive, with each crew cussing
and badmouthing the other. The DJ would put on
instrumental tracks and we would 'ride' them, which meant
we would rap and sing across the tracks. It was a really
vibrant underground scene, and that was what we were all

into – we wanted to be successful at making great urban music.

The gigs we played were often underage raves and grotty garage clubs, but the first shows we did were for a Metropolitan Police Crimestoppers tour for under-eighteens. The first time I performed on stage was in a school hall which had been converted into a teenage rave, and I was really nervous – we all were. There was another more established garage act on the bill, so we were only supporting, but we actually went down really well. We performed a song called 'Bad Man Riddim' among others, and the young kids watching us seemed to really like us. The more gigs we did, the more the kids got to know the songs, and eventually we noticed the audience singing along to our lyrics – I can remember clearly how good that felt.

Uncle B always used to make me channel all my anger into writing songs, and he often didn't have time for my sob stories about bullying, however real and scary they were for me.

'You think you're so hard done by,' he'd shout at me. 'There's people dying in this world. You need to stop moaning and get off your arse and do something.'

I wasn't all that keen on his tough love back then – in fact, at times I hated the way he was so hard on me. Looking back, though, I suppose Uncle B didn't really know all of the facts about how bad things had become for me on the streets. I tried to hide it all from the adults around me. Even when I went to stay with my dad, I kept all my anger and fear inside as much as I could. I felt like it was something I had to deal with on my own.

Once, when I was upset and complaining about Mum being ill yet again, Uncle B had a proper go at me at the studio.

HONEST

'All this shit that's doing your nut in at home – why are you bringing it to the studio to do *our* nuts in?'

Looking back, I now know that B was simply trying to get me to fight back rather than give in, just like my dad was, but in a more constructive way. B wanted me to make something of myself rather than give in to self-pity, and I guess that was his way of getting me to knuckle down in the studio and forget my problems while I was there.

Unfortunately, Dappy, Richard and Uncle B weren't around all the time, and as soon as I was on my own and out of the studio environment I was depressed and vulnerable all over again.

Some nights I would sit in my bedroom at home, crying my eyes out and praying. I even made regular pacts with God, telling Him that I didn't care how many times I got beaten up, how many times my heart got broken, or how depressed I got, as long as I could have music in my life and make a success of it. Just give me music! If I could just have that, I could cope with anything. One night, in despair after breaking up with Carlos, I even started banging my head against my bedroom wall through the tears, promising God that I would trade in love and happiness for a successful music career. When I look back now, I sometimes think He must have heard me, because my music career really has been plain sailing in comparison to my personal life, which has always been full-on drama. Everyone who's close to me can see it too, and they're all a bit confused by it. They don't understand how somebody can be enjoying such success while still living life as if they're in an episode of *Eastenders*. I sometimes think I might have made a pact with the devil by mistake – I'm not sure God goes in for making pacts.

My frustration and depression at that point in my life led to the formation of some strange and damaging habits that stretched right into my adult life. At one point Mum was going through one of those phases where she was particularly anxious, and every time I turned around, there she was right behind me, whatever I was doing. It was bad enough feeling trapped and isolated at home anyway, but having my mum constantly fretting and fussing around me wherever I went was making me as anxious as she was. These are the times I would lock myself away in the bathroom, just to get away from her. On one occasion, when Mum was having a particularly bad day, I shut myself in the bathroom and began scratching and picking at a tiny little spot on my chin. It was a strange feeling, and hard to describe, but concentrating on getting at this little spot seemed to distract me from the situation at hand. So after I'd picked away at that spot for a while, I found another spot, then a small blackhead, and then a tiny mark that wasn't even a spot, and after an hour I felt extremely relaxed. The only thing was, I'd picked and squeezed non-existent spots all over my face until it looked like I had really bad acne.

This became a regular thing. Picking at my face was my way of zoning out, I guess, and sometimes I would go into the bathroom and just pick at my skin for hours, not realising that I'd developed an anxiety disorder of my own: dermatillomania. As far as I was concerned, it was just something I did to get away from my mum, but it got so bad that eventually I was tearing into my face with nail clippers and tweezers, just to get at any minute blemish or invisible little bump under my skin. At times I caused absolute catastrophe on my face, leaving gaping, weeping holes that must have looked horrendous. I was extremely lucky that my skin always healed quickly and without too much scarring.

I did this almost every day for years, and it's only three years ago that I started getting my dermatillomania under control. Even when I was having success with N-Dubz, I would have spells of picking and digging at my face when I felt under pressure or anxious. If ever I went to stay with my mum for a few days, for instance, I'd always find myself picking at my skin again, and there was nothing I could do to stop it. The last time it happened severely was while I was filming a documentary called *My Mum and Me* in 2010. The documentary was about young people who had parents with severe depression and bipolar or schizophrenic disorders, and specifically about my relationship with my mum. All throughout the weeks of filming, I went back to picking at my face again, and I'd often be late for the filming because I'd spent two hours in the bathroom by myself and hadn't realised what the time was. At the time people thought I was being difficult and stroppy – turning up late for work or sometimes missing it altogether – but the anxiety of reliving all that stuff with my mum had sent me back to my old tried and trusted habit. I wasn't a troubled teenager anymore, though; I was a successful recording artist, which made what was happening even harder to accept. I became very distressed and I Googled the condition, sending links to my management and the people I was working with, just to prove to them that I wasn't making it all up and shirking my responsibilities.

'This is what's wrong with me,' I told them. 'It's a recognised condition.'

But nobody had ever heard of it, and even once they had, they struggled to understand it. And what's worse, I hated myself for letting it happen. It got so bad one day that my personal assistant Gareth found me sitting on the floor, rocking back and forth, in tears. Why was I hurting myself like this?

'I hate myself for being weak,' I told him. 'I need to go and see someone about this. I want to try a session with a hypnotist.'

The strange thing was, after seeing the hypnotist, I went home and tore my face up worse than I ever had before, but once it had healed, I finally managed to get it under control. Let's hope it stays that way.

Back when I was fourteen, however, this routine destruction of my face wasn't enough for me, and I took to harming myself in other ways. One day, through a friend, I met a girl who had bandaged wrists, and I found myself intrigued and itching to know why. It turned out that the girl had tried to slit her wrists. I didn't know exactly why, but it sent my mind racing. I couldn't stop thinking about her. I'd never had any thoughts of suicide or hurting myself before, however bad things had got for me, but for some reason, after meeting this girl and talking to her about how she cut herself because she was depressed, the possibility suddenly occurred to me. How would it make me feel? Would it make me feel any better? Would it change anything? I certainly didn't want to commit suicide, but I was intrigued nonetheless – that was how dark my world was back then.

When I first cut my arm with the scissors, there was a part of me that enjoyed it. That small line of blood across my arm and the sharp pain felt sort of good. Looking back, I can see how badly I craved some kind of attention, but back then I felt like I was trapped in my own head, screaming, and when I cut myself it was a way of conveying that anger. At least I'm feeling something, I told myself, and it feels real.

'Yes, I am screwed up, and this is my way of expressing it.'

This too became a regular thing with me. I harmed myself with knives, or scissors, or anything sharp I could get my hands on, to the point where Javina and some of my other friends would notice the damage and comment. I kept it hidden from Mum, though, covering my arms with long tops and jumpers. I never wanted her to know.

The self-harming went on until I was around sixteen or seventeen, and unlike the face picking, which was subconscious and almost involuntary, cutting myself was very deliberate. I knew exactly what I was doing. On one occasion, when I was sixteen, I took things to a whole new level while I was house-sitting for my dad, who was away on holiday. Instead of cutting my arm in an ordered line, as usual, I started slashing madly at my wrists with sharp scissors, causing the blood to pour rather than seep. I didn't want to kill myself, but I also wasn't scared of dying if that's what ended up happening. All I remember thinking at the time was that I was so unhappy and so far down a dark hole that I needed to hurt myself badly, to go further than I'd ever gone before. I wanted to see what would happen if I let myself go completely.

Within minutes of starting this, my arms were covered in blood, and I think I must have suddenly come to my senses because I started to feel very freaked out and afraid. Suddenly the possibility that I might die did feel scary. I thought I was going to bleed to death, so I grabbed a towel and held it over my wrists until the bleeding stopped. I thought about calling one of my friends I was so scared of what I'd done, but I couldn't face a big scene, so I just sat on my own in the bathroom until I was OK again. It disturbs me very much when I think about it now. Did I want to kill myself that day? Was I that far gone? It was like a madness coming over me, and I was too scared to talk to anyone about it, especially my dad. I thought that he would assume I was mentally ill like my mum. I was certain that he'd freak out and have me sectioned if he found out about me cutting myself. Once again, I kept it all in.

It's a really sad thing to say, but when I think back on those teenage years, the only times I ever felt happy were when I was either in love or being loved. Despite promising God that I would be content without love if I became a successful singer, I was desperate for people to love me, especially men. This longing for love and recognition had started when I was as young as eleven, but it just grew and grew as I got older. In fact, as well as all the violence I'd suffered on the streets and the craziness I was facing at home, some of the relationships I got into also led me to self-harm during that period of my life, especially if I felt rejected. Nowadays I'm so much more in control of my emotions and the way I deal with guys and relationships, but back then I was naive and desperate to feel wanted, so I made some truly terrible mistakes as far as men were concerned.

Chapter Nine

When I broke up with Carlos, the first guy to grab my attention was my Lickle Rinsers bandmate Richard, who by now had adopted the street name that he's still known by today: Fazer. I don't know where the name came from, but it certainly suited him. Whenever the three of us were working in the studio he seemed to drift off into a world of his own – fazing out, we called it.

It had been obvious to me from day one that Fazer had a crush on me, but, as I said, I wasn't that interested at the time. Fazer had persevered though, and in a good way. He was a great friend to me, and he always treated me well and thought highly of me, despite the fact that I would never give in and go out with him back then. He still thought the world of me and wasn't afraid to show it.

Suddenly, when he was about fourteen, Fazer shot up in height and became more appealing almost overnight. His style changed too: he was no longer the little dude in the smelly green GAP jumper. Now he was wearing the coolest trainers and he would match his caps with his sharp outfits perfectly. He had a certain swagger about him, and suddenly girls started to notice him. *I* started to notice him.

When I heard that Fazer had a new girlfriend it didn't really bother me at first, but after a while it started to niggle at me more and more and I couldn't work out why. Was it jealousy? After all, up till then I'd always been the number one girl in Fazer's life, and I knew it. Even when he was hanging around with other girls, it was still pretty obvious that Fazer was obsessed with me. Ever since I was twelve, he'd been telling me that we were going to get married one day – he was like my little safety blanket. Now, suddenly, I started to feel like Fazer's obsession might be waning slightly and I didn't like it. Yep! I was jealous! Luckily for me, his new relationship didn't last too long, and as soon as Fazer broke up with his girlfriend, I got straight in there and we started seeing one another. I can remember our first kiss quite clearly because Fazer had been eating salt and vinegar crisps and that's all I could taste. Still, it obviously didn't put me off at the time.

At that time it was all quite innocent, and pretty casual too. I was still a virgin then, so Fazer and I would just hang out together, holding hands or kissing. At the same time, Dappy was going out with Javina, so the four of us would go round to Fazer's house for little double-dating sessions. We'd watch a film and drink alcohol, and it felt like a really safe and relaxed environment for me, which I know sounds crazy, bearing in mind how young I was, but at least I was away from the madness on the streets or the stress of home. I was still drinking pretty much every weekend then, but by now it was beginning to take its toll and make me feel ill. In fact, I'd been drunk so often since the age of twelve that sometimes I couldn't even smell booze without wanting to throw up. Eventually, Javina came up with a solution.

'I smoke weed,' she said. 'Why don't you give that a go if you don't like drinking?'

It was a way to get high without feeling sick, as far as I was concerned, and besides, Dappy, Fazer and Javina were all doing it, so why not me? I loved the buzz right away.

HONEST

The trouble is, after a while I was ready to start drinking again as well, and so the two ended up going hand in hand. It could get quite messy at times.

Back then Fazer had bunk beds in his room and I remember the two of us would be on the top bunk while Dappy and Javina took the bottom one. We just smooched for hours, like high school kids do, and we became quite the cute little foursome. I remember having so much fun on those date nights. They were good times, but it didn't last forever. Over the next few years Fazer and I would casually see one another, on and off and then on again. We'd date other people in between and then we'd hook up together again for a while, and all through it the band kept going. Sometimes when he didn't have a girlfriend, I was with another guy, and sometimes when I wasn't dating, Fazer had a girlfriend. So it was always there and not there – that was the way it was with us for years.

I can still count on my fingers and toes the number of guys I've slept with in my life, but a good percentage of those encounters happened between the ages of fourteen and seventeen, and that felt like a lot, even at the time. Now I really regret losing my innocence at such a young age. Despite my street-girl persona, I was totally into the idea of fairy-tale romance: that's what I thought I was looking for in a man. I wore my heart on my sleeve and I was ready to give my all if I thought I was going to get love in return. Of course, it wasn't the right way to go about things, because any attention and affection I got from those men was usually only temporary, but it took me a while to learn that lesson. Maybe I was searching for something I felt was missing from my childhood. Maybe I wanted to find the security I never got from my parents. I don't know, but my overwhelming craving to be loved led me into some very bad relationships.

'You're so beautiful – I'll take care of you.'

'I can't believe the way you've been hurt, I'd never do that to you.'

I was a sucker for lines like these from guys, and I heard them – or something like them – time and time again, often just before the guy in question tried to get me into bed. What's worse is, I bloody believed them, no matter how many times they turned out to be lies, probably because I wanted to. I hoped that if I slept with a guy he would look after me and make me feel loved, and I wanted to be looked after and loved more than anything. This foolish thinking on my part led me to sleep with too many guys, too soon, and it became a pattern I repeated over and over: a guy would promise to look after me, I'd sleep with him, and then he'd leave me. And when it was all over I would be all the more desperate for it not to happen the next time. By the time I was seventeen, I had gone through this so many times and dated so many wankers that I was starting to get the measure of it, but by that time the damage was done.

It all started when I was fourteen and I began dating a good-looking seventeen-year-old from around the area where I lived. As I said, I'd progressed from drinking alcohol to smoking weed by then, and Jono was the dealer who supplied me. All the girls fancied Jono. So much so that even if they could get their weed from someone else closer to hand, they would always call Jono because he was fit. Anyway, I started hanging out with him, sitting in his car, talking and sometimes kissing. In the end I became quite obsessed with him, although I wouldn't describe it as love. I was a little intimidated by Jono, because he was older than me, and he was sometimes very quiet around me, but I didn't let any of that stop me and pretty soon we were meeting up fairly regularly.

After about eight months of Jono regularly dealing to me and hanging with me on and off, one day he drove me to a little bed and breakfast hotel in Kentish Town, and before I knew it we were alone in a room. Lying down on the bed together, we started kissing, which was nothing I hadn't done before in his car, but then he started to take my clothes off as he kissed me. I didn't stop him; I don't think I would have known how to or what to say. I just went with it, knowing that I was about to lose my virginity, and knowing what a big deal that was. Jono didn't ask me if I was ready to take that step or if I was OK with what was happening, he just went ahead and undressed me and we had sex. Afterwards, I felt slightly numb, knowing that I'd just lost my virginity. Was that it?

All the time I was on and off with Fazer, he really wanted us to have sex, but he was a gentleman about it. He'd never have put me in that position, and now I'd given myself away to someone else. I very much regret this now, and I wish that Fazer had been my first, but it wasn't to be. A little while after I slept with Jono, I found out that he had a 'proper' girlfriend, so things went downhill pretty fast after that and we didn't see one another anymore.

Of course, once I'd lost my virginity, there was no getting it back, so at fourteen I saw no reason not to sleep with a guy if that's what he wanted to do. Most of the guys I dated after Jono were older than I was, so I often felt quite intimidated by them. This meant that if a guy jumped on top of me and started yanking my clothes off, I just didn't know how to say no. Why would I? I wasn't a virgin anymore, so they'd be expecting me to have sex with them, wouldn't they? I felt awkward and I was usually too afraid to stop it, even if I wanted to, so I just went along with it.

I don't know what was wrong with me, looking back: it's quite bizarre. Maybe I was just scared that if I didn't do what a man wanted, he might reject me, and there was nothing worse than that as far as I was concerned. Or maybe I was just too young to deal with what was happening to me. I certainly didn't have anyone to talk to about it. It wasn't something I felt I could share with my mum or my aunts, and because it was all happening while I was in-between schools, I had no teachers to advise me either. I think that because of all this I've actually become more prudish about sex as I've become older. I'll only sleep with someone who I'm in a relationship with now, or perhaps when a relationship is about to blossom. I'm just not interested in casual sex.

A little while after Jono, I started hanging out with one of Dappy's friends, Daniel, who was seventeen but quite mature, with a high-profile job for his age, in the entertainment industry. Daniel was gorgeous, and the girls all fell at his feet, but it was me that he seemed to take a shine to, and I liked him too. He became the second guy that I slept with, and right after I did, he did the dirty on me and disappeared. Yes, he pissed off after he got what he wanted. It wasn't until a year or so later, when I was fifteen, that we met up and started dating, and this time we fell into a full-on relationship. It was the first time I experienced real love for a man, but it was an obsessive love that turned sour quite quickly. It was the first and last time I let a man take me over completely. At the time I was content to let Daniel control me, which is exactly what he did.

Quite soon into my relationship with Daniel, I realised that he wasn't the easiest person to be with. He would get jealous and possessive to the point of violence, and it could happen at the drop of a hat. If I ever got a text or a phone call from a guy he didn't know, he'd freak out and accuse me of cheating on him without even giving me a chance to explain who it was that was texting. There were times when Daniel would lock me in his flat because he thought I might leave him if he let me out, and there were other times when he'd get so angry that I'd be the one locking myself in the toilet. I remember him standing outside the locked bathroom one day, banging on the door and telling me that if I didn't open the door he was going to break it down and kill me. Still I stayed with him. Like many abused women, I mistook his jealousy and possessiveness for love, and I felt that I was in love with him. I wanted so much for my relationship with Daniel to work that I was prepared to put up with things that I would never stand for today.

One night we were both sitting on the couch in the living room having a seemingly normal discussion about whether people are born with great singing voices or whether it is something you can learn. My opinion was that you either have it or you don't, and a great singer has a gift that they are born with. Daniel didn't agree, and after a while the debate got fairly heated – or overheated. In the end, he got so furious that he kicked me hard in my back, sending me flying off the couch and onto the floor.

At other times he would hold me around the throat, or slap my face, or just threaten to kill me, but I did nothing about it. For me, it was the closest thing I'd ever had to any sort of discipline, and that's something I thought I desperately needed. In my mind, any form of attention, whether it be violence or aggression or jealousy, meant that somebody cared about me. I suppose that's the case with a lot of women in abusive relationships, especially if they don't have very much self-worth. You end up taking whatever you can get, and when things get bad, you don't know how to stop it or how to walk away.

In the end, Daniel broke up with me to be with somebody else, and I was devastated. But a little while later, when it suited him, we got back together, and because I loved him – or thought I did – I let the same thing happen all over again. On the day he broke it off for the second time, he was especially cruel.

'You're scum, you're not even attractive.'

The things he said to me destroyed me. Only a week before he'd been telling me how much he loved me.

'You're mentally ill, just like your mother.'

While I was screaming and crying, Daniel took a call on his mobile phone and shoved me across the room.

'My girlfriend's on the phone,' he said coldly.

And he locked himself in his bedroom and started chatting away casually to his new girlfriend, leaving me virtually hysterical outside the bedroom door.

At this point something in me snapped, and I ran to the kitchen drawer and grabbed the first thing that came to hand, which was a hammer, of all things. I really have no idea what I intended to do with it, but it seemed like a good idea at the time. I started to bang the hammer on the wall in fury until Daniel came running out of the bedroom in a mad temper. He picked me up, literally lifting me off my feet, and then dropped me onto the floor, smashing my spine against the hard wood. Then, to finish the job, he slapped me in the face.

'You're nothing without me, and you never will be. You'll never amount to anything.'

These were the words ringing in my ears over the next few months after we broke up for the last time. I even started to believe Daniel when he told me I was ugly, such was the control he had over me.

Alone and back at my mum's house, I tore into the medicine cupboard and started to open various bottles of my mum's medication. I took a handful, not even knowing what they were, and washed them down with alcohol. I felt dizzy and sleepy almost straight away, but luckily for me, I also felt sick, and ended up throwing everything up. I don't think I even registered what I was doing at the time, I was in such a reckless and irresponsible state.

Over the years, of course, I've grown and changed so much as far as relationships go, and I guess that comes with maturity and confidence, but also from bitter experience. These days I'd never let a man treat me like Daniel did back then. In fact, I quite often notice that the guys I'm dating become more attached to me than I am to them, and I think that's because I find it hard to let my guard down and trust men in the way that I used to. There's always something inside me that stops me from falling fully head over heels. Sure, I can mirror a guy's emotion and enjoy being with him, but there's a constant invisible barrier that I find hard to cross. It's like I'm holding up a shield or wearing a protective suit all the time: I'm an armadillo!

It's still true that I am much happier when I am in a relationship and feel loved, so I do tend to jump from relationship to relationship. Now, though, I understand myself a lot more: I know why I do it and I also know how to survive when I *am* single. I can't imagine letting myself be controlled again in that way by a boyfriend, or anyone else for that matter, and there are plenty of guys who find that kind of strength attractive. In fact, if a relationship wasn't going well now, I'd be the first one to put an end to it, because I don't want to get my heart broken anymore. These days, I do the dumping.

Chapter Ten

When I was fifteen I fell in with a new crowd of girls around Camden who were more serious faces in the area. The girls were older than me by a year or two, and not exactly well behaved. I'd seen these girls around for a couple of years, but they weren't playing out, like a lot of the other kids: they were older, more 'gangsta' types who kept themselves to themselves – and most people in the area were afraid of them.

It all started when my old mate Mercedes called me up to patch up our troubles. We'd been close once, but she'd turned on me after believing some of the many terrible rumours about me that had been circulated a year or so earlier. Now she wanted to put the past behind us, and I was glad. The band was going great and I loved hanging out and making music with the boys, but up until then we hadn't had any success, and although I really believed that it was eventually going to happen, sometimes it seemed a million miles away. I'd missed having Mercedes around. She was such an independent spirit and I admired that about her.

'I'm sorry I did what I did,' Mercedes told me. 'I don't have any bad feeling towards you, why don't you come and see me?'

I was really happy to get this call. Mercedes had been a really good friend, and still is now. Anyway, during our time apart, Mercedes had started hanging around with the aforementioned gang of girls, and once she and I had got together and made our peace, Mercedes took me to meet them. This was the start of a whole new phase in my teenage life, and although I ended up going down a very bad path, hanging out with this tough crew did have its upsides.

For a start, I suddenly felt like I belonged again. I had a group of mates, and nobody would dare mess with me while I was with them. I felt safe and I liked the feeling of being with them. These girls were another level of bad, and even the way they looked was bloody intimidating. It was certainly enough to scare the shit out of most people.

Our uniform was matching black tracksuits, Avirex jackets and bandanas over our faces. We dressed, walked and talked like guys, and our whole demeanour was intended to intimidate. In fact, to this day, if I saw that group of seventeen-year-old girls coming towards me in the street, I'd think, Oh fuck, it's all about to kick off. We looked like a girl-gang, even though I thought of us as just a group of girls who hung out together, causing a bit of trouble. I never thought of myself as being in a gang, although looking back I can see that actually I was.

These girls really took a shine to me, and as time went on I was introduced to more and more people from a wider area. Eventually, we were a group of about twenty girls who came from Camden, Kentish Town, Tottenham and everywhere in between. Some of the girls were as old as nineteen and a couple of them already had kids. There was one particular older girl I remember hanging around with who ended up in Holloway prison for conspiracy to murder.

As is usual with groups of kids causing trouble, the main motivation was boredom. I think a lot of the girls had felt insignificant and powerless in their lives and coming together that way and having solidarity with one another was a form of empowerment. For me, it was like having a family that I could rely on and who both protected and cared about me. I'm sure many of the other girls felt the same.

A few years before, I'd got a buzz out of all the kids at Haverstock liking me and wanting to be my friend, but by now, after everything that had happened to me, I was much more into the idea of people being scared of me. I was no longer scared of all those girls whom I'd spent months hiding from – now I was the aggressor, not the victim.

Most of the time we would get drunk or high, and then we'd get on a bus and head to the 'hoodest' area we could find where there was a good house party or a rave going on. We'd play loud garage and grime music, like early Dizzee Rascal and Wiley at the back of the bus and drive all the other passengers nuts as we'd rap and 'spit' our own lyrics over the tracks. At the time I thought of it as having fun rather than causing trouble, but I'm not sure the people we were harassing saw it that way.

As we needed ID to get into some of the raves and parties we went to, I had to get creative. One evening I sat in my bedroom trying to work out how I could turn the 1988 on my passport into 1986. Eventually, I came up with a plan. I found an Argos catalogue and, scanning through it, I realised that the numbers on some of the prices were exactly the same size as the numbers in my passport. I took a small pair of scissors and cut around a number six from the catalogue with absolute precision, right up to the outline. Then I took some warm wax and rubbed it on the back of the tiny number, laying it precisely over the eight.

I knew I couldn't use glue, as it was messy and would have seeped through the paper. It just had to be something sticky enough to hold it. Once I'd done that, I took an extremely pale pink nail varnish and lightly brushed over it, to blend with the colour of the passport. And finally I put sticky-back plastic over the number, so even if somebody rubbed or scratched it, it would feel smooth as if it was part of the passport. Hey presto! I was eighteen, born in 1986.

In fact, it looked so convincing that I soon had my own little business on the go. Kids I knew would bring me their passports and I'd charge them a fiver a pop to doctor their birth dates and make them old enough to get into a rave or buy alcohol. I even put together my own professional little fake ID kit, with tiny, sharp scissors, sticky-back plastic, a glue stick, nail varnish and, of course, an Argos catalogue. Within a week or so, there were about twenty kids who went from being fifteen or sixteen to eighteen or even older. And, luckily for me, I never got nabbed!

After a full year of being out of school I was forced to go back when the authorities got involved. My mum had been getting letters informing her that if I wasn't going to attend school then she would be liable for prosecution. She sent me to a school called Quintin Kynaston, which was a mixed school in Swiss Cottage, but this time I went in full of swagger. I decided that nobody was going to mess with me or bully me, and my approach was completely defensive. In truth, I was really scared of being seen as weak again, but this fear shone through as aggression. After my past experiences I knew that I had to fight and be tough to survive, and so I was ready to battle with anyone who tried to intimidate me or stand in my way.

'If you've got a problem with me, let's fuckin' 'ave it!'

That was my attitude, and it seemed to serve me well. I settled into the school without too many problems, although it was quite a shock to the system after a year without any school rules and regulations.

Although I got on fine with most of my new classmates, some of them warned me about two sisters who were a bit older than me who I should fear and avoid. It wasn't long before I bumped into them and found myself surrounded by them and a group of their friends in the corridor during break time.

'So what, you're the new girl then? What're you sayin'?'

The girls were scoping me out, trying to work out if I was easily intimidated, and I knew it, so I came back at them with a calm confidence and self-assurance that said, 'Don't even try it. I'm not having it. Not this time.'

'Yeah, I'm the new girl,' I said cheekily. 'And what?'

It worked. The girls thought I was funny and bold, and they liked my cheekiness.

'Look at this one,' one of the girls laughed. 'She's a brave 'un.'

And I knew everything was going to be all right. These girls actually appreciated my cockiness, and they soon took me under their wing – it was a huge relief. Suddenly I was in with the hardest chicks in school, and everybody liked and respected me. Sorted! I never had one single problem with fighting or bullying for the whole time I was at Quintin Kynaston.

Unfortunately, my relationship with the teachers at the

school wasn't quite as rosy. With this new-found confidence, in and out of school, I was a proper cocky little fucker, and as far as I was concerned, nobody could teach me a damn thing I didn't already know. I was over it. You have to remember that although I was still only fifteen, I'd been out of school and living without boundaries for a whole year, just like any adult. I was making my own music and I was out every night, with no real parental control. In fact, with my mum's illness, I often took on the role of the parent myself. I'd also been practically living with my boyfriend Daniel on and off for quite a while, having a full sexual relationship. All in all, I'd been living the life of a free spirit and then suddenly I was thrown back into the education system. My attitude was, 'What the hell am I doing here? I'm not having some teacher who doesn't know anything about my life telling me what to do.'

Even something as simple as a teacher asking me why I wasn't in class yet was insulting, as far as I was concerned – I was on another planet. During the first week of school a teacher challenged me about something and I remember answering back with hostility.

'Excuse me, who the fuck do you think you're talking to?'

The aggression was terrifying and extreme, but it came straight from the world I was living in. I didn't live my life like a child. I didn't have boundaries or curfews. I didn't have people telling me what to do and when to do it, and as far as I was concerned, I didn't need to be in school either. In fact, in terms of education, there really was no point in me being there at all, to be honest. I was so convinced I was going to be a pop star that I simply refused to go half the time, and when I did go I used to either fall asleep in class or just sit there listening to music on my iPod. I was probably one of the worst students in the school. Consequently, I missed out on a hell of a lot, and that's something I regret. Now that I don't feel it's being forced on me, I know how important knowledge and education is, and I love the idea of learning more.

Back then, though, all of the teachers at Quintin Kynaston saw me as a lost cause – all except one. Miss Shield was from Sheffield, where my mum grew up, and was about thirty years old, of Somali descent. She was actually not one of my class teachers but my head of year, and when she noticed how frequently I was bunking off school and how wayward I was she started checking into my background and making it her business to find out more about me. The authorities all knew about my mum's mental health problems, and the school knew about the background I'd come from, but Miss Shield was the one person who actually connected the dots and realised that my bad behaviour and my circumstances were probably tied up together, so she decided to try to help me see sense.

One afternoon, to my surprise, she turned up at my mum's house to find out why I wasn't in school. She asked me why I wasn't attending and made me promise to come in the next day, trying to get across to me how important it was for a bright girl like me to get an education. She even offered to come and pick me up the next morning and take me to school in her car. She did this on a number of occasions, and said she wasn't going to give up on me. I really liked and respected her for that, because she was the only teacher that didn't just dismiss me. Miss Shield wanted to give me a bit of hope and encouragement, and because she was nice to me I didn't bitch and talk back to her, like I did to the other teachers. She was one patient woman, offering me love and support rather than punishment. She knew that, deep down, I was a soft and loving person, despite my aggressive bravado, and she knew that I felt guilty about all the bad stuff that I did. So when she'd look me directly in the eye and ask me, 'T, are you all right?' or when she'd softly touch my arm and say, 'I care about you', it was enough to make me break down and cry. In the end, I could never refuse Miss Shields when she asked me to please come into school, because I felt like she really did care.

'Do it for me, please, T!' she'd say. 'Even if you don't want to be in lessons for the whole day, just come in and sit in my office.'

'Do you know what, Miss?' I'd say. 'I will, I promise.'

Sometimes I did just that: I'd get bored in a lesson and I'd go and sit in Miss Shield's office and answer the phone for her, like a secretary. And as long as I was in school, my mum wasn't going to get into trouble with the authorities. Miss Shield was a smart cookie. I sometimes wonder whether I might have had a different kind of childhood altogether if I'd had more people around me like that. As it was, my mum was in and out of hospital, and I was basically running wild. Even my dad had realised by then that I'd gone way beyond the point of parental control, so the only thing he could do was work with me as best he could to stop me going off the rails completely.

Outside of school, I was getting in deeper and deeper with my gang of girlfriends, and the criminal activity I was getting involved in started to get a lot more serious than just creating fake IDs. Sometimes a few of us would head to the richer areas in north London, like Hampstead or Swiss Cottage, and snatch handbags from well-to-do

women and even men! I was never the instigator of this
kind of activity, and I was much too scared to actually
snatch somebody's bag myself, so I used to be the lookout,
or the one who hid the bag once it had been stolen.
Usually the girls would snatch a bag near a street corner,
so I'd be waiting just around the corner, ready to conceal
the stolen bag as they threw it to me, while they carried
on running. The idea was that anyone chasing them would
ignore me and continue chasing them down the street.
Meanwhile, I would head off in a different direction and
meet up with the rest of the group later. As I was the only
white girl in a group of tough-looking black girls, this plan
usually worked effectively. If anything did go wrong and we
were approached by the police, I would always be the one
thrust forward to do the talking, putting on a posh
speaking voice and sounding as innocent as I could. The
thinking behind this was that nobody would suspect the
innocent-looking, blue-eyed white girl. I was known as
'Whitey' or 'the white one', and although the girls all loved
me and I had equal standing within the group, this was my
role, and I was much more comfortable with that than I
would have been actually snatching the bags myself. I also
felt terribly guilty every time we did it, but unfortunately
the feeling of security and power I got from being with the
group always overrode that guilt. I felt safe with these girls,
and I knew that they loved and respected me. I didn't want
to give that up, even though it meant committing crime.

The most dangerous activity I remember from those
days was some of the rip-off scams we pulled on guys
that we met. To this day, the thought of what we did
scares me, because the sort of guys I'm talking about were
gangsters and drug dealers, older than we were and
basically people you'd never want to mess with in any way,

shape or form. These guys would often meet up with us, thinking they were going to take some of us on a date, or perhaps have sex with one of us, or something like that. The scenario was that once we were at one of the guy's houses or flats, we would wait until they were distracted or drunk or asleep, and then leave on the pretence of going to the shop to buy something, taking their phones, wallets, jewellery and anything else we could get our hands on, never to return.

On one occasion, one of the toughest girls in the group actually beat up a guy who attacked her. He came back for her later, though, and slashed her across the eyebrow with a knife.

This wasn't unusual: as I got older, I saw more and more weapons come into play and witnessed some scary violence. It wasn't always a knife either – pretty much anything could be used as a weapon. I remember one night, when a group of us girls were fighting with a rival crowd, suddenly one of our gang – one of the hardest bitches I've ever met – took off her new Timberland boot and started smashing one of the rival girls in the face with it. Then, when the girl was crying and bleeding on the floor, the girl from our gang started screaming at her.

'You fuckin' bastard! Look! You've got blood all over my new Timberland boots!'

At the time, I suppose, I was hardened to it. It was normal life. I'd gone much too far off the rails to have any qualms about it then. Nowadays I'm making records and appearing on TV and staying in nice hotels and doing all those glamorous things that go with being a pop star, but even now I'm not really shocked when I hear about the violence that goes on in the areas where I grew up. Sad, yes, but not shocked.

Me enjoying a day out with Uncle B, aged 6

Early pictures of me.

Here I am bonding with Dappy (right)

Opposite and above: Christmas at Uncle B's **house**

Below: In the studio with the boys recording our early material

Above: Lickle Rinsers photo shoot

Below: Me and Adam at a family christening

HONEST

Although I have changed massively as a person, I'm still very much aware of what goes on because some of my friends and family are still living it. I still get calls from people I know telling me that their brother or their cousin has been stabbed or shot. I still know people who know people who are involved in crime. I may have changed for the better, and I appreciate the fact that people can see that, but the bad shit hasn't gone away, and it's very difficult for me to look on it all with horror and just turn away, wanting nothing to do with it. I know that way of life is not right, but it still seems very normal to me. The only difference is, now I see it for what it is, and I'm glad to be out of it.

Not everyone I came across back then was a truly bad person. Like me, many of them were simply products of their environment, and although most people are very quick to generalise and judge the people who live in that dark world they only hear about on the news, you can never understand it properly unless you've lived it. The truth is that if I hadn't been saved by music like I was, I'd most likely be living with a drug dealer on a rough council estate.

I recently visited some of these girls and, like me, their lives have completely changed; they've grown up to become good people. A lot of them are mums now, and they're not into that scene at all anymore. When we chatted about old times and the things we used to get up to, the girls all laughed and told me that they thought I was jumping on the bandwagon at the time – just to be a part of the group. I was never really the instigator of the criminal activity, but the fact is that I was involved, and that's something I can never change. I'm not proud of some of the things I did back then, and if I could take back the hurt I must have caused, I would, but of course that's not possible. All I can do now is show young people, through being the person that I am today, that there is an alternative to a life wasted on crime and violence.

It seems to me that each generation of parents gets weaker and kids seem to have less and less discipline. My parents' generation were having kids at a young age, and my generation are having them even younger. To me, it's kids bringing up kids, and the morals and guidance that young people are supposed to get from their parents seem to be disappearing. Knowing what I know and having been through what I have, I really believe that parents need to show a firm hand when it's necessary. I also think that schools should be stricter and that teachers should have the power to discipline kids when they misbehave. In fact, I sometimes think that teachers and parents need to have lessons on how to impose discipline. Twenty years ago, when kids got a wallop if they played up at school, they were too afraid to run riot like some of them do now. I think we need to get some of that back, otherwise who knows what it's going to be like in another twenty years? It's a kid's natural instinct to look to an adult for guidance, and it's a parent's job to teach them right from wrong.

I realise now that however much I thought I knew at fifteen, I was still a child and had so much to learn, both mentally and emotionally. I think I only did the things I did back then because I knew I could get away with it. I had no fear because I had no discipline. Perhaps if I had, I'd have been a better person when I was a teenager, who knows? As it was, my fearless nature and lack of guidance often led me into some pretty terrible situations, one in particular that I've never really spoken about before.

HONEST

When I was sixteen I went along to a rave with some boys I knew from my local area. This was nothing unusual really; the boys were all mates, or friends of friends, and I often hung out and went partying with them. On this occasion, though, I noticed that a couple of them were dropping pills in one another's drinks while we were at the club, so I gave them a stern warning.

'Guys, don't even think about putting anything in my drink. I don't want any part of it.'

I think I lied and told them I had a heart condition, just to make sure nobody tried any funny business, and they all promised to keep me out of it. An hour or so later, though, while I was chatting away to one of the boys who I knew but wasn't close friends with, I started to feel abnormally drunk. It was like I was off my face, and I knew I hadn't drunk anywhere near enough to feel that out of control. Before I knew it, I was dizzy and I could hardly stand up, so the guy I'd been chatting to took me outside the club to get some air. The next thing I remember was waking up, lying in the back of a cab and seeing the street lights whizzing past me through the window. I felt completely out of it, and I blacked out again. When I came round again, I was in a bedroom, and my so-called friend was on top of me, having sex with me. I couldn't even move, let alone get up or speak, and once again I just blacked out. When I finally woke up in the morning, I found myself in a strange house, obviously in this boy's bedroom, and there was his mum, standing over me with a cup of tea. It was as if I was just a girlfriend that he'd invited home, yet I couldn't remember anything apart from the vague flashbacks I'd had in a few moments of consciousness: staggering out of the club, being in the back of a cab, and waking up to someone having sex with me. And now here was this guy's mum offering me tea.

I felt so embarrassed and ashamed that I couldn't bring myself to tell her that I actually hadn't consented to any of this, even though I knew that there was no way I'd got so drunk that I'd blacked out like that. I knew I'd been drugged. I went into the bathroom and burst into tears. Then I pulled myself together, got dressed, and left without saying another word, crying all the way home. I spoke about it to my mates, but I never reported it to the police or told anyone in my family, and I still haven't to this day. I realise now, of course, that I'd done nothing to be ashamed of and the boy in question should have been prosecuted, but I was young and confused and not strong enough to speak up. As much as I'd like to, I can't go back and change the way I reacted to the situation that day, but I've learned to come to terms with it, and I'd like to see someone try that with me now!

Chapter Eleven

By the time I was sixteen, The Lickle Rinsers had recorded about three albums' worth of material – and we were good. In fact, for three teenagers who were essentially writing and producing their own material, we were very good indeed. By then, Uncle B had been sending our songs and photos to radio stations and record labels for a couple of years, and eventually we started getting meetings with some big industry players. Nothing ever seemed to come off, though. We would be called in to meet A&R managers, and we'd hear all sorts of exciting promises from them, only to be let down a bit further down the line. One minute someone would be telling us they were going to make us the next big thing, and the next minute it was a different story.

'You're not ready' we kept hearing. 'It won't work.'

Even Darcus Beese, president of my current record label, Island Records, turned us down back then (I've never let him forget it!). We just couldn't get a foot in the door. Every time someone at a record company was enthusiastic about our music, we'd get all excited, only to be let down once again. It was very disheartening.

One of the things that the labels didn't seem to like about us was our name. Many of the industry people we met thought that the name Lickle Rinsers was much too garage or urban – too ghetto. There was a lot of negative press about UK urban music around that time, with acts like So Solid Crew being accused of glorifying guns, and several outbreaks of violence at concerts by urban acts. I'd experienced that violence for myself first hand, with gunfire and bloodshed at some of the raves and clubs I'd been to. I'd even witnessed someone pull out a gun and point it at someone in a club. It was rampant on the scene back then, and because of this, many people were saying that UK garage music was dead and that we should distance ourselves from that scene if we wanted to make it in the business. Eventually, we came up with the name NW1, which was the postcode of the area we all came from, Camden, and a bit more commercial. Maybe that would work for us.

Around that time, there was a new satellite TV music channel that everyone was talking about, Channel U. The channel was playing upcoming UK grime and hip-hop music and was featuring artists who weren't even signed yet, like us. We suddenly felt as though we might have a platform to get our music out to the public, even though we didn't have a deal. First, though, we had to have a video. Step up Uncle B. He'd been working six days a week cutting hair to make some extra money to keep the studio running, and he decided to spend £500 to make a video of one our songs, 'Every Day of My Life'. First, he found a young student filmmaker from Bournemouth called George Burt, who was really keen to shoot it for us, and then, with one little hand-held JVC video camera tied to a makeshift trolley on the back of a car, off we went.

The song was about a lot of the bad shit that we saw going on around us on a day-to-day basis, and the video introduced me, Dappy and Fazer performing the song in different locations around London. It also featured many of the friends we hung around with at the time. We were really happy with the result, but although it did get some night-time plays on Channel U, it didn't really get us the attention that we needed to make the record companies take notice, and we were back to square one.

It was then that we decided on yet another name change. We'd only changed our name to NW1 in the first place on the advice of some of the record labels, and we still hadn't been signed. On reflection, we all thought the name was too poppy for us. After all, whatever anyone else thought, we were an urban act, and we decided that we wanted to do things our way and not listen to anyone else's opinion about what we should or shouldn't be. We rechristened ourselves N-Dubz, which is a play on the postcode we came from, NW It was much more edgy, much more urban, and much more us.

We were still playing lots of shows at this time, and I suppose we were quite well known on the circuit, even though we didn't have a deal. It was around this time that I struck up a friendship with a girl called Ny, who I met through a friend. Her full name was Naomi Grey and she was hanging out with a more musical crowd: a lot of underground MCs and rappers – mostly boys – and specifically a crew known as SLK. Ny was a very wise girl, and a calming influence on me to a certain extent. I bonded with her very quickly. She knew that some of the people I'd been hanging around with were trouble, and she clearly wasn't afraid to tell me what she thought.

'What are you doing with these people?' she'd say to me. 'They're surrounded by trouble, and you need to stay away from it.'

I guess I knew she was right, because as I got more and more excited about music, I began to gravitate towards a new group of friends who were making music rather than making trouble. As it was, a lot of my friends in my old crew of 'hard girls' were calming down quite a lot too. Some of the older girls had babies, and others had just grown up and realised that the way they were behaving was wrong. The group just fizzled away, although I'm still friends with some of the girls today.

I had my music to keep me busy now, and I wanted to put everything I had into that. Seeing our video get played on Channel U, plus the reaction we were getting at our gigs, convinced me that we were in with a shot if we could just get the right break.

Meanwhile, through Ny, I met a guy called Adam Bailey – aka Van Damage – at a friend's birthday party. Adam was a garage MC and part of the SLK crew, and this particular crew were really flying at the time, so he was at the point in his musical career that I was trying to get to. I was immediately attracted to Adam, which was unusual, as he definitely wasn't my usual type looks-wise. More often than not, I liked mixed-race boys with green eyes – that was my thing – but Adam was a white boy with shaved blond hair, although he did have a similar sort of style and demeanour to a lot of the mixed-race and black guys I knew. I guess because of the environment I'd been in for the last few years, I'd just never really dated white boys, but here I was falling for a guy with bright blond hair and blue eyes, who was twenty, almost four years older than I was. Of course, me being me, I lied about my age and told him I was eighteen.

Everything about Adam was cool, as far as I was concerned: the fact that he was a garage MC, the way he looked, the way he dressed. It's funny, because in some way I think I was also drawn to him because he was in a similar situation to me: he was the white guy in an otherwise black and mixed-race crew, just like I'd often been the only white girl in my groups of mates. There was always a big gang of people hanging around with SLK, but the actual band only consisted of three people: Adam, his sidekick Flirta D, and a mixed-race girl called Lady Envy – almost identical to the set-up N-Dubz had – but these guys were at a much higher point in their music careers than we were. Right away, I set my sights on Adam, and before long the two of us were hanging out and dating. At the time, SLK had a song out, 'Hype Hype', which was a massive underground hit, and I would go and watch him MC on the mic at garage raves, performing with his crew. I was really besotted.

Unfortunately for me, but not really surprisingly, Adam, who was seen as a bit of a bad boy on the music scene, wasn't exactly the settling-down type. Consequently, I had to resign myself to the fact that I wasn't going to be the only girl in his life, at least not then anyway. Adam was enjoying the groupie vibe, and there were always plenty of girls surrounding SLK. Still, the two of us had a very definite connection, and we enjoyed hanging out together, despite the fact that he was having sex with other girls, and I knew it. It's certainly not the way I'd conduct a relationship today, but back then I thought it was something I had to accept if I wanted to be with him, even though *I* wasn't seeing anybody else but him. We called it 'a link'. This meant that you were seeing someone – you were linked to them – but it wasn't exclusive.

That's not to say that I didn't have plans to change the situation. Around that time, I really felt like I was growing up and turning from a girl into a woman. I certainly wasn't in the market for the sort of abuse I'd suffered with Daniel, and I was starting to feel more confident as far as men were concerned. I was even learning the fine art of female manipulation. So I guess I looked upon Adam as a sort of challenge: maybe he wasn't completely mine yet, but if I worked on him for long enough, he would be. I decided that no matter what stood in my way, I was going to have him, and that's all there was to it. For the first year and a half of our sort-of relationship, though, I put myself through a huge amount of tears and drama. I was madly in love with Adam, but his attitude was still casual. It was very frustrating, and there didn't seem to be anything I could do to change it.

When we were first together, I can remember always desperately trying to be terribly cool and sexy while I was around Adam, and there was one occasion when this went hilariously wrong. We were at his dad's house one night, watching a movie, when Adam pulled a joint out of his pocket. Now, Adam didn't smoke weed very often, and I'd started having panic attacks whenever I had more than a couple of puffs on a joint (I was known as Two-lug Tula), so I wasn't blazing at all, and I wasn't particularly keen on the idea of trying it again.

These panic attacks had started a year or so before, when I was bunking off school with some mates. I'd just come back from a long holiday in Greece, where I'd been visiting my grandparents, so I hadn't had any spliff for a month. Consequently, when one of my mate's brothers offered me a twos (the second half of a joint) inside the block of flats where we were hanging out, I jumped at the chance. I couldn't wait to get high again. Anyway, after chuffing it down quite quickly, I felt somewhat dizzy, but I just merrily carried on and tried to fight it. Then I felt faint and my eyes started to close, but I was buzzing madly at the same time. All of a sudden, and this was something

which was told to me after the event, I started fitting while
I was standing up – actually having a fit. The other kids I
was with thought I was mucking about – body popping of
all things – because it looked so weird, but then I fell
down onto the ground and went into a full-on fit. Of
course, all the kids I was with panicked, but all I remember
is everything going black and knowing something was
very wrong. My first thought was that I was dying. My
eyes were open, but all I could see was pitch black, and
then, quite suddenly, the black became a bright white
light: yes, I was definitely dead!

'This is it, I've died, haven't I?' I said to myself. 'See ya
later, Mum!'

In truth, the kids I was with had dragged me from the
darkness of the block we were in out into the sunshine.
They were slapping my face and throwing water over me,
but I still didn't feel it. As far as I was concerned, I was
dead. Slowly, other objects started to come into focus as I
lay on the ground: tower blocks, railings, concrete. 'Well,
this can't be heaven can it?' I thought to myself. I wasn't
dead after all.

'Fucking hell, what happened?'

'You just fell down and started fitting,' one of the kids
said.

It was all pretty alarming, but it didn't stop me blazing
and getting high again, not straight away anyway. After a
few more of these incidents, however, including one when I
ended up in an ambulance after blacking out and falling
off a bike while I was cycling through Camden with a
friend, I had to accept that my blazing days were over. It
was bloody scary! All of a sudden, I just went dizzy, and I
don't remember anymore until the ambulance arrived.
What was even scarier was that I hadn't even smoked any

weed that day, so God knows why I'd blacked out. In the end, the hospital didn't find anything conclusive, so it was all a bit of a mystery. Still the panic attacks continued spasmodically, and for quite a while, even after I'd stopped smoking completely.

So that night at Adam's dad's house, when he offered me some weed, I wasn't keen, but at the same time I didn't want him to think I was being a pussy or uncool, so, eager to impress him, I decided to have just a couple of drags. After all, I had my asthma pump in my bag and I could usually handle a couple of pulls – what the hell could go wrong? Quite a lot, was the answer to that one!

After I'd had a couple of pulls on the joint, I got brave and decided to have a third. Bad move. Straight away I started to feel my heart beating faster and the panic in me rising. Oh shit! I was about to have a panic attack in front of Adam – the man I loved – maybe even a fit. Adam was the coolest person I knew and he would sometimes laugh at me if I did or said something he thought was uncool or daft, like I was some kind of adorable geek. I just could not let this happen.

As I began to feel more and more breathless, I pulled my asthma pump out of my bag, all the while trying to remain calm, and put it up to my mouth, inhaling deeply into my lungs. What I didn't know was that a cigarette had broken inside my bag, and a massive wad of the tobacco from it had somehow made its way inside the mouthpiece of my asthma pump. So when I inhaled, the huge chunk of tobacco shot down my throat and lodged in my windpipe. One minute we were sitting on the sofa, nicely relaxed after a few drinks, and the next I was choking and gagging loudly and flailing my arms about wildly, with Adam looking on in wide-eyed horror. I couldn't breathe at all, so

HONEST

I started punching Adam on the shoulder and pointing at my throat while making the horrendous death-rattle sound of someone who is choking to death. Adam, who was as high as a kite by this time, had no idea what to do, but eventually he grabbed me around the waist and threw me into the air, trying to perform the Heimlich manoeuvre, as if I had a piece of steak stuck in my throat. He pulled me backwards and crushed my stomach over and over, while I continued to choke and flail my legs around wildly. It was like that scene in *Mrs. Doubtfire* when Robin Williams tries to save Pierce Brosnan from choking in the restaurant, and they're falling all over the place – completely mental!

Eventually, I got a little gasp of air and I managed to swallow the tobacco, but afterwards I was hacking and coughing for a good twenty minutes in front of my beloved – it was not a good look, I'll tell you. I was trying so hard to be cool and it couldn't have gone more wrong, but what made the situation even more hilarious was the sight of ultra-cool Adam swinging me round like Mrs Doubtfire, while I was punching him and waving my arms and legs about all over the place, choking half to death. It really wasn't my most glamorous moment.

———————

Just before my birthday in 2006, we'd had a bit of a row and weren't on speaking terms, because by this time I was getting pretty fed up with Adam's casual attitude towards our relationship. Anyway, out of the blue one day, Adam called me up and asked me what I was doing and if I fancied going out somewhere. I guess it was his way of making up.

'OK,' I said. 'Why not? It's my birthday today.'

'Oh cool, you're twenty today,' Adam said.

'Eighteen.'

'What?'

'Eighteen. I'm eighteen.'

I think he was shocked that I'd lied to him for so long, but I also think that knowing the truth helped Adam make sense of some of my more immature character traits.

It didn't change anything much: we carried on seeing one another and Adam continued to be very casual about the whole situation. But as time went on and I started to turn from a girl to a woman, I became less and less satisfied with the arrangement. Something was going to have to change.

Chapter Twelve

Just before my eighteenth birthday, Dappy, Fazer and I went on holiday to Greece. We spent two weeks in the village where Dappy's mum and grandma came from, Platanos, and we had such an amazing time, just chilling out with people from the village. This trip was during the period when Adam and I weren't speaking, and so, unsurprisingly, Fazer and I rekindled our on/off romance once more while we were there. Dappy stayed with his grandma, and Fazer and I got a little hotel room of our own. It's funny really how the two of us always seemed to gravitate towards one another whenever we were both single. I guess it was convenient, but it was also very comfortable.

Ever since I was a kid, I'd been coming to Greece for holidays, first with my parents and then later on I'd either go on my own or with Dappy. My nan and granddad lived in a place called Lagonissi, and it felt so good to be in the sunshine and away from London, especially during my tough early teenage years. The only problem was that I tended to go to Greece whenever I was running away from something back home, and although the holidays were wonderful, I always knew that I'd have to go back to London and face the world eventually. As far as my nan and granddad were concerned, however, I was just their innocent granddaughter: a normal girl going to school and living a normal life. They never knew how bad things had been for me at times, and they knew nothing about the life I was living.

Still, it was always fantastic being there, and during the time when Dappy, Fazer and I were there together, we really connected as a group. We'd sit by the sea, talking about our ambitions and our dreams, and then we'd have a swim or lie in the sun. It was two weeks of bliss.

One afternoon, Dappy dared me to jump into the sea off a rock known as The Lion's Head, assuring me that everyone did it, unless, of course, they were a pussy. This huge rock comes out from under the main highway and juts out into the sea in the shape of a lion's head, and I have to say, it didn't look all that scary to me until I got up there on top of it. Then, just like when we were kids, Dappy started taunting me.

'You can't do it because you're a girl! You may think you're hard, but you're not.'

He knew that this would piss me off, and he was right. Not only did I jump off the bloody thing, but I went up to the very highest point to do it. The higher point jutted out a bit further, and I thought the lower ledge was too close to the rocks. Unfortunately, I landed in a bomb position, and what seemed like a ton of seawater shot straight up my bum. It was excruciatingly painful, and the boys thought it was hilarious.

At the same time as I was making music with the band, I also got myself a part-time job in a music management company through my Aunt Maria's best mate, who was working in the accounts department. I never thought of myself as a waster or a bum, and I wanted to be as independent as I possibly could, financially. Even a couple of years before, while I was running around acting like a proper little hood, I always knew that I wanted to amount to something. A life sitting on my arse collecting benefits was definitely not for me. A lot of my mates signed on when they left school, but I never wanted to. I wanted to work for my money, and just in case I didn't become a world-famous ghetto star, I thought I'd better have some sort of back-up plan.

When I was fifteen I'd had a job in a hairdresser's, sweeping up and helping out, and now I was working as a secretary in a music company called Sanctuary three days a week. The company looked after big acts like The Who and Led Zeppelin, among others, and I only got paid about £250 a month. Still, that paid for my cigarettes and socialising, and it made me feel good to know I was making my own money. I didn't mind the job, but I eventually got sacked when I forgot to send off an important cheque for forty grand. I think the people I worked for knew my heart wasn't in it, and that I was more suited to performing songs than I was performing office chores.

Meanwhile, after all the disappointments we'd had with various record companies and the lukewarm reception we'd had to 'Every Day of My Life', the boys and I were starting to wonder whether we were ever going to make it big. Uncle B was a driving force behind us, though, and he wasn't prepared to let us give up.

'If you get knocked down, you've got to get up again,' he insisted.

He held us together, because as far as he was concerned, quitting wasn't an option. I knew full well that B hid a lot of negative feedback from us and only fed us the positive; sometimes he even invented 'good news', which turned out to be utter rubbish, just to keep us all going. There was a method to his madness, and it worked. He was always very proud of what we were doing.

Eventually, we decided to make another video using the same director as before, but now bigger and better than the first one. Uncle B had already formed a record company for us, LRC (which stood for Lickle Rinsers Crew), so we could release the track on our own label; we had to – no major record company would come near us. We wrote and recorded the song, we scripted the video ourselves and we rented a much better camera. The track was called 'Better Not Waste My Time' and it turned out to be N-Dubz's first taste of fame.

I was eighteen years old now, and all of a sudden our video was being hammered on Channel U – it was huge. Of course, it wasn't a mainstream pop kind of thing, it was more an underground buzz – with the track released as a download-only single – but it was exactly what we'd been striving for. Our hits on Myspace rocketed and the internet buzz about the song went crazy. As time went on, more and more people started voting for the video on Channel U, until eventually, in the summer of 2006, 'Better Not Waste My Time' got to number one in their chart, and stayed there for weeks and weeks.

It was then that N-Dubz finally got the break we'd been waiting for. Colin Barlow at Polydor Records offered us a development deal, handing us £25,000 to record some new material or make another video; it was basically our money to do what we thought best with. Just like before, we decided to release a brand-new record on our own label, LRC, but this time we had a bit of financial support behind us, and that made all the difference in the world.

The song we decided to put out was called 'I Swear' and it was N-Dubz's defining track, blowing us up to the point where people in the music industry really started to sit up and take notice. It was like: 'What is going on here?

Who are these three little ghetto kids?' Colin and the people at the label obviously saw that we had something, but they wanted to see how we would develop on our own, given a shot of cash. Their thinking was: here are these young kids who clearly have a bit of talent and who don't mind doing it all themselves – let's sit back and see what happens. We were a bit like hamsters in a cage being observed really, but that suited us fine.

With a lot more money to play with for the 'I Swear' video, we spent £3000 on a proper HD camera, £2000 on lighting and another £1000 on someone who Uncle B employed to work on promotion. On Uncle B's advice, with the rest of the money, we bought all the studio equipment we needed to be self-sufficient and to keep making our own records, just in case it didn't work out with the label.

Once again, we used George Burt to direct the video, and we came up with the idea for the treatment and scripted it ourselves. 'I Swear' is a song about a guy who's being cheated on by his girlfriend, and the video we made reflected the lyrics. The fans loved it because we added a storyline to the treatment as well as just performing the song. Kids seemed to love the fact that we shot our video from three separate perspectives, Fazer's, Dappy's and mine, with different love interests and outcomes. Again, it went down a storm on Channel U, but this time the track also started to get played on KISS 100 FM – our first mainstream radio plays. It was really exciting. Finally we were starting to break outside the underground scene.

Unfortunately, while all this good stuff was going on with the band, things at home weren't going well. Around the time when my music career started kicking off big, Mum had a very long period of illness – probably around a year in all – and she ended up in hospital for about five months. It was always the same pattern. One minute she was stable on her medication, and the next minute I'd be coming home from the studio to find her sitting silently in a corner or behaving erratically. As soon as I could see that she was about to have another episode, I would alert the hospital, hoping they might be able to nip this one in the bud, but because the hospital was always so stretched, they would usually leave it to the last minute before intervening. By that time it was too late. Mum was always too far gone and would end up in hospital for months.

Of course, Mum's latest bout of ill health put me on a proper downer too. It seemed like no matter how well my music career was going, there would always be something to drag me down. Yes, I was feeling sorry for myself, and sometimes I'd slack off from the studio to hang out with my mates instead of doing what I should have been doing, which was making music. Uncle B, of course, was always the one who put me straight. There were times over the years when he'd come and find me wherever I was hanging out and literally drag me into the studio to work. I remember once, after a particularly bad day with my mum, I was really feeling down at the studio, and it was evident to Dappy and Fazer how depressed I was. I'd been slacking off big time, and once again Uncle B had been forced to round me up off the streets and drive me to work.

Much later that night, Uncle B dropped me off at home, but he had a few things to say to me before I got out of the car, and I guess I needed to hear them.

'Listen, T,' he said, 'I don't think it's naturally in your blood to be a depressed person like your mum, but unfortunately, because you've been brought up in that environment, it's made you depressed. I think you do suffer from depression. I can see it. But instead of wallowing in it, you need to accept it as a fact and deal with it. You have to say to yourself, "Yeah, I suffer from depression sometimes, but you know what? Fuck it! I'm just going to learn to live with it."'

It was a bizarre thing for an uncle to be telling his teenage niece: not to get help or to take medication, but to accept the fact that I had these mood swings and then try to control it. Deal with it. But the truth of the matter is, that is exactly what I've done ever since. Yes, I have dark moments, and sometimes I feel completely lost, but now I accept that that is a part of who I am, and I just wait for the storm to pass and then move on. Nothing and no one can control my mind better than I can: no doctor, no medication, nothing. Of course, this wouldn't work for everyone, and there are lots of people, like my mum, who simply can't get by without medication and the help and guidance of doctors. But for me, this train of thought has always worked well. Uncle B made me see it when the two of us were alone in his car that night, after all those years of torturing myself. I'll never forget that he did that for me.

As it looked like Mum was going to be in hospital for quite some time, I decided to move in with my dad, and that worked out really well. We were more like flatmates than father and daughter half the time, and Dad tended to just let me get on with things without too much hassle. I felt comfortable and content with the arrangement, and with my life in general: I'd got myself together, my music was beginning to happen, I'd started seeing Adam regularly – though still not exclusively – and I didn't have my poor mum to deal with every day. Although I was still worried about her, I felt a sense of security and I was strong again. It was a nice place to be.

In April 2007, N-Dubz played a gig in Camberley in
Surrey. 'I Swear' was by now a huge hit on the
underground scene, and we were booked to perform at a
rave with about two thousand teenagers in the audience.
When we walked onto that stage, we were completely and
utterly blown away by the response. The whole crowd
went flippin' mental. Absolutely everyone was singing the
words to the songs, girls were screaming, guys were trying
to grab at Dappy and Fazer or touch my hand – it was
mayhem. We had never experienced anything like it, and
we were gobsmacked. We still didn't even have a proper
record deal – in fact, if a record company executive had
walked into the show that night, they'd have probably
thought to themselves, 'Who the hell are these kids? Why
haven't we signed them?' We were the UK's rough
diamonds, urban music's best-kept secret, and the kids
who were fast becoming our fans loved that. They loved
the fact that when they went home and raved about
N-Dubz to their parents, those parents didn't have a clue
who they were talking about.

'What the hell are N-Dubz?'

It made us all the more appealing to the people we
were trying to reach. Our buzz just got bigger and bigger,
like some sort of underground epidemic, and it was
exactly what Uncle B had been hoping for.

That night in Camberley, the audience screamed out the
words to our songs at the top of their voices, word for
word. The crowd showed so much love to us, and Dappy,
Fazer and I were over the moon. It was magical being up
there, and such an amazing buzz. I wanted more of it.
When we came offstage, it was clear that we weren't the
only ones feeling that way. B was smiling and shouting to
us over the screaming: 'We did it guys, we fucking did it!'

HONEST

He was so ecstatic. Uncle B had worked so hard for us, and he finally felt like he'd taken us to where we needed to be. It was like we were fulfilling his dream as well as our own. We were safe at last, in his eyes – we'd made it.

'Now you can go all the way,' he told us. 'You're gonna be stars!'

Just two days later, Uncle B was dead.

Chapter Thirteen

The day that I heard Uncle B had died started off a happy one. I was on set, getting ready to film my very first scene in a television show called *Dubplate Drama*, and I was really excited about my first proper acting job.

Before I'd landed the small role of Laurissa – who was the baby-mother of an already established character called Bones, played by Adam Deacon – I'd already watched the Channel 4 show, and I was a big fan. It's funny, because I distinctly remember seeing the show, which followed the story of a female MC and the people surrounding her, and thinking, 'Wow! That's not a million miles from the world I live in. I could be on that show. I could totally do that.' A few weeks after that, someone from the production company who made the programme got in touch with Uncle B through the N-Dubz Myspace site and asked if both Dappy and I would go and audition for roles in the show. I guess they'd seen our videos on Channel U and thought that we'd suit the style of the show, which had quite a gritty, urban vibe.

I was into the idea straight off. I'd always loved the idea of acting, and one of the things I'd set my sights on if my music career took off was getting into film or television off the back of it. For the audition, I'd been told to learn a scripted scene, but when I arrived at the studio, I was also asked to improvise or freestyle a scene to camera. I was asked to play out my reaction to finding lipstick on my boyfriend's collar, but instead of a male actor, I had to rant and rave at another girl who was standing in as the cheating boyfriend. Anyway, while I was going nuts at this girl and acting my little heart out, I saw Luke Hyams, who was the show's director, jumping up and down behind the camera with apparent excitement as he watched me. He loved it.

The original plan was for me to play a character who was quite slutty and ghetto, but after my audition it was decided that I would be better in a more emotional role, hence my landing the part of Laurissa, who has to cope with the murder of her baby's father. It was only a very small role, but I was really happy when I got it because I knew it could well be the first step to more acting roles in the future.

The day before Uncle B died, I was on set preparing to film an incredibly emotional scene where I discover that my child's father, played by Adam Deacon, has been killed. I remember sitting there thinking, 'How am I going to do this? How am I going to cry convincingly and portray that kind of terrible loss on camera?' After all, I'd never really lost anyone close to me before; I really had no idea what it felt like. It was my first acting role, and I wanted to get it right.

Dappy also had a cameo role in the series, and after we'd both finished work that day, we decided to get in a cab with two of the other actors in the show, Big Narstie and Solo, who were also MCs. Dappy and I just fancied a drive out of London instead of heading straight home in our own cabs, and Narstie's cab would have to come back into London after dropping him off anyway, so we knew we'd be able to travel back. I love long journeys in cars listening to my music: iPod time, I call it, and everyone who knows me is accustomed to seeing me zone out and immerse myself in my music. While we were heading out of town, I decided to listen to some sad, emotive tracks to get me into the right frame of mind for the following day's dramatic scene. Once again, I began to think about how I was going to play the scene, but then those thoughts turned into questions about how I really would be affected if, say, my mum, or dad, or grandparents died. I thought about it long and hard, and all of a sudden I felt incredibly sad and emotional and I started to cry, turning my face away from Dappy, Solo and Narstie, so they couldn't see the tears. It was like it had already happened, like I was grieving for someone but I didn't know who or why. It was an extremely powerful force and I couldn't make it go away.

The next day I went into work at the studio and, prepping myself for my big moment, I put on my iPod and listened to Mariah Carey and Boyz II Men's 'One Sweet Day', which contains the line 'I know you're shining down on me from heaven'. And I immersed myself in sad thoughts again, just to get into the right frame of mind for the sad, dramatic scene I was about to film. As it turned out, it went brilliantly, and although it was my very first scene in front of a camera, I still consider it one of my best: crying my eyes out and having a very convincing breakdown. I was chuffed with the result, and so too was Luke, the show's director.

Straight after the scene, we broke for lunch, and one of the show's producers came over to me and said that Dappy had been trying to get hold of me, that he needed to speak to me urgently. My phone had been turned off because I was filming, but as soon as I turned it on there was a whole bunch of texts from both Dappy and Fazer. Immediately I began to panic. This wasn't normal. This was weird. What the hell was going on? Of course, I tried to phone straight away, but neither Dappy nor Fazer were picking up. I tried calling another close friend of ours, Mazer, but again there was no reply. Then another message was relayed to me by one of the show's producers while I was sitting at a Chinese buffet in the middle of a food court in Hendon, near the studio.

'Dappy's on his way down to see you, T. He wants to speak to you in person.'

'Somebody's died!' I told my mates in the cast. 'I can feel it.'

Shystie, who played *Dubplate*'s lead character, Dionne, and Adam Deacon both tried to assure me that it was probably nothing and that I was overreacting, but I wasn't convinced. Finally Dappy called me.

'Where are you?' he said. 'I need to tell you something.'

I told him where I was, but before I could get anymore out of him, he just hung up the phone. Then I really started panicking and I got straight on the phone to my mum.

'Are you OK, Mum? Is everything OK?'

'Yes, why?'

Then I called my dad, but he didn't pick up either, so I tried my grandma, who was over in England at the time.

'Is everything all right, Grandma?'

'Yes, everything's fine, why?'

Maybe I *was* overreacting. I mean, if something bad had happened, surely my mum and my grandma would have known? Then I saw Dappy stride into the open square of the food court, with Fazer and Mazer in tow. I rushed over to them.

HONEST

'What the fuck is going on?'

'I think you need to sit down, T,' Dappy said.

By this time I was in a really agitated state, and I was furious at being kept in the dark.

'I don't want to fucking sit down,' I shouted angrily. 'Now just tell me what the hell is the matter.'

Dappy looked at me blankly.

'B's dead.'

I knew that I couldn't have heard right. 'What?'

'B's dead,' Dappy said again. 'He died last night of a heart attack.'

Suddenly my mind was all over the place. Sure, I'd known something was terribly wrong that day. I'd even convinced myself that someone had died: my mum, my nan or my granddad – all of them had crossed my mind – but I had never imagined for one second that it was my Uncle B. I felt my heart beating faster and faster and I thought I might have a heart attack myself. I couldn't accept and process the information – I just couldn't take it – and I blacked out. Our friend Mazer caught me under the arms and sat me down on a chair, and then as I came round, I heard this terrible wailing sound which turned out to be coming from me.

Fazer and the boys led me out to a space outside the food court, holding onto me in case I fainted again, and they sat me down on a nearby bench. I was devastated and quite hysterical for a while, but then I looked up and saw Dappy next to me. All of a sudden it struck me that however distraught I was, B was Dappy's dad. Dappy had lost his dad. I threw my arms around him and pulled him close to me, still sobbing uncontrollably. I remember that he was almost pulling away from me, and that he wouldn't cry – like he was numb. So I just kept saying, 'I'm so sorry,

I'm so sorry.' When Dappy pulled away from me, he was just shaking his head sadly, and I felt such pain for him. It was a terrible moment.

Later, once I'd calmed down a bit, Dappy asked me, 'What are you going to do now, T, once you've left the studio?'

'I don't know,' I said. 'I was just going to go home, but I've got no plans, obviously.'

'Can I just be with you?' he said.

'Of course.'

Later that day, one of the crew from *Dubplate Drama* drove Dappy and me back to my mum's house in a convertible car, just the two of us, with Fazer and Mazer following in a cab behind. We drove home with the roof down, and I remember there was the most beautiful sunset that evening and a gorgeous cool breeze hitting us as we travelled. Dappy and I just sat there, head to head and holding hands so tightly that it hurt, silently grieving. That night, after delivering the awful news to my mum, who hadn't yet heard, we both headed to our studio, which was now in Finsbury Park. The two of us just sat there with some of Dappy's mates, Fazer and Dappy's brother, Spiros. That was our place with Uncle B, and we all wanted to be there.

B had died of a heart attack the evening before, while Dappy and I were driving around with our friends, Solo and Big Narstie. When Dappy got home that night he didn't have any keys, so he'd rung the doorbell but got no answer. Dappy's mum was due back from Greece the next day, so she wasn't home. There were a few things Dappy couldn't understand, like why his dad's car keys and phone were clearly visible on the kitchen table when he looked through the window, and why his mum's dog was locked in the house alone, and why his dad's van was parked outside the house if he was out.

Eventually, he'd given up trying to get in and gone round to stay at a friend's house, but when he arrived back with Fazer the next morning, he discovered his mum, my Aunt Zoe, standing on the doorstep with her suitcases, unable to get inside. Uncle B was supposed to have picked her up from the airport. It was clear by then that something was very wrong, so Fazer broke into the house and went into the living room, where he found B. He was sitting on the couch with his hands behind his head, as though he was just relaxing, but Fazer said he knew straight away that B had passed away. Meanwhile, Dappy and his mum rushed into the room behind Fazer, despite his attempts to stop them, and poor Dappy was faced with the sight of his dad, there on the couch. B had died watching television, Channel U, waiting for our video to come on.

The following night we had a show scheduled, but Dappy and I were unsure about doing it. Fazer was the one who changed our minds.

'B died waiting to see our video. We can't not do this; we have to do this for him.'

It was a hard thing to do, and one of the most emotional experiences of my life, but we got through it and we were all very glad that we'd forced ourselves to get up there and perform. Dappy made a short speech to the crowd about his dad, and we all shed some tears.

Uncle B had been everything to us, and especially to Dappy. B was not only his dad, but also his best mate and our manager: he was Dappy's whole world. I'm not sure if he's ever really grieved properly, but I know that B's death changed him. Dappy is one of the most adorable little souls I've ever known, but I often think he's too vulnerable for his own good, and he often lets himself be drawn into situations and dramas that would be best avoided, especially now that his dad isn't around to guide him. One thing I'm certain of is that if it weren't for Uncle B, there would have been no N-Dubz, and I almost certainly wouldn't have the life I have now. He was so fiercely passionate about the group, and he went through so much stress, putting himself under a huge amount of pressure to push the band forward and make us a success. There had been a fair few arguments between B and the boys, and also between B and me, leading up to his death. He wanted us to work our arses off and he pushed us to the max. He wanted to inspire us, and he did.

It might sound odd, but looking back now, I sometimes wonder whether B knew that he was going to die, because in the weeks before it happened, he said some strange and fairly ominous things to each of us.

'You're going to have to do all this on your own soon,' he'd say, or 'I'm not going to be around for long. You may hate me now, but I won't be here to look after you soon.'

I'd gone through a particularly rough patch with B in the weeks before he died, arguing about different aspects of the band – in fact, we were barely speaking right before it happened. Then, just a few days before he passed away, he called me up for a chat out of the blue.

'Fuck the music, T,' he said. 'Fuck the business and fuck the money! I just want to go back to being your uncle again.'

'All right, cool, B,' I said.

As usual, I was too stubborn to give too much back

emotionally, but I think he knew that it *was* cool and that I accepted what he was saying to me. I'm very glad now that we had that conversation. I loved him very much and I miss him every day.

Chapter Fourteen

Not long after my Uncle B passed away, we suddenly found ourselves going from street kids to honoured guests at the 2007 MOBO awards, nominated for the Best Newcomer award. The awards ceremony was an amazing and electrifying night, and we all found it hard to believe we were there. I was very proud and excited, even though I didn't necessarily think we were going to win. For me, it was just an amazing buzz to even be there, let alone to be nominated for an actual award.

MOBO stands for Music of Black Origin, and the awards are given to artists that make and perform black music (R&B, dance, dubstep, grime, etc.), whatever their skin colour. The event that year was at the O2 Arena in London, and although we were all thrilled to be there, Dappy was incredibly nervous and on edge. We were up against some big competition, particularly Mutya Buena, previously of the Sugababes, and Tinchy Stryder, but Dappy was convinced that N-Dubz deserved to take the prize, and he wasn't going to accept any other result. Fazer and I were a bit more realistic about the whole thing. Mutya had been huge that year and we hadn't even released an album or had a big hit single yet: our success was very much an underground thing. Dappy wanted to do it for his dad, though, and as the evening went on, I could see him becoming more and more uptight and nervous. As the time for the Best Newcomer category got closer, I looked across the table at him and I noticed that he was crying – actually shedding tears – because he was thinking about Uncle B and what this accolade, and even just us being at the MOBOs, would have meant to him. My heart went out to him, but I was convinced that he was going to be disappointed with the outcome.

'It doesn't matter if we don't win, Dappy,' I told him. 'Fuck it, we're here. It's still an amazing achievement.'

But at the same time, I knew exactly where he was coming from. We'd had such a rough ride of late, culminating in the loss of our mentor and beloved family member; surely we deserved this one little bit of luck and glory. I knew that's what my cousin was thinking, and though I didn't think there was a chance of it happening, I guess I felt the same. We all did. Dappy's mum was there at the table with us that night, and so was our brand-new management team.

Not long before Uncle B had died, a large and well-respected company called ROAR Global had approached him about the possibility of taking over the management of N-Dubz. At first B was having none of it, but towards the end I think even B realised that he might need help, as there was always so much to do and think about, and the responsibility and strain of the day-to-day management was starting to take a toll on him.

Soon after B died, a guy called Rich Castillo, who worked for ROAR Global, approached us again. He'd been to a few of our gigs before – in fact, there had been an altercation between him and Uncle B at one gig, because B felt like the company was trying to poach the band away from him, but that actually hadn't been the case: Rich had just been there to find out if B needed the help of a professional management team. Now that B had gone, Rich turned up to chat about our future management situation. It was a no-brainer for us, to be honest. Jonathan Shalit, who ran ROAR Global, was a hugely successful music business manager, and although we weren't the type of act he was known for managing, he could obviously see something in us, and I think Rich helped to convince him that we had the potential to make it big. So, in early summer 2007, we signed with ROAR, and they have represented us ever since.

Finally it was time for the MOBO Best Newcomer award, and by this time Dappy was holding my hand tightly under the table. All that day the three of us had been begging our new manager, Jonathan, to tell us whether or not we'd won, but he wouldn't say a word, even though he knew the result. The actor Wil Johnson was presenting the award and as the huge screen on the O2 stage flashed clips of all the nominees, including a clip from our video for 'You Better Not Waste My Time', Dappy squeezed my hand even harder.

'And the winner is . . . N-Dubz!'

I could hardly believe it when Wil Johnson said the words, and suddenly I realised that Dappy wasn't holding my hand anymore, that he was already heading for the stage as a huge scream went up in the O2.

We'd won the MOBO, and I jumped up and headed towards the stage, running to keep up with my cousin. I was ecstatic, and all I could think about was how proud my Uncle B would have been if he could have been with us right then. I was completely overwhelmed and emotional as I stepped onto that stage.

Dappy spoke first, shouting out for everyone to chant the N-Dubz trademark phrase: 'Na Na Niii'. He thanked his mum and our new management team, headed by Jonathan, and then finally he thanked his dad 'most of all'. When he handed me the microphone, it was all I could do not to start blubbing, I was so overcome. I thanked all of our fans and my mum and dad, and, of course, Uncle B for putting his heart and soul into N-Dubz. Meanwhile, the crowd was going nuts for us; it was crazy. This was going to be the start of something amazing for N-Dubz: a whole new world for me. It was one of the best moments of my life.

After the huge buzz surrounding 'I Swear' and our next self-released single, 'Feva Las Vegas', Polydor had finally decided that they wanted to put out an N-Dubz single. They'd monitored the success we'd had putting our own tracks out, and now they decided to get in on the action themselves. The only problem was, the label didn't seem to like any of the songs we brought to them – well, not enough to release them as singles, anyway.

'No, that's not a single. No, neither is that. No, we don't think that's strong enough.'

We were turning out material that we knew our fans would go for, but they never seemed to be good enough. Eventually, the powers that be at Polydor, who didn't really seem to have a clue where our music was concerned, decided that we should re-release our first single, 'You Better Not Waste My Time', but as a major release on Polydor rather than just a download-only single on LRC records. We were horrified. I remember us having a conversation with the label's MD, Colin Barlow.

'We need to release a fresh single. Our fans have already

got 'Better Not Waste My Time' – they ain't gonna buy it again. We've been to concerts and seen two thousand kids singing this song: trust me, they've already downloaded it.'

I told Colin that we would be automatically losing out on thousands of sales if we re-released that song, that it would be career suicide, but he was adamant.

'Trust me,' he said. 'There are loads of people who haven't heard it. Let us do this. I know what I'm talking about and I guarantee it's going to work. If I turn out to be wrong, then we do it your way next time.'

At the end of the day, we didn't have a choice, because we didn't have any other record deal. Whether we liked it or not, N-Dubz's first major single release was going to be 'You Better Not Waste My Time'. As soon as it came out, there was an online backlash from the fans.

'What are you doing? Your first big release and you give us what we already know.'

'Give us fresh music!'

'What is this shit?'

'You're selling out!'

It was tough for us to have to read that stuff, but we'd all known it was going to happen. Polydor had completely underestimated how big our fanbase was. When the record went to number twenty-six in the chart, we were left wondering how well we might have done if we'd been allowed to release something new. Sure, it got us into the top thirty, but it wasn't good enough as far as we were concerned. We wanted to make it big, and there was no room for compromise.

To make things worse, after 'You Better Not Waste My Time', Polydor decided that they wanted to re-release 'I Swear'. Now we were really pissed off! We'd won a MOBO for fuck's sake; surely they'd have a bit more faith in us now? The answer was no, they still weren't feeling any of our new material.

'This is career suicide. I'm not doing this shit!'

I was adamant that this was the wrong thing to do, and Dappy and Fazer were right behind me.

While all this was going on, we'd presented the label with some great potential singles, like 'Ouch!' and 'Papa Can You Hear Me?', which was dedicated to Uncle B, but they just wouldn't listen to us. Instead, they put us in the studio with pop writers and producers who'd had success with artists like Kylie Minogue, George Michael and Leona Lewis. This just wasn't right for N-Dubz, so I laid my cards on the table with the label executives.

'If you want to find three urban-looking kids off the street and turn them into pop tarts, then go out on the street and find them. Pick 'em up now and stick 'em in the studio and see what happens. I think that's what you're looking for, at the end of the day. When you first signed N-Dubz, you liked us because we were doing our own thing, our own way. You told us that you liked us because we weren't manufactured and we were staying true to ourselves, and now you want to strip away everything you liked about us in the first place.'

Polydor wanted us to appeal to a wider market, I suppose, but we knew that our sound wasn't going to appeal to people in their thirties, and that wasn't who we were aiming at anyway. We wanted to make music for kids and teenagers like us. There was no point in trying to capture a market we weren't right for, or trying to please people who were never going to like us anyway. I felt that the band were at a real high point, especially after winning the MOBO, but I was worried that the fanbase we'd built up was going to be obliterated if we went down the route that Polydor had planned for us. We felt that N-Dubz had something real and unique that was working, and if Polydor wasn't willing to let us 'do us' then it just wasn't the right label for us anymore. Time was marching on, though, and while all this fighting was going on, we had no records coming out. It had been well over a year since the buzz of 'I Swear', so the fans had heard nothing new from us apart from a re-release of an old song. One day, when we stopped at a service station on our way to a gig, a young girl came over and said to us, 'I remember you guys. You're those kids who had that song out ages ago.'

That did it for all of us, and we knew it was time to take drastic action. There was still a lot more fighting back and forth behind the scenes, but in the end we know that there was no way that Polydor Records and N-Dubz were going to be able to work together in the future. We asked them to let us go, and eventually they did.

We were gonna have to do it on our own again.

———————

Once we'd parted company with Polydor Records, we decided to put some of the money we had into another self-released record – one that we believed in. The song was called 'Ouch' and, once again, we used our friend George Burt to direct the video. As in our previous videos, there were strong storylines, and although it was the slickest and most expensive-looking video we'd made to date, it only cost seven grand. 'Ouch' was lyrically like 'I Swear' Part Two, only this time around it was the girl who was being cheated on.

Once again, the buzz was crazy around the release and the video got something like four million hits in its first month of release. Suddenly we were getting calls from Polydor asking us how we would feel about releasing 'Ouch' with them. We could hardly believe our ears. What? The song that they'd told us had no chorus? We asked our new management to tell them, as politely as possible, to shove it. It's funny to think that three years after N-Dubz left Polydor, the new president of the label, Ferdy Unger-Hamilton, tried to sign me as a solo artist. He seemed like a good guy, but I wasn't interested. I don't believe in going backwards.

I suppose that after winning the MOBO we expected record labels to be biting our hands off, but that wasn't the case. I think that a lot of major labels just didn't really have a clue what to do with us, despite our underground reputation. But all of a sudden, in 2008, there was a label that did seem to get us, and they offered us an album deal – at last! The label was All Around the World, an independent run by two guys up in Blackburn called Matt Cadman and Cris Nuttall, and they seemed to have the same vision for us that we did.

Financially, it wasn't the huge advance we'd been hoping for, once the money was split three ways and we'd paid management commission and tax, but what was more important to us was that we were offered so much more creative control: over how we were presented as a band, over how the marketing money was spent and, most importantly, over the songs we released. Cris and Matt put so much faith in us and invested a lot of money into our next release, 'Papa Can You Hear Me?', and the album that followed it, *Uncle B*. That album had been a long time coming and was finally released in November 2008. We'd been recording tracks for it for the past three years, and it included our earlier singles 'You Better Not Waste My

Time' and 'I Swear'. It hit the album charts at number eleven, and as the weeks went by, we watched the sales going up and up, until *Uncle B* went platinum, selling over half a million copies. We'd done it. N-Dubz had finally hit big, just like Uncle B always told us we would.

Chapter Fifteen

All the time my music career was on the up and up, my on/off relationship with Adam Bailey continued. I guess the reason we kept gravitating back to one another was the similarities in our background. We were both only children, both living with our dads at the time and both the only white kids hanging out with large groups of black and mixed-race kids. There was a very definite connection there, and we were always friends as well as being a couple. In fact, we're still good friends today.

The trouble back then was that Adam had been too casual about our relationship for too long, and I wanted more than just a hook-up. I'd had enough of casual relationships and flings: I wanted to be with someone for keeps – that's just the way I'm made. For the early part of our so-called love affair, I would constantly be throwing tantrums and getting into fights with Adam, knowing that he was often seeing other girls when he wasn't with me. In fact, there was one girl Adam used to see who I felt meant more to him than I did. That really cut me up and it made me even more determined to go for all or nothing with Adam. Either we were going to be together or we weren't – it was that simple. It's funny, these days I'd never let myself get into such a vulnerable position like that with a guy – it just wouldn't happen. And looking back now, I think this was the turning point. It was when I finally found my voice as far as men and relationships were concerned.

I was changing from a girl into a woman, and as I shed my girlish skin and found confidence in myself, I started to put up with Adam's nonsense less and less. If he didn't turn up to meet me when he was supposed to, then I didn't answer the phone to him for the next week. If I found out that he was hanging out with another girl, I just refused to talk to him. After all, screaming and shouting hadn't got me anywhere, so now my attitude was more like 'Fuck you!'

The ironic thing was that it was Adam who was always encouraging me to stand up for myself where other people were concerned.

'You shouldn't let people talk to you like that,' he'd say when I complained about this or that altercation. 'Don't hang around with those types of people.' Or he'd tell me, 'Don't ever let a guy treat you badly.'

He was quite protective of me, in a funny way, and he often schooled me on how to act in a given situation, because he was older and supposedly wiser than me. I learned so much from Adam, because I idolised him in many ways, but what he didn't realise was that he was creating a monster, and that everything he was teaching me would soon turn right around and bite him on the arse. I remember him calling me up very late at night once, to tell me he wanted to see me asap.

'What the fuck do you think you're doing?' I snapped down the phone. 'What time do you call this? It's twelve o'clock at night. Don't be calling me up at midnight, thinking I'm your booty call. You can go fuck yourself, mate!'

There was a very definite change in me, a more womanly confidence and strength, and Adam seemed to find it attractive. I guess I'd stopped believing that a guy would give you his heart if you gave yourself to him. There's a slang word my friends and I often used about girls, 'stush', and I guess that applied to me at that time. To a man, stush means uptight and frigid, but to us girls, it meant being choosy and not putting out.

During one of the periods when I wasn't getting along with Adam, I met a guy called Justin Edwards in a nightclub called The Opera House in Tottenham, and we started dating. It wasn't a serious relationship at first – I guess we were just finding our feet really – but when Adam found out about it, he was none too happy, despite his cool attitude towards me. As it turned out, my little flirtation with Justin was quite short-lived, but after that I really started to notice a change in Adam's attitude. He was a bit more thoughtful, more attentive all of a sudden. It was at that point that I took the bull by the horns and sat him down for a talk about how I felt. I had a couple of drinks first, for a bit of Dutch courage, and then I went to see him at his dad's place and laid it on the line once and for all.

'I don't like the way you've been treating me. I don't like the way you randomly ring me up once a week, whenever you want, and refuse to stay in touch with me on a day-to-day basis. I'm tired of how casual this whole thing is, and do you know what? I'm not doing it anymore. If you want to be around me and you want to see me, you better get your act in gear.'

I wasn't finished either.

'I want to go out for dinner next week, so you can set a date and a time and then call me, 'cause I won't be calling you.'

It was quite funny to see his reaction to this declaration of independent womanhood. It was sort of: Woah! Who is this?

Unfortunately, my moment of glory didn't last too long. Right after Adam had told me how strong his feelings were for me, and how important I was to him, and how he was going to try to make 'us' work, his dad, Joe, came up the stairs, calling the name of the other girl Adam had been seeing. When Joe entered the bedroom and saw it was me and not 'the other woman', he was suddenly flustered and blurted out more than he probably should have.

'Oh, T, sorry!' Joe spluttered. 'I didn't realise it was you. It's just that she was here last night and they had a big argument and I thought she'd come back and . . .'

Meanwhile, I was glaring at Adam, who was clearly horrified.

'Oh yeah, Joe? Tell me more,' I said through gritted teeth.

'No, T, it's not like that,' Adam said. 'I had a row with her and we broke up. I do want to try to make it work with us, honestly.'

I wasn't having any of it.

'Do you know what? Piss off!' I said, and I spun around and marched out of the bedroom and out of the house, vowing not to ever call him again.

Later that day, one of our tour managers, Mark, who looked after us for ROAR Global and had also become a good mate, happened to be attending the same wedding as Adam. I didn't realise at the time but he and Adam were actually part of the same circle and knew one another well, even though both were unaware of their mutual connection to me. They were now sat at the same table, and my name came up in conversation. Adam had already left me eight or nine messages that day, which I'd ignored, but then Mark called me from the reception to tell

The opening night of the Against All Odds tour

Picking up our O2
Silver Clef for winning
'The Digital Award'

The picture below was taken on tour when Gareth and I had just met. As you can see, we've been inseparable ever since!

Top: Chilling at the studio in Atlanta recording tracks for my debut solo album

Bottom: Backstage on the   tour

Being interviewed on *This Morning*

Top: Me, Gareth and NY the morning before my first meeting with Simon Cowell in LA

Middle: In the studio with Jean-Baptiste in LA recording a track for my album

Bottom: Living it up in the south of France while filming the Best Behaviour video.

me how devastated Adam was that I didn't want to know him anymore.

'Since he found out I work with you, he's not stopped going on about you,' Mark told me. 'He made me promise I would talk to you and get you to speak to him. He's desperate. Just pick up the phone to him, T, please.'

Of course, I loved it. This guy who I'd been so mad about for so long, and who'd treated me so poorly, was now begging me to give him another chance. Eventually, we talked and Adam promised to change. We were a proper couple at last. In fact, at the end of 2008, we got engaged.

I suppose it wasn't the usual get-down-on-one-knee proposal, but it was a proper commitment nonetheless. Adam had bought me an eternity ring for Christmas that year, and when he gave it to me we got talking about relationships and marriage. Eventually, one thing in the conversation led to another, until we decided that we might as well make the ring an engagement ring. We weren't planning on tying the knot right away – not for a couple of years – but still, there it was: I was engaged.

When things were good between Adam and me, they were brilliant, but little did I know when we got engaged the kind of shit we were going to go through the following year. On Adam's twenty-fourth birthday in 2009, the two of us were out with Dappy when we got into an altercation with a group of lads at a shop in Finchley Road. Later on that night, one of this group of lads was stabbed, and because Adam, Dappy and I were in the area, we were arrested on suspicion of GBH with intent, and Adam was eventually charged with the offence.

Adam had driven back to the store a fair few hours after the row to buy some alcohol, and Dappy and I had

gone in my car, parking up opposite the store.
Unfortunately for us, the same crowd that Adam and
Dappy had clashed with earlier were still hanging around,
and suddenly I saw a large group of guys gather and start
throwing things at Adam's car as it drove by. I jumped out
of my car to see what was happening, and suddenly I was
watching Adam's car flip over in the street, like something
out of a movie. I was horrified. Looking at the state of the
car when it came to rest, I was sure Adam must be dead
and I screamed, going into a complete panic and running
towards the scene. The car was practically upside down;
how could he have survived that?

The next thing I saw was Adam staggering out of the
car, looking dazed and confused.

'Get in the car!' I screamed at him, and when he was
safely away from the gang of men and in my car, we sped
off, leaving his upturned car where it was. There was no
stabbing. That was something we only heard about the
following day.

I knew full well that Adam hadn't been party to any
GBH with intent, despite getting into a row with these
guys, and I'd said as much to the police, so I was to be
called as a witness at the upcoming trial. It was a terrible
time, and Adam faced a long prison sentence if he was
convicted. I wanted to do everything I could to help him,
and if that included standing up in court then so be it, but
he became very depressed leading up to the trial, and the
cracks in our relationship started to show. It also put a
huge strain on my relationship with Dappy.

Before the incident, Dappy and Adam had always got
on really well. The first altercation in the shop had only
started because Adam had come to the defence of Dappy.
But as the legal process went on, Dappy became less and

less happy about being dragged into the drama of it all. He had a serious mistrust of the police, and he had been in enough trouble himself, so he just wanted it all to go away. He didn't want to go to court, he didn't want to be a witness, and he hated the fact that I was going to be involved in the court case. I was stuck between my fiancé and my cousin, and it went on for months. I knew full well that the press was going to be all over this case, and I knew that I might be risking my career by getting involved if it went the wrong way, but the fact was that Adam was innocent, and I couldn't stand by and let him go to prison for something he didn't do.

What complicated matters more was that Adam's legal team didn't exactly fill me with confidence and they just kept telling him that things 'didn't look good'. I was terrified that he wasn't getting the best representation available, and so I went to see a music publisher I knew whose son had been in a similar predicament to Adam. I asked him who their lawyers were, and then put up every single penny I'd saved from my earnings and advances, £100,000 in all, to employ their services. I knew that once Adam was acquitted, I would get my money back, but at the time this put a terrible strain on our relationship.

I was spending most of my time with Adam at his dad's at that point, and between my stress about the situation and his constant anxiety about the impending court case, we started to argue more and more. Eventually, I stopped having sex with him, which didn't go down too well, as you can imagine. I couldn't face it, though, and of course this made him even angrier and more depressed. Then I heard from some random girl I knew that she thought Adam was cheating on me. She sent me a message saying that Adam was in my car, which he'd been borrowing, with another girl. Then she sent me a picture of the car, parked up, with them in it – including the car's number plate. I confronted him in the pub later, but I didn't go nuts. No, I was a bit more devious than that. I remember it was a lovely summer's afternoon, and there I was engaging Adam in a long but relaxed chat about the state of our relationship, and how we might sort things out. Then, once I'd lulled him into a false sense of security, I quietly went in for the kill.

'Look, I know how things have been between us, but I think the best thing is for us to get everything out in the open and be honest with one another. I guess I'd understand if you'd been with someone else. But just be honest with me about it. Tell me. I'm not going to freak out.'

'Yes, I have been sleeping with someone else,' Adam confessed.

I burst into tears in the middle of the pub, and then I went ballistic.

'You fucking bastard!'

I walked away . . . and that was the end of my engagement to Adam.

––––––––––

On the day of the trial, I was absolutely terrified. Despite the fact that we'd split up a couple of months before, I still couldn't stand the thought of Adam going to prison for something he hadn't done, and I also had a lot of personal investment in him being acquitted. What scared me the most was the fact that Adam was relying on me so heavily. I was his key witness, but I was worried that my nerves were going to get the better of me and that I was going to somehow make a mistake or say the wrong thing in court. Maybe I wouldn't be a believable witness if I came across as being too nervous. The one thing I had to keep telling myself was that Adam was innocent – however much the prosecution said otherwise, he didn't do it. I held on tight to that fact.

Strangely, by the time I came to give evidence, my nerves had started to evaporate, and after a few minutes I felt confident about what I was saying and doing. That's not to say that the prosecutor didn't give me a hard time – he did. The prosecution's take on it was that we'd plotted the whole thing and I was involved. I wasn't having it, though, I was angry. One of the things I hate most is being accused of something that I haven't done, and as the prosecutor challenged me I had a moment of clarity and answered confidently and articulately back.

Finally, the barrister put it to me that we had planned the whole thing together and had gone to the area specifically to commit the crime in question.

'What would you say to that?' he asked.

'I would say that I'm here because there's an innocent man in that box who could spend years of his life in prison for something he hasn't done,' I replied. 'You're here because you're being paid to be.'

Some of the jury giggled. The poor guy really got a run for his money.

Mercifully, Adam was found not guilty of all charges, I got my money back and suddenly the huge weight of it all was lifted from all our shoulders. Still, there was no chance that Adam and I were going to get back together. For a start, we'd had one row too many and there was too much water under the bridge, and besides that, I had started seeing Justin Edwards again.

We didn't really speak or see one another for well over a year – not until my relationship with Justin had ended.

Further down the line, though, Adam and I did start talking again, and as soon as we did, we realised what a strong bond there was between us. No, we weren't in love with one another any longer, but each of us still had love for the other. Eventually, we became the closest of friends again. In fact, at one stage, I actually moved in with Adam, as a flatmate. It was an odd situation, I guess, but it worked. We even slept together in the same bed quite often, but the only physical contact between us was the odd hug now and again. If Adam had a girl coming over, he'd simply ask me if I minded going to stay with another friend, and I happily would. That was how cool our relationship had become.

Adam and I are like family these days, and whatever man comes into my life, I will always have time for Adam. It's just something that whoever I am with will have to accept. It isn't a sexual relationship, or even romantic love, but Adam and I have an understanding and there's a link between us that will always be there. He 'gets' me in a way that nobody else does, and I don't think that will ever change.

Chapter Sixteen

The one bright spot on the horizon through the stress of the trial and my break-up with Adam was that I was back working on another series of *Dubplate Drama*, and I was loving it. After my small appearance in the second series, I'd been asked to appear in the third series, but this time my role was to be a major one. I had a few meetings with Luke, the director, and he told me that he really wanted to develop the character of Laurissa and build a lot more of the action around her. Now I was going to be playing the enemy of the lead female character, Dionne, and I was chuffed to bits. I'd really enjoyed working on the show before and now I'd have a proper chance to shine. Of course, on this series of *Dubplate*, I'd have a lot more to do and a lot more lines to learn, and I remember feeling quite nervous about it. It was a big challenge for me, and I was determined to get it right and to be good, because I really wanted to act as well as sing.

One of the things I loved about being on *Dubplate* was the fact that I got to work with some really great, seasoned actors, as well as the younger cast members. I'd already acted opposite Adam Deacon, but this new series saw me teamed up with Ricci Harnett, who'd starred in movies like *Rise of the Foot Soldier* and *28 Days Later*. Ricci was playing my character's boyfriend, an unscrupulous music manager who was trying to force Laurissa into the music industry after discovering she could sing. Laurissa ends up hooked on cocaine, and getting in a right old state, snorting drugs off toilet seats and trying to survive a really abusive relationship. Ricci was brilliant to play opposite. He was a very nurturing actor and I learned a lot from him. He guided me through the process and taught me how to act like a real professional.

He was also great at calming my nerves and giving me the confidence I needed to get the job done, and as a first-time actor, I never once felt intimidated working alongside him. Eventually, we became great mates off-set as well as on. It's funny, because while the cameras were rolling, the pair of us would be screaming and swearing in one another's faces, and then as soon as Luke yelled 'cut' we would both fall about in hysterics. This sometimes made it hard to conjure up all the emotional distress I had to portray at a moment's notice. So if I had to cry in a particular scene, I'd usually sit there with an onion held to my nose for five minutes, and at other times, when I was supposed to be miserable, I'd try to work myself into a really depressed state before the cameras rolled. Sometimes I'd be sitting around the set looking really miserable and various cast members would come over to me with looks of concern on their faces.

'Are you all right, T? Are you sure you're OK?'

'Of course I'm all right, I'm trying to get into character. Leave me alone. I'm acting!'

When *Dubplate Drama* finally aired, I remember watching my performance with mixed feelings. There were definitely some scenes where my inexperience and nerves came through – at least I thought they did – but generally I was pleased with my work and what I consider to be a pretty natural performance. So despite the fact that I sometimes found the whole process quite nerve-wracking,

HONEST

I decided that acting was most certainly something I wanted to pursue, and I'd love to do more of it in the future. I have fond memories of doing *Dubplate*, and having Ricci around to keep me laughing and joking on set was fantastic. We've stayed friends ever since.

———————

I should have been enjoying my career with N-Dubz – and all the success that came with it – as much as I was enjoying my acting. However, there were a few cracks beginning to show, and they were getting bigger by the day. Dappy was clearly deeply affected by his dad's death, and he seemed to be constantly angry and depressed, causing him to overreact to anything and everything. Consequently, the two of us started to argue, and the more time we spent together, the worse it seemed to get.

This unfriendly atmosphere between us really started to get to me, and sometimes I just didn't even want to be around him. I found him really difficult to reason with, as I'm sure he did me, but I'd already had enough drama outside the band.

During this time, we were rehearsing for our first tour, which was named after the album, the Uncle B tour, and it was a sell-out. The trouble was that at the same time as I was in rehearsals for the tour, I was also filming *Dubplate*, which meant that I had to cram all my filming for the series into two weeks before the tour actually started. Everyone was tired and frazzled, but once the rehearsals were done for the day the boys could go home, whereas I had to go and film for *Dubplate*, sometimes until 4 a.m., so by the time rehearsals rolled around the next day I was completely knackered. Don't get me wrong, I was thrilled that all this exciting stuff was happening to me at last, but at the same time, my constant tiredness meant that I was sometimes on a short fuse and very snappy. Then I was even more sensitive to Dappy's more annoying habits. He would often make snap decisions without consulting Fazer and me, like changing the order of the songs in the set. More often than not, I'd disagree with him, whether it was a decent idea or not, just because we couldn't stand the sight of one another at the time.

'No, we've set and rehearsed this – you're not fucking changing it!'

'Oh, piss off, T!'

The truth was that I still loved Dappy very deeply, but I found his attitude and manner unbearable. Some days we didn't even acknowledge or say hello to one another when we arrived at the rehearsal studios, and the first time we spoke would be to yell and argue. Half the time I was just as pissed off with Fazer, too, because he always sided with his mate and I had to battle against the pair of them. There was a very definite division: them and me.

As far as I was concerned, Dappy didn't seem to know how to conduct himself as somebody in the public eye, no matter how well known we were becoming. There was incident after incident where I felt he'd made the band look bad. One particular incident caused a huge press storm, when Dappy threatened a young woman who had texted into the Chris Moyles Show on Radio 1 while N-Dubz were guests. The girl, who was called Chloe, had sent an abusive text message to the studio, calling us losers and saying that I was a slag and Dappy was repulsive, and unbeknown to the show's producers – and me – Dappy made a note of her telephone number. The next day he sent a personal message to the woman, telling her that she was going to die. Of course, he hadn't meant any real threat to her, he was just pissed off because this girl had sent in such a nasty message for no reason. However, it was the wrong thing to do, and the press had a field day. As a result of this, we were dropped from a government anti-bullying campaign that we'd been involved in, and I was enraged. I didn't want to be seen as a negative role model for young kids, and I objected to the fact that we were all being branded with the same bad name because of Dappy.

This wasn't the only episode either. Dappy just didn't seem to have any media savvy or know what was acceptable in society and what wasn't. It didn't matter that he was now a pop star, he just continued acting like the hood ghetto kid from Camden, swearing and cussing on live radio shows, being caught on CCTV taking the drug mephedrone (also known as miaow-miaow), being charged with assault – his antics went on and on, and I just didn't understand why he couldn't see the damage it was doing to his own band. I think I understood why it was happening, though. Still, knowing that didn't make his tantrums and his mood swings any easier to deal with, and I felt like all the fights and unnecessary drama were ruining what should have been a great time for us. What's worse is that Fazer would often follow suit if Dappy got involved in something dodgy, and so I'd end up being pissed off with both of them.

Sure, I was happy for the band to be seen as a gritty young urban group who had something to say, but now I felt we were being portrayed as horrible little shits from Camden who'd just got lucky. The media saw us as naughty little chavs who didn't deserve the success we were having, and that's not what I wanted for myself at all.

I'd had a difficult childhood and I'd made mistakes, but now I was making something of myself. I guess, for someone who doesn't understand the kind of world I grew up in, that's hard to grasp, but I felt that I'd earned the right to a successful career. All Dappy's wild antics and brushes with the law were just making all that bad press harder to combat, and it made me angry and resentful. I saw his actions as a reflection on me, and I wanted to distance myself from them. I wasn't the little hood girl anymore, and I didn't want to be. We were in the public eye now, and there were young kids looking up to us, so I felt like I had a responsibility to behave in a certain way. Yes, we still had an edgy urban style, but that didn't mean we should come across like ignorant hoodlums.

As time went on, even the writing and production process of what we were doing started to stress me out. It became very clear that Dappy saw himself as the star of the show, and he became very dominant and protective about his music and wanted to control every aspect of it, even down to what happened during the live performances. I suppose I don't blame him: he was passionate about N-Dubz and it was in his nature to want to shine. Unfortunately, it's also in my nature to want to be the star of the show. I'm no back-up singer, and I didn't appreciate being treated like one. We were now clashing about absolutely everything. It was like a war.

Poor Fazer, meanwhile, was piggy in the middle, and it made our working environment virtually unbearable. Everything was a drama, and anyone that came into contact with us could see it. Friends who knew us would ask me how I managed to cope.

'How can you be in that environment day in, day out, T? It's so intense. I don't know how you deal with it.'

HONEST

To be honest, I didn't really know how to answer them. Outsiders would come to work for us, either from the management or the record label, and would quit after a week or so, because they couldn't handle the stress. It pained me so much to be going to work knowing how lucky I was and how grateful I should be that we had achieved all that we had, yet still feeling miserable and anxious the whole time and wishing I wasn't there. It was hard to know where it was all going to end.

I suppose the thought of going out and playing live in front of an audience made all the shit I was going through with Dappy seem worth it, because I just loved to perform. However, before the first show in Wolverhampton, I was absolutely petrified. This tour was on a whole new level to the shows we'd done before. We were now playing famous venues like the Shepherds Bush Empire, and for the first few gigs, my nerves really kicked in. I think half of it was because I couldn't take it all in – none of us could really. We had fought so long to find success and now, with a platinum-selling record and our own tour, we'd been propelled into a whole new world. We were pop stars.

Once I got over my initial nerves after the first couple of shows, I loved it, and so did the boys. The arguments and fights disappeared as soon as we hit the stage – they had to. We had to look like a gang, however hard it was. We usually pulled it off, too, and when we were all up there, singing our hearts out, it was almost as if we were a real team and were all happy again. The crowds at our shows were pretty amazing too. We've always been lucky with our fans – the N-Dubletts as we called them – they make so much noise, and they're real screamers. It was always a pleasure to perform in front of an audience like that.

We still didn't have much money while we were doing

the Uncle B tour, but although it wasn't super-glamorous behind the scenes, we would always find an excuse to party and have fun. It didn't matter if we were at a club after the show or just on the tour bus, N-Dubz liked to party! This was what it was all about, as far as I was concerned, and despite all the arguments, there were moments of real togetherness as a band on that first tour. We all felt like this was meant to be, and that we were all out there doing it for Uncle B.

At the 2009 MOBO awards, which were held in Glasgow, N-Dubz picked up the awards for Best UK Act and Best Album for *Uncle B*. I felt like we were on a roll, as if there was absolutely no stopping us now. Despite the rows within the band, it was a brilliant time and a fantastic experience, something I will treasure for the rest of my life. Something to tell the grandkids.

Chapter Seventeen

N-Dubz had much the same game plan for 2010 as we'd had for 2009: record an album, make the videos for the singles, promote the album and then tour. While I was excited and grateful for all the things that were happening to me, I was also exhausted by N-Dubz's ridiculously packed schedule. When I think about it now, it just seems like a complete blur, because all we did was graft, and as much as I was enjoying being a pop star, I sometimes felt like I was being worked into the ground. There were periods when we worked for weeks on end without a single day off, and to me it seemed abnormal and excessive. Sometimes we would get to bed at 4 a.m. and then be expected to be up again for early TV appearances three or four hours later. Sure, that's OK now and again, but this would be a regular occurrence, and we were endlessly knackered. This only added to the friction within the band, and I'd sometimes get annoyed with our management for not realising that we were only human and we needed some downtime every now and again.

Still, we were on a definite roll. Our album *Against All Odds* had gone platinum and the first single from it, 'I Need You', went top five. We'd followed this up at the start of the year with a song we wrote with Mr Hudson, 'Playing with Fire', a song that eventually became everybody's favourite N-Dubz tune – or so it seemed.

Still, despite a seemingly endless run of wonderful

success, there was a real lack of glamour around N-Dubz, as far as I was concerned, and I used to complain about it all the time. In fact, until I started working on *The X Factor* there was virtually no glamour coming my way at all really. Sure, I've always been a bit of a tomboy, but sometimes it was as if N-Dubz was made up of three guys, the way we were handled. Nobody in the N-Dubz camp seemed to realise, or even care, that I had something to offer as a woman and that I wanted to make the most of my femininity and milk the glitz and glamour at least a little bit. In the first few years of the band, there was never enough in the budget for me to have hair and make-up people when I was on tour, and even on photo shoots I'd often be expected to glam myself up with not much help. Sometimes I barely had enough money to go down to Camden Market and get myself an outfit, which is why I was always in a tracksuit with my hair tied back. The chavvy look was nice and cheap to achieve! As a result of all this, I was just treated like one of the lads most of the time, and so eventually I started to behave like one – especially when we were on tour.

During our second big tour, the Against All Odds tour, which started in March 2010, we were all pretty wild. This was a much bigger tour than the Uncle B tour, taking in venues like the Hammersmith Apollo. And while all the lads were partying and welcoming various girls onto the tour bus along the way, I'd match them by inviting all my mates to join me for drinking sessions and late-night parties. It was like a rave on a moving bus most nights, with everyone getting completely smashed. I suppose we behaved more like a rock band than a pop band when we were on the road – in fact, we always used to take Jack Daniels on stage with us in cups, instead of water. We were usually merry before we got on stage and pissed by the time we came off.

I suppose it was during this time that I realised that I was starting to lose sight of my femininity, and I was behaving more and more like a lad. The way I carried myself, how I walked, talked, and even the way I interacted with other people, was really macho. I guess I was just unconsciously copying the behaviour of all the people around me, but soon other people started to notice too. Guys who knew me would find this contrast both intriguing and disturbing all at the same time. They couldn't understand how somebody who cared so much about looking feminine and sexy most of the time could also come across as so blokey.

Still, there I was every night after a gig, straight into my tracksuit bottoms, relaxing with a bottle of beer or a fag in one hand, with the other hand stuffed down the front of my trackies, like the rest of the lads. That was what being in N-Dubz did for a girl. I was surrounded by boys the whole time, so I just became more and more like one. Once I'd reached that stage, it was hard to go back, and I quite enjoyed my more masculine persona for a while – it made me feel strong. Mind you, if there was an attractive guy on the scene, I could always switch back into girly, flirtatious mode at the drop of a hat – I never had a problem with that. Once the guy in question had disappeared, though, I was straight back to being one of the lads again. I don't think that side of me will ever totally disappear.

By the start of the Against All Odds tour, my relationship with Justin was all but dead in the water, at least for me. It hadn't been good or right for a long time, and I knew it. I'd tried to convince myself that it was true love for the longest time, because that was my way and that's what I ultimately wanted, but Justin had a dark, controlling side, and it just never sat right with me.

When Justin and I had first started dating again, in the run-up to Adam's trial, it was as if he'd come along at exactly the right time. I felt like he was almost some kind of saviour, that he was rescuing me from a bad situation. Things got pretty intense quite rapidly, and he told me that he loved me and wanted to be with me for keeps very early on in our relationship. Looking back, I know I had love for Justin, but I'm not sure I was ever really *in* love with him, and despite the fact that we made all sorts of plans about the future, there always seemed to be something inside me that prevented me from throwing myself into our relationship wholeheartedly.

I guess I was living in some kind of romantic fantasy for a while – a bubble – but eventually Justin's temper and possessive nature began to emerge. Plus his attitude towards women was bloody terrifying and went against everything I believed in. Justin didn't believe in equality between the sexes. He thought that women were inferior to men, and that I was inferior to him, and he let me know it too: he actually told me that! As far as Justin was concerned, he was the man and he was the dominant force. So the qualities in me that he was attracted to in the first place – my fieriness, my independent spirit – suddenly became a burden to him.

The funny thing was, Justin was more than happy to accept a woman's help when it came to his career – my help! He didn't seem to mind me having the upper hand then. Justin was an up-and-coming MC who went by the name DJ Ultra, and during the course of our relationship, I persuaded our management to work with him, our record label, All Around the World, to put out his single, and I even got him a support slot on our upcoming Against All Odds tour. That was all fine and dandy, as far as he was concerned.

As my boyfriend, though, Justin wanted to mould me and change me – to own me even. And he spent far too much time telling me what he thought was wrong with me and how I might improve myself by changing. He even kindly offered to help me to change all the things in me he didn't like. As you can imagine, I wasn't too keen on being dominated, and I believed that I was a pretty OK person already. Sure, I'll take on board what someone is saying, but when that person is telling me what I can and can't do, I'm not having any of it. In fact, on the very day that Justin told me that he felt he was above me, just like all men were above all women, the relationship died for me. Yes, it dragged on for another few months, but for me, it was done. You don't say shit like that to the Female Boss!

The only problem was that however much I distanced myself from Justin, he simply didn't get the message. By the start of the tour, I'd really backed off; I'd hardly seen him and we hadn't slept together in two months. Once the tour was underway, however, Justin was acting as if everything was cool between us, and it just seemed like the further I pulled away from him, the closer he tried to get to me. I didn't want to hurt him, but in the end, I couldn't take it anymore. One night, early on in the tour, I had to spell it out for him.

'I think it's time for me to be on my own for a while,' I told him.

Who was I trying to kid? I hated being on my own, but it was the best way I could think of to let him down lightly.

'I feel very down, Justin, and I just don't think it's working between us.' This much was true; I had been feeling very low during the last few months with him.

I could see that he was pretty devastated, and I felt bad for him, but at least now I'd been honest. I suddenly felt relieved.

The very next day, however, Justin was acting as if nothing had happened – completely delusional!

'Babe, it's all right! I know you didn't mean what you said last night,' he told me. 'I know we can sort everything out.'

'No. I did mean what I said last night,' I said, somewhat gobsmacked. 'I don't want to be with you anymore, Justin.'

After that he switched over to full-on emotional/crazy: crying his eyes out, getting dramatically drunk and acting like it was the end of the greatest love story ever told, which it most certainly wasn't. His behaviour made me want to run away even more, because I just couldn't handle all the drama. After all Justin had said about men being the superior sex, I'd hoped he'd at least 'be a man' about it and take it on the chin, so to speak, but no. Although he had no choice but to accept the fact that our relationship was over, he was clearly very bitter about it.

I started hanging out with our dancers while we were on tour, and one of them became more than just an on tour drinking buddy, ending up as my personal assistant and best friend. When I first met Gareth Varey, I wasn't actually that keen on him. He was with someone I know at the MOBOs' after-party towards the end of 2009, and I remember thinking that he came across a bit 'music-industry bitchy', making smart comments about some of the people around him. I later discovered that Gareth has quite a dark sense of humour and he'd actually been taking the piss out of all the catty music-biz types, having a bit of a joke about the way they behaved. The second time I met him was when he was cast as one of our dancers on the tour.

This time I got on a lot better with him, but he still wasn't exactly my cup of tea as a potential friend. Remember, I'd been used to hanging out with bad boys and an urban or ghetto crowd for the longest time. Gareth definitely isn't ghetto. I could get on well with anyone, but I couldn't exactly visualise myself hanging out with him if we hadn't been thrown together on a tour, even though we got along fine. I mean, up until then, I'd never really had any gay friends before. In fact, I'd barely had any white friends, and Gareth was both, so it was a whole new experience. It's not like I had a problem with somebody being gay – or white – it was more that I was only just starting to open up to all different kinds of people, instead of sticking with the same crowd all the time, and that had to be a good thing, as far as I was concerned. One night Fazer, me and a bunch of the dancers, including Gareth, got completely smashed and started banging out tunes from my computer. We were dancing and laughing and having a typical wild on-tour party night. It was then that I really clicked with Gareth, and I told him.

'I like you,' I said.

'I like *you*,' Gareth said.

It was as simple as that, and after that we started chilling together or having a goss – it seemed as though we always had something to talk about, and it was great to have someone bright and funny to chat to. We clicked! I brought out the more ghetto side of Gareth, and he brought out the bitch in me – all in a light-hearted way (I'd never take the piss out of someone anymore than I'd take the piss out of myself). Of course, I had no idea then just how close Gareth and I would eventually become, but after a drunken night out raving together, we became even closer. That night we got completely hammered, and the drunker we got, the more jokingly vile we became, and the more we made one another laugh. We had a very similar sense of humour and seemed to share the same carefree approach to life. We also both swore like troopers, so I felt as though I could just be myself with Gareth. He was a great listener too, and I felt like he was an honest and caring person. I decided that I needed someone like that in my life, and from that night onwards, we've been virtually inseparable.

Meanwhile, me being me, the one thing I was missing was some positive male attention. As I said, Justin and I hadn't been intimate for a couple of months at least, and once the Against All Odds tour was in full swing, I was craving a bit of tenderness and affection – and yes, that means sex too, in case you were wondering!

As it turned out, it was Fazer who I ended up leaning on after the break-up, which wasn't unusual: he had often been the one I turned to in the face of any emotional turmoil. Of course, I left a respectable full twenty-four hours between breaking up with Justin and turning to Fazer (well, I'm just being honest!). We started hanging out a bit together, just as friends at first, laughing and joking with one another and chilling out on our own whenever we had some downtime.

With Fazer, it was so easy for me to pour my heart out about all the problems I'd been having with Justin, and I tried to explain to him how all the other stresses around me – including all the in-fighting within the band – were getting me down too. Suddenly everything was coming out: the long build-up to Adam's court case and our break-up, Justin's controlling ways, Dappy's reckless behaviour. It made me realise just how low I'd felt for so long. In turn, Fazer told me about the hard time he was going through in his current relationship: he wasn't in a good place either. His girlfriend was living in his flat and he was supporting her financially, but he told me that he had fallen out of love with her.

'She's doing my nut in, but I can't get her out of my house,' he told me. 'I sometimes feel like she's leeching off me.'

When we weren't complaining about our dismal love lives to one another, we were reminiscing about our childhood and the time we'd spent together as kids. When Fazer and I were alone like that – away from all the stresses and strains of N-Dubz – it was as if time had stood still and nothing had changed from when we were fourteen.

As I spent more and more time in his company, I began to notice how much more mature Fazer had become. He'd changed so much in the past year, and all the little things that I'd found irritating about him in the past seemed to have disappeared. Fazer wasn't a boy anymore, he was a man, and I suddenly started to see him in a whole new light – a romantic one. I was attracted to him all over again, and there didn't seem to be anything I could do to stop it. It was blindingly obvious to both of us that we had very strong feelings for one another, and, of course, the inevitable happened. We ended up together one night on the tour. I guess it was bound to happen, but it was romantic nonetheless. In the morning, I remember getting up to sneak back to my hotel room while Fazer was still asleep. I bent down and kissed him on the cheek, and he opened his eyes, lifted his head off the pillow and said, 'T! I love you.'

That was the thing with me and Fazer. It was never just a roll in the hay; it was always more meaningful than that. We cuddled and we talked, and when we did have sex it was always very passionate.

Still, I was very aware that Fazer was already in a romantic situation, however broken, but he told me that he now knew that he wanted to be with me, and that he was going to end things with his current girlfriend just as soon as he could.

As the tour rolled on, though, this much-talked about break-up still hadn't happened, and I started to feel uneasy about the whole thing.

'I think you're trying to have your cake and eat it,' I said to him one night.

Once again, Fazer swore that it was me he loved and wanted to be with, but still the promised break-up didn't happen. Eventually, I knew that I had to put a stop to what was going on between us. At the end of the day, Fazer had a girlfriend, and I was just kidding myself. His heart wasn't solely mine anymore, and I wasn't the type of girl to play second fiddle to anyone. I just had to accept that my tried and trusted safety blanket had finally disappeared. I didn't like it, but that was the way it was. Still, there were nights on the tour when I would get drunk and he would be all over me and I would weaken, hoping against hope that he would finally make the break. As time went on, that seemed less and less likely.

Then – right in the middle of the tour – *News of the World* columnist Dan Wootton 'exclusively' reported the story that Fazer and I were an item. I was furious. At the time, everything was all up in the air and uncertain, so I decided to try to squash the story as quickly as I could. I was aware that Dan was just doing his job as a journalist, but we weren't ready to go public about what had happened on the tour. It wasn't the time. Apart from the fact that Dappy hated the idea of us as a couple, as he thought it would alienate our fans, Fazer still hadn't broken up with his girlfriend. I felt guilty about that, and although I wanted Fazer to leave her, I didn't want her to find out about us by reading it in a newspaper – that would be awful. So, because of all those things, we denied it. I hate to say that I lied, because telling the truth is something I pride myself on, but I did. I went onto Twitter and told everyone that what Dan was reporting was completely untrue. There was quite a war of words on Twitter about it, actually, and I felt terrible, but I was under pressure and I didn't know what else to do. I couldn't face the drama that I knew would result in my confirming the fact that Fazer and I were in love, and I just wanted my private life to remain private.

Looking back, it may have been the worst-kept secret in showbiz, but because Fazer and I were always so close, it was easy to keep our love affair under wraps. We hadn't even told Simon Jones, our publicist, or many of the people who worked for us and with us. People were used to seeing us chilling out, or sharing a hotel room together as mates, or dancing together, so it was just standard. There had been countless times when Fazer had been a bit tipsy, telling everyone 'I'm going to marry T one day', and then getting overly affectionate with me. People were just used to it.

Despite everything, at the end of the tour, Fazer told me that he just couldn't face breaking up with his girlfriend. He hated the thought of hurting anyone's feelings, and he just couldn't face breaking her heart, even though things weren't right between them.

'You can't see me and live with her at the same time,' I told him. 'I'm not having it.'

It made me sad, but I knew I was doing the right thing. I'd had such an amazing time with Fazer while we were on tour, but once it was over, I just had to accept that he was going to go back to his girlfriend and that was that.

Chapter Eighteen

Along with all the daily drama of me and Dappy constantly at one another's throats, plus the on-going sexual tension between me and Fazer, the last thing I needed was a camera crew following me around 24/7, but that's exactly what I got when we agreed to take part in a fly-on-the-wall documentary series for Channel 4 *Being N-Dubz*. The show was meant to be an intimate, behind-the-scenes look at the band, capturing all the fun and excitement that surrounded us, plus, of course, some of the drama. A lot of the filming took place during the time when I was pissed off at Fazer for not having the balls to break up with his girlfriend when it was clear that he wanted to be with me, and if you were to watch the series back now, I'm sure you'd notice my frustration and animosity towards both him and Dappy simmering just below the surface the whole time.

Sometimes the show was quite enjoyable to film, because there were some genuinely fun moments between the three of us, but at other times, I found it stressful having a camera shoved in my face all day long – I think we all did. Let's be honest: the real drama going on within the band was not something I particularly wanted our fans to witness on a bloody prime-time TV show!

There was one particular incident that happened while the cameras were rolling where my anger and frustration were laid bare for everyone to see. We had flown to

Greece to appear at the MAD Music Awards, which are a bit like the Greek version of the Brits, and I was so looking forward to getting out of the country for a week or so.

The day after our performance, I was heading out to Ibiza with my new best mate, Gareth, and some other friends, and I was well up for a good time. Anyway, the trip didn't start off that well when Dappy wandered off while we were checking in at the airport and nearly missed the flight, so I was already a bit annoyed with him. Then, on the morning of the show, we were due to do some filming for *Being N-Dubz*, jet-skiing from a harbour by the sea. Well, I'd had about an hour's sleep, as I'd stayed up drinking with Gareth the night before, so I was quite late for the filming. I also had a vile hangover and my head was banging. As soon as I got there, Dappy started laying into me about how late I was and how unprofessional I was, but after all the crap I'd put up with from him, I didn't think he was being very fair. Then, while we were all hanging out by the water, Dappy decided that it would be hilarious if he and his mates picked me up and threw me into the sea, fully clothed. I went ballistic!

What annoyed me the most was that Dappy would have never dared do it if the cameras hadn't been rolling, because we were in no way cool enough at that point. We weren't having the fun and jokey kind of relationship where it would have been funny for him to chuck me in the sea. I climbed out of the water, looking like a drowned rat, enraged and upset, and I completely lost it with Dappy, stomping off along the harbour, shaking. When Fazer came over with Gareth to make sure I was all right, I just yelled at him.

'Do I look like I'm fucking all right? Do I look like I

wanted to get my hair completely soaked and mascara running all down my face?'

When I thought about it later, I knew I'd overreacted, and if it had simply been an isolated incident, then OK. But once you've had ten years of that sort of crap the novelty wears off, I can tell you.

There were other times on the show when I was portrayed as a 'mother hen' type of person, very protective and nurturing of the boys. Huh! I guess there was some small grain of truth in that, but to be honest, I needed to be a pretty fierce mother hen to keep Dappy and Fazer on the straight and narrow. It was exhausting, and I often felt like an overwrought parent of two fifteen-year-old kids when they were together, shouting and screaming at them the whole time to behave and focus and not to plunge N-Dubz into any scandals or controversies while the eyes of the country were on us.

Being N-Dubz wasn't the only TV show I took part in in 2010. The BBC approached Jonathan Shalit with the idea of me taking part in a documentary about my relationship with my mum, and specifically about how I had coped with her mental illness as a child. When Jonathan first put the proposal to me, I really wasn't keen. For a start, it was putting a very personal area of my home life out there, which was not something I felt comfortable with. Plus, I never wanted to be one of those people who come across all 'poor me, this is my sad and tragic life story'. Yes, I had talked about my mum's illness and the problems I'd had as a teenager, but I'd always tried to put a positive, and hopefully encouraging, spin on the story. As in: 'Look at me now! Haven't I come a long way?' I was worried that this programme might make me sound like a whinger, and apart from all that, I certainly didn't want my mum to be seen in any sort of negative light.

Eventually, the documentary-makers talked it through with me a bit more and helped me realise how many other kids there were out there caring for parents with bipolar disorder, schizophrenia and severe depression. They thought that someone like me taking part in such a programme could really help a lot of other young people and bring awareness to a cause that had been virtually ignored in the UK. Then, after talking to my mum to make sure she was OK with the concept, I agreed to do it.

I wish I could say that I appreciated and enjoyed the whole experience. In many ways I did, but it was tough. I'd spent my whole childhood immersed in and surrounded by mental illness, and this was a sad reminder of how hopeless it can feel at times. I met several young people who were caring for depressed parents, and I saw how it affected their entire lives. I had complete empathy with them, and for their parents, but their distress and despair was very upsetting for me to witness.

These kids were trapped in terrible situations, with very little help from anyone. It was the sort of existence that I'd been lucky enough to escape from, to a degree, because although I still had a close relationship with my mum, it wasn't something I had to cope with day to day anymore. Being in the midst of it all again had a very strange effect on me, and I suddenly felt like I was fourteen again. Before long, I was picking at my face and feeling anxious during the filming. Even just thinking about it now makes me apprehensive. I guess, if anything, doing the documentary highlighted what a big effect Mum's illness had had on me, but I never compared the depression I'd suffered to the sort of thing Mum goes through. My down times and mood swings were almost always triggered by something specific. I'm not bipolar or schizophrenic. That's something completely different.

I was actually very proud of the reaction that I got from doing the documentary. Apart from all the awareness it helped to raise for a good cause, I also think it helped many people to see me in a different and more positive light, and I really appreciated that. I was also very proud when *My Mum and Me* won a MIND media award, which are given for the best portrayals of mental health in the media.

In the midst of all this, I moved into the new house I'd bought in Watford. My very first. I was looking forward to a fresh start, plus Gareth had promised to move in with me down the line.

The two of us were together all the time now, so it just seemed like a natural progression. I felt like Gareth and I were on the same page all the time, and it was a nice feeling. We could laugh and muck about together one minute and be sad and emotional together the next, plus I felt comfortable telling Gareth all about what had gone on between Fazer and me. He became a brilliant shoulder to lean on, and in turn I would try to help him make sense of some of his romantic dilemmas.

He told me stuff about his life that he'd never told anyone, and there were times when we both sat crying in one another's arms. I'd never had that with anyone else before, and pretty soon it was obvious that this was more than just a passing or faddy friendship. We were in this for life – like two peas in a pod – with Gareth automatically slipping into a kind of motherly role, worrying about me all the time and showing real concern if ever I was upset or sad. He even seemed to be able to get his head around my occasional bouts of depression and my mood swings, and he was sensitive to the fact that I hated being on my own.

Whenever he was around, in fact, Gareth would undertake little tasks that needed doing and would help me out without being asked. It's the reason I knew he would make such a fantastic personal assistant for me. I trusted him, we adored one another, and if Gareth was my P.A., I knew he would be able to come absolutely everywhere with me. I was chuffed to bits when he agreed to take the job.

Anyway, for the first few days in my new house, it was all very exciting; in fact, I felt very grown up finally having my own property. I love to decorate and the idea of turning a place into a proper home, so I was really looking forward to picking out furniture and paint colours for the house. Sure, I could have got decorators in, but I was so excited about moving in that I started doing all the painting myself. Some nights I was up till all hours, painting a bedroom for me and another for my mum, for whenever she came to stay.

The shine soon wore off, however, when large groups of young fans started to appear outside my lovely new house, making themselves known. I don't know how they found out I was living there, but I suspected it was because the front of the house was featured on our TV show, *Being N-Dubz*. Suddenly there were kids outside my house at three in the morning shouting 'Na Na Niii'– great!

HONEST

Then some of them decided it would be fun to ring on my doorbell too. I love my fans, but this was a bit over the top – I was well pissed off! The final straw came when, in mid-July, N-Dubz performed at GuilFest, the annual music festival in Surrey. I got a call while I was on the tour bus informing me that my house had been broken into. Luckily, at the time, there wasn't much in there to nick, but the thieves had cracked the TV trying to get it off the wall, and then had seemingly been disturbed and fled before finishing the job. After that, I knew that I couldn't live there anymore – not on my own. Gareth wasn't quite ready to move in yet, and I decided I couldn't wait any longer, so I put the house on the market.

The prospect of moving back in with my dad wasn't that appealing. I felt as if I'd be going backwards, like I was a kid all over again, despite our relaxed relationship. So instead, I moved in with my ex-boyfriend, Adam Bailey, purely platonically. No love affair, no sex – we were just mates. And for a while I was quite happy there. Adam and I had put all of our past problems behind us, and it was lovely to be able to hang out without having the complication of a relationship between us. We would just talk and laugh and chill out together. We had respect for one another, and it was a really good time. Eventually, though, the situation with Fazer reared its head again.

It was bound to happen, I suppose. N-Dubz performed at quite a few festivals throughout 2010, including the Isle of Wight Festival and T4 on the Beach. We also played Glastonbury, which was a momentous thing for me, because it's such a world-famous event. Every band dreams of playing Glastonbury. Consequently, Fazer and I were together quite a bit: at rehearsals, at gigs, in hotels and on the tour bus. Sometimes, knowing that he was sleeping next door to me or in the next bunk was torture, because I badly wanted to be with him, but I wouldn't allow myself to go there. Some nights I would just lie there in bed thinking about Fazer; it really wasn't a good situation. One night he even knocked on my hotel door and asked if he could stay in my room with me – not for sex, just for a cuddle.

'You have a girlfriend,' I told him. 'I can't do this, I've told you.'

It was obvious to both of us that our feelings for one another were much more than they should have been, but as far as his home life was concerned, nothing had changed. He still didn't have the guts to break it off with his girlfriend, despite telling me that he wanted to be with me. So that was that. Fazer stayed with his girlfriend and I became more and more resentful because I couldn't be with him. It was madness really; Fazer knew he was going to have to end it with her sooner or later. As far as I was concerned, dragging it out was only going to end up hurting the girl even more in the long run, but right then, he just couldn't do it.

Despite this, Fazer would still persist in trying to get close to me at any and every opportunity. It caused a very negative energy and a lot of anxiety between us for a while, and it came to a head late one night when I'd fallen asleep on the sofa in the lounge of the tour bus, while everyone else was kipping in their bunks. Fazer decided to creep out of his bunk and snuggle up next to me on the sofa, with his arms wrapped around me, pulling me close to him. When I woke up and found him asleep next to me, I went absolutely mental.

'Get away from me! Get off me!' I screamed. 'I don't know what you want from me – you've got a girlfriend and you're not gonna leave her. What do you want from me?'

I was really upset, almost breaking down.

'You're always worrying so much about hurting her, telling me how vulnerable she is. Well, I'm not just some cold bitch who doesn't have any feelings, you know. What about me? What about my feelings?'

Fazer was just staring at me, clearly in shock, but still I went on.

'Do you know how hard it is seeing you every day and not being able to be with you? And then you go and do something like this. It's just selfish.'

By this time, I'd started to cry.

'Don't you get it? I'm in love with you.'

Fazer had told me that he loved me a hundred times, but that sudden admission from me, which had been such a long time coming, shook him. I saw a single tear fall down his cheek.

'I'm in love with you too,' he said. 'It's you I want to be with, T.'

It was a very intense moment. We were both still woozy from the alcohol we'd had earlier, both upset, both emotional, but in that moment, we'd finally declared our love for one another, and I felt so happy that night.

Chapter Nineteen

Once Fazer and I were official, at least with one another, I moved straight out of Adam's place and into Fazer's flat. Literally within days after he broke up with his girlfriend. What was the point in hanging around? We knew one another well enough. We were happy, we loved one another and we couldn't stand the thought of being apart – so we just did it. To be honest, we'd spent so much time together on tour, living in one another's pockets on the bus and in hotel rooms, that there wasn't going to be much of a difference anyway. We were just over the moon to finally be together, and there was a long period when I was very content. I'd been lonely for such a long time, and now I'd finally got what I wanted – Fazer.

I guess I'd always known it would happen eventually. Even when Fazer went back to his girlfriend after the Against All Odds tour, I remember having one of my famous premonitions and announcing to Gareth: 'You mark my words. I may not have him now, but I will have him. He'll come back to me and I will get him.'

As far as I was concerned, mine and Fazer's love for each other was pretty much unconditional. I don't think anyone has ever loved me as much as Fazer did then. When things were good between us, I felt like he would do anything for me and that I could tell him anything. I felt loved and protected and it truly was one of the happiest times of my life. All my friends noticed and commented on the change in me, because it was so obvious how content I was. They were happy to see me happy.

The other great thing about Fazer and me as a couple was that we laughed at the same stuff and had similar thoughts and feelings about so many things. We also really enjoyed one another's company, whether we were just chilling out, watching a movie, or playing combat and football games on the PlayStation together. Fazer was also mad for my cooking – all of it – which was a definite bonus, because I love to cook and I thoroughly enjoyed cooking for him every night. I was a proper little housewife, and I loved it! Plus, we'd known one another since we were kids, so it was always very natural when we were together. We were like the ultimate best friends in love. It was real.

Now, moving in together was great, but there were a few tricky obstacles that Fazer and I had to navigate too. For a start, there was the continuing issue of keeping our relationship a secret from almost everyone, at least for a while. As I said, Dappy thought our relationship would alienate our fans. This meant that we had to be very clandestine about the whole thing, not being too openly affectionate in front of other people, or even going out on proper dates in case the press spotted us and put two and two together. Keeping such a big secret was getting harder and harder, though, especially as we were now living together and both experiencing such a deep and intense love.

The other problem was that despite the fact that Fazer had broken up with his girlfriend, he didn't want to add to her pain by letting her find out that he was now in a relationship with me. All very commendable, but he handled the whole thing quite badly, leading his ex to believe that Fazer was still single for quite some time after the two of us got together. Consequently, she was determined to chase him down and win him back, calling and texting him constantly and thinking up reasons why the two of them needed to meet up.

For the first few months she kept coming over to the flat, and I'd have to go out, which seemed ridiculous to me. Then, instead of being upfront with me about the situation, Fazer thought that the sensible thing to do was to avoid telling me whenever he went to meet her or even spoke to her. He was extremely good at barefaced lying to me, and he made the mistake of doing that quite early on in our relationship, when he didn't need to.

'Please, just be honest with me,' I'd say to him. 'Look me in the eye and tell me the truth. If we're not honest with one another now, we're going to regret it in the future.'

Fazer could be very convincing – I reckon he should have been an actor – and there were quite a few occasions when he looked me straight in the eye and lied to me about what was going on with him. Of course, most of the time, I'd find out the truth and be duly enraged. The stupid thing was, I didn't really care whether or not he'd met up with his ex-girlfriend to sort stuff out or hand her back some of her possessions, but I did care about the fact that he'd lied to me about it. It shook my trust in him right away.

To add to the problem, there were the odd times when I'd spot a flirty text from a girl on his phone and that would just make me feel worse, even when it was probably something innocent. I found myself feeling quite insecure and more jealous than I'd ever felt in any other relationship. It was paranoia, pure and simple, and whenever it took hold, there was no shaking it. I knew that Fazer loved me, and it wasn't like he didn't show it, but I guess my past bad experiences with men just wouldn't allow me to relax and enjoy it sometimes, despite the fact that I loved him very much.

'Phone check!' I'd randomly (and regularly) demand, holding out my hand.

Fazer would be expected to hand me his phone, so I could scan it for texts or messages from his ex or anyone else I might not approve of.

'Why aren't you answering that?' I'd say to him if he ignored a phone call. 'Who is it?'

At the time, I didn't see anything wrong with the way I was behaving. Fazer had been dishonest, so I had a right to be suspicious. It was quite destructive, and I'm sad to say that it never really went away, despite the fact that Fazer did his best to prove himself to me all the time. I think the main problem was that I knew Fazer better than anyone. As far as women were concerned, Fazer would generally rather lie than face any kind of confrontation, and it's got him in a lot of trouble over the years. I'd always known that he was capable of bending the truth in a relationship, because he hated the idea of hurting people, but of course it never bothered me before because I wasn't the one on the receiving end of it. Well, now I was, and I had all that knowledge and insider information turning over in my mind. My friends often said to me that I knew too much for my own good, and they were right.

'It's different with you, T, because we're friends,' Fazer would say. 'I'd never hurt you, it would be like hurting my family.'

I really wanted to believe that, and I think most of the time I did, but throughout our two-year relationship, there were many moments when I lost faith and went off the deep end.

HONEST

'I love you, but I don't trust you.'

That was my mantra, as far as Fazer was concerned, and I was quite open about it.

'You'll never trust anyone,' he told me once. There was a chance he might be right, but I truly hoped he wasn't.

Anyway, in the end, I got so fed up with him not telling his ex-girlfriend about us that I phoned her up and told her myself. Well, it was getting ridiculous! I got tipsy, called up and delivered the news in person, so there was absolutely no grey area.

'I'm not doing this to be spiteful, but you need to know,' I told her. 'Fazer should have told you long ago why he broke it off with you, and I don't know why he hasn't. It's getting ridiculous now. It's affecting our relationship and it's not fair on you. The reason Fazer left you is because he's with me.'

The silly thing was that when Fazer found out, he didn't really say much at all – he just cringed a little. After all that!

I felt better once I'd done it and it was all out in the open, of course, but because of all his ducking and diving early on in our relationship, I could never just relax and trust Fazer, even though I loved him very much. It was just something I had to push to the back of my mind as much as I possibly could. I truly hoped he might finally change his ways . . . just for me.

Chapter Twenty

N-Dubz were really keen on the idea of cracking America. We all believed that the urban flavour of our music had the potential to go down really well in the States, so when Max Gousse, who was the senior vice president of A&R at Def Jam records, said that he was interested in seeing one of our shows, we were more than a little bit excited. Originally, we'd heard that Max was only interested in me as a solo artist, but Jonathan Shalit met up with him in America and persuaded him to come to the UK and see the N-Dubz vision for himself. Max came to see our gig at the Shepherds Bush Empire at the end of 2009 and loved it, and soon after that, Dappy and I were on a plane to LA to meet with Def Jam chairman L. A. Reid. It all happened very quickly, and it was really exciting.

When I arrived at LAX airport and saw America for the first time early in 2010, it was like I was in a film. It was all very bizarre. Everywhere we went, I felt like we were on some sort of giant movie set, and I could hardly take it all in. The whole thing felt so important, because it was everything we'd been working for – trying to crack America. Every single minute seemed essential, and it all felt so exciting and life-changing.

The funny thing was, though, that once I got used to being there, I didn't actually like Los Angeles all that much. Everyone I met seemed a bit la-la, a bit superficial, I thought, and besides that, I didn't cope well with being away from my home and friends in London. I'm a proper homebody at heart. Still, we were there for an important meeting that could take N-Dubz to a whole new level of success, and that's what I had to focus on.

When Dappy and I met with L. A. Reid, I really wanted to make as good an impression as possible. I think I work best under pressure, and in a situation where there's a lot riding on something, I only tend to be nervous beforehand. Once it's actually happening, I usually stay calm and focused. This was the case at that meeting. I wanted L. A. Reid to see me as a star and to have confidence in my ability as an artist. When we walked into the room, I could feel his presence right off. He had the aura of a powerful businessman, and although he seemed quite reserved, he was also straight to the point.

'I like you kids,' he told us. 'I think I'd like to sign you.'

As the meeting progressed, I felt like both him and Max 'got us', which was an important factor, after all our artistic differences with Polydor. We were chuffed to bits to be signing to such a cool label in America – home of artists like Rihanna and Kanye West, among many others – and we came home very happy and optimistic.

In May of 2010 we signed a five-album deal with Def Jam records. Max Gousse was always a great supporter of N-Dubz, and he was quoted at the time as saying, 'I signed N-Dubz because they're great entertainers and speak to London's youth unlike any other band. We want to bring their message to the rest of the world.'

He always had the best of intentions for us, but unfortunately that's not quite how it worked out.

When it came down to it, Def Jam had a plan for N-Dubz that didn't fit in with our vision, especially Dappy's.

HONEST

When we headed back out to LA in the summer of 2010 to start work on our third album, *Love. Live. Life*, he found it very hard to fit in with their method of working. We were hooked up with several big-name writers and producers like Jean Baptiste Kouame and Salaam Remi, who've worked with artists like The Black Eyed Peas and Beyoncé, but we just weren't used to other people writing and producing our music – that was what Fazer, Dappy and I had always done. It just didn't work very well for us.

For a start, they didn't understand some of the very British urban slang that we often used in our songs, and they didn't think that it would work in the US, let alone globally. Of course, we didn't want to lose our British flavour completely, so there had to be a compromise, but it was definitely something we had to bear in mind while we were in the studio writing. Aside from that, we just seemed to have different views about what made a hit song. Our sound was always very specific and unique, so it was hard for us to suddenly be expected to change so radically just to fit a certain marketplace.

I think it would have been fine for me as a solo artist, working with different production teams, but not for N-Dubz. The whole process was a struggle, and not something we enjoyed very much. Dappy, in particular, hated every minute of it, and was miserable working there. Trying to get him to focus to even write a verse was a tough task.

We did ultimately get some tracks recorded, but it was a long and gruelling process, and once again we found ourselves in the position where nothing we came up with seemed good enough for the label. We were eagerly waiting to have a first single release in the US, but all we kept hearing from Def Jam was: no, that's not the one; no, that's not the one; no, that's not the one either. They couldn't hear a worldwide smash. It was really frustrating to have done all that work and still not get a single out of it. We all wished we'd just recorded the album in London and kept the sound more N-Dubz.

Once we'd finished the initial recording sessions in America, that's exactly what we did, and back in the UK, we produced some new tracks and did them the way we wanted to do them. We'd still have to finish off the American album, but this version would be perfect for the UK fans. We ended up releasing the album in Britain with a mix of our new tracks plus the ones we'd finished in the US.

Love. Live. Life came out in November 2010 and went straight into the top ten, and we followed it with a top-five single, 'We Dance On', plus three further hit singles from the album. We also ended the year by picking up another MOBO award. This time it was Best Single, for our collaboration with Mr Hudson, 'Playing with Fire'. It was a great time for me. N-Dubz were really flying high, and I was finally in a happy, loving relationship with Fazer. Life was good!

Max Gousse still really wanted to make it work with N-Dubz in America, so it was decided that we would head back out to Los Angeles early in 2011 to record some more tracks. The idea was to re-package the *Love. Live. Life* album for the American market, and we all really wanted to make it work. In February, Fazer and I flew out to New York with one of our managers, Rich Castillo, to do an interview for a music TV show. Dappy had caught a stomach bug and had been throwing up everywhere, so he wasn't able to travel with us. The plan was that we would meet up with him in Los Angeles a few days later. Tagging along with us on the trip was the *Being N-Dubz* production team. The show had been picked up for a second series, which would feature our recording trip to the States plus the lead-up to our first ever arena tour, set for the spring of 2011. And although I hadn't been overly fond of the cameras following us around the first time, I also couldn't ignore how successful *Being N-Dubz* had been.

As it goes, the TV interview in New York went pretty well, and Fazer and I came across with plenty of swagger about conquering the US market, but underneath I was nervous. It was still such a big thing for us – or any British band – to break big in the States. I was so aware of the fact that nobody there knew us, and it made me feel a little insecure. Fazer, on the other hand, was so excited to be in New York. It was freezing, but I think it was exactly how he'd imagined it would be, and we had such a great time hanging out together without having to worry about how pissed off Dappy would be. Then we were off to California, which was gorgeous and sunny. We were due to record in Los Angeles for three weeks, and we hoped to come up with that elusive smash hit that our A&R man Max was hoping to hear. 'Three and a half minutes of magic,' Dappy christened it.

One of the things that was really nice about that whole trip was that Fazer and I got to spend a lot of time together away from London. Dappy had one of his mates with him in LA, so during downtime from the studio, they would hang out together, leaving Fazer and me to do what we wanted. We went for romantic dinners or chilled out together around the hotel pool or in our lovely room – it was fun.

We were still trying to keep our relationship very quiet,

however, for several reasons. For one, Dappy was still very unhappy about the prospect of Fazer and me as a couple – in fact, he hated it. This made the energy between Dappy and me even more spiky than usual, if that were possible. At times, it felt like we were at breaking point as a band, and now, when Dappy and I got into an argument, Dappy had no one to back him up and take his side against me, which is how it had been for so many years. Dappy felt that if our fans found out that Fazer and I were together, it would ruin their image of N-Dubz as a gang or a team, and he was absolutely adamant that we should never go public about it. I had my own reasons for wanting to keep my love life private: I just couldn't stand the thought of all the press attention.

I looked at some of the celebrities who constantly seemed to be flaunting their relationships – whether it was on a reality TV show, or chat-show interview, or selling their wedding pictures for a magazine deal – and I just didn't get it. One minute they seemed to want everyone to know every little detail about their romance, then the next minute they were complaining because there were all sorts of people talking bollocks or making up stories about them on the front of all the gossip magazines. All of a sudden, they were craving privacy, when all the time they were the ones who had made their relationship a big public hoo-ha in the first place.

As far as I was concerned, my relationship with Fazer was my private life, my world. If people wanted to scrutinise and criticise the things I did in my work life, then fine, but I didn't want them digging into my personal life and turning it into a pantomime for everyone's pleasure. Kind of ironic, I guess, as I'm now telling my life story in a book, but that was how I felt at the time.

HONEST

The mad thing was that, back in the UK, we had actually bought an apartment together in Finchley by then – we had a joint mortgage. So despite all the secrecy, I'd been busy making a proper home for the two of us, and that was something I thoroughly enjoyed doing. I loved running around all the shops in Camden Lock and picking out different themes for the various rooms I was decorating. A banana-skin lamp for my African-themed room, a chandelier and dining table for my black and white room – I was so into the design and look of everything, and I loved being a homebody. I always have. I even got Fazer bitten by the shopping bug, and when we weren't working, he would often come shopping with me to choose stuff for our new apartment. We really got into it.

Still, we kept ourselves to ourselves. And while we were working in America, it was even easier, because nobody really knew us there. That's what made our time off from the studio so cool.

Unfortunately, the business side of things didn't go so well stateside. At one meeting, Max suggested to us that we launch ourselves in America off the back of a reality TV show. I was all for giving it a go – after all, we'd had a big hit with our UK TV show, why not in America? Dappy was violently opposed to it, though. He wanted the music to speak for itself and wasn't in the slightest bit interested in being a reality TV star. I think he was also pissed off with me, because in principle I agreed with the concept. Meanwhile, in the studio, things didn't go much better. Although we did some cool sessions in LA, nothing mind-blowing came out of it, and having the *Being N-Dubz* camera crew in the studios just caused stress and arguments between all of us. To make matters worse, the chairman of the label, L. A. Reid, decided to leave Def Jam to go and be a judge on the brand-new American *X Factor*. After that, we were all utterly demoralised by the whole N-Dubz–Def Jam situation, especially Dappy.

Love. Live. Life never did get released in America, and after a long drawn-out silence from the label, we parted company in August of 2011. It was widely reported that we were dropped by Def Jam, but it was 100 per cent our decision to leave. In the end, it doesn't matter how high-powered, amazing or successful something is, if it doesn't work for you, it doesn't work, and that's that. Still, at the end of it all, I maintained a good working relationship with Max Gousse. He'd always had a vision for me as a solo artist, and although I didn't quite know it then, that was where my career was headed.

Chapter Twenty-One

Pretty soon, we were rehearsing for the biggest tour we'd ever done, the Love. Live. Life tour, which took in huge venues like the Manchester Evening News Arena and the O2 Arena in London. Rehearsals were a bit rushed, because we'd been in America, but I was really excited about stepping out onto those massive stages in front of such enormous crowds. N-Dubletts on a massive scale. I'd also have Fazer with me, and Gareth, who was not only my best mate and personal assistant, but also assistant choreographer on the tour. It was all going to be brilliant – wasn't it?

Certainly the experience of those shows is something I'll never forget. They were real moments. Walking out onto the stage at the O2 Arena on 30 April 2011 was like some sort of dream. The spotlights flying about above us, the phone-cameras pointed at us, glowing in the dark, and almost 20,000 people, screaming and cheering and singing the words to our songs – it was magical. I felt it was what my whole life had been for, for moments like that. Even one moment like that. I actually cried on stage, I was so overcome with emotion. Then away we went, performing old stuff as well as new: 'Ouch!', 'Better Not Waste My Time', and, of course, 'Papa Can You Hear Me?' They were all in the set list. It was amazing, and I loved every second of it.

Backstage, things weren't quite so much fun. Dappy

and I were arguing constantly. We couldn't agree on anything – it was a nightmare. Apart from all the usual stuff we argued about, Dappy was convinced that my relationship with Fazer had signalled the end of N-Dubz, and he just didn't seem to want to know anymore, despite the fact that we were enjoying such an amazingly successful tour. One day, in the catering room during lunch before one of the shows – I think it was at the MEN – Dappy dropped an absolute bombshell on all of us.

'Fuck you,' he said to me in the midst of one of our all-too-regular slanging matches. 'I'm going solo anyway.'

Yes, it was said during an argument, but there was something about the way he said it. It was obvious that he'd been thinking about it.

'Yeah?' I said indifferently. 'Well, fuck you too then.'

I was shocked though. Really shocked. What the hell would happen if N-Dubz were no more? Even after we'd both calmed down, Dappy was saying the same thing. He'd decided. N-Dubz was over for him, and when I really started to think about it, I realised that he might be right. I couldn't deal with the band any longer either. I was at breaking point. It turned out that Dappy had already had meetings with our management and record label about a possible solo career, without even telling Fazer and me. I wasn't surprised, I guess – that was Dappy. That's just the sort of thing he did.

As the news sunk in, I wondered whether this was my chance to have a solo career too, but I knew how hard it was going to be. It always is when bands break up and certain members go solo – quite often it doesn't work out. To tell you the truth, I was shitting myself!

Then fate stepped in, in a big way. Just a few weeks

earlier, I'd had an interesting but slightly surprising call from my manager, Jonathan Shalit.

'What do you think about having a meeting with the producers of *The X Factor* about you working on the show?' he'd asked me.

I hadn't really been expecting to hear that while I was in the middle of rehearsing for a tour, I have to say.

'What, you mean presenting *The Xtra Factor* or something?'

'No,' Jonathan said, 'as a judge on the main show.'

'WHAT? Replacing who?'

'Cheryl Cole. She's leaving to be a judge on the American show with Simon Cowell, and Simon is considering you as her replacement in the UK.'

I had to let this sink in for a second. Me, judge on *The X Factor*? The biggest show on television? It seemed like it was too good to be true.

'OK, get me the meeting,' I said eventually.

I was intrigued and excited all at once, and completely bowled over that Simon Cowell was considering me to replace Cheryl Cole, who was probably the biggest female pop star in the country.

Jonathan warned me that this was all extremely confidential, and that if word got out that I was even being considered for a judge's role, I would almost certainly lose it. So, yes, I kept my mouth shut, but nobody seemed to be in any particular rush to interview me for the job or even bloody meet me. The first meeting with the show's producers was cancelled, and then after a couple of weeks, so was the second appointment. And I don't mean postponed as in re-organised for a later date; I mean cancelled, as in they didn't want me anymore – there was no job.

'I'm sorry, T,' Jonathan told me. 'They've changed their minds; they're no longer considering you.'

I was devastated, naturally, but then a few weeks later – after Dappy's shock announcement about going solo – I heard that the show's producers *did* want to see me again after all. Wow! It was a bit like being on a rollercoaster, to be honest, and now that I'd had the carrot dangled in front of me not once but twice, I wanted it badly. This would be perfect for me, especially as I was soon to be out there on my own for the first time, with no Dappy and Fazer by my side – no N-Dubz.

After another long wait, I finally got to meet the show's main producers, Mark Sidaway, known to his friends and colleagues as Sid, and Beth Hart, and I decided to go in with all guns blazing. I told myself that this was my moment, and that I had to show Sid and Beth why I was the right person for the job, and exactly what I could bring to that table. I felt pretty confident, despite the random on/off nature of the job offer, and I have to give myself ratings for the way I handled it. I felt I was pretty good, even if I do say so myself. While I was talking away, I could see Sid and Beth glancing at one another, as if to say, 'Yep! This is the one.' I came out feeling very excited, and I was whisked straight over to ITV to meet a few more people who were involved with the show.

Before I knew it, literally within a couple of days, I was on my way to Los Angeles to meet Simon Cowell during a short break in the tour schedule. I'd never met him before, although our paths had crossed when I was a guest on *The Xtra Factor*, when I vividly recall him staring at me as if I was some sort of alien life form, somewhat intrigued. Not in a sexual way, more along the lines of: who the hell is she? Like he was trying to get the sum of me. I think

HONEST

Simon found me interesting, and I think that was precisely why I was now headed for a meeting at his house in LA.

Before I left London for the meeting, I had a T-shirt made – a white V-neck, Simon's signature look – and on it I had printed a picture of the man himself with the words 'THE MALE BOSS' emblazoned across it. I'd been known as 'the Female Boss' for quite a while, so I thought it might be funny. My nickname had originally been 'the Bitch'. Not *a* bitch, *the* bitch! That's what Dappy, Fazer, Rich and all the guys called me for ages, because I was always laying down the law and usually got my own way. The boys tried to avoid using it in interviews, thank God, but actually it wasn't meant as an insult – it was more a nod to my female power. In fact, if anyone ever called me a bitch in jest, I'd always come back with: 'I'm not a bitch, I'm *the* bitch!' What the guys meant was that I was a woman with balls, and I didn't mind that in the slightest.

The polite version of that nickname was the Boss, because I was usually running the show, despite the fact that I was surrounded by a bunch of alpha males.

'Speak to the boss,' they'd tell everyone. 'T's the boss.'

As I was the only female, my nickname then morphed into the Female Boss. It was a lot more user-friendly than the Bitch, and it sort of became my alter ego. Whenever I had to be strong or make tough decisions, I would always talk about 'bringing out the Female Boss'. I guess it meant showing my strong side, my tough outer shell (I am a Cancerian, after all), and my claws too. They come out when they need to, and they're serious fuckers. That's the Female Boss. I've now famously got it tattooed on my arm, and it's also the name of my very own signature perfume.

Anyway, I was hoping that my comical little gift for

Simon Cowell would break the ice and make him laugh. I wanted him to see how cheeky I was. It was a big part of my character and had often stood me in good stead. When I finally sat down with Simon, the conversation seemed to flow quite easily – I liked him. I felt like I was talking to someone who I'd met before, and I didn't feel at all anxious. Just like the previous meeting with the producers, I decided to leave Simon in no doubt as to what an asset I would be to the show, and why I was perfect for the job, and while I chattered away, he took out a cigarette and started puffing.

'Do you mind if I have a fag, Simon?' I suddenly said mid-conversation. And the two of us sat in his house chuffing on cigarettes and talking like old mates.

'I'm honest,' I said, 'and I like to say what I think – as you know – but I'm also emotional. Now that you're not going to be on the judging panel anymore, who's gonna be the judge to tell people that they're rubbish when they are? Now that Cheryl's gone, who's gonna be the judge that brings the emotional edge to the panel? The one who will really react to a beautiful performance that moves them. I'm both of those judges,' I told him, 'and with the pair of you gone, you're gonna bloody need that.'

At the end of the meeting Simon stood up and shook my hand.

'Congratulations, I think you're going to be great. Let's get the contracts drawn up,' he smiled.

'OK, great, yeah, cool.'

I was as blasé as I dared be until I got outside, where Gareth and my friend Ny were waiting for me in a cab.

'What happened, what happened?'

They were much more excited than I was; I was slightly stunned, to be honest, because it had all happened so fast.

'Er . . . I think he just gave me the job,' I said.

I really wasn't sure once I'd left the house – Simon had delivered the news in such a throwaway manner.

'WHAT?' Ny and Gareth both screamed.

'Yeah, but I'm not completely sure . . .'

I was baffled, and I could hardly let myself believe it had finally happened.

Sure enough, a week or so went by without me hearing a thing again and, back in the UK and on tour, I was a wreck all over again.

'Nah! They've fucked me over,' I told Gareth. 'How can they do this to me after offering me the job on a plate in LA?'

I kept saying to myself, 'Simon wouldn't do that. He can't do that . . . can he?'

After seeing how the whole *X Factor* machine worked, I'd started to believe that anything was possible. A couple of weeks later, though, as I walked into my lawyer's office to sign some papers, I got the call. Yes! I had the job; it was confirmed . . . or was it?

A few days later, Gareth delivered yet another titbit of interesting news.

'Cheryl has been sacked from *The X Factor USA.*'

'What?'

'Apparently, they can't understand her accent. She's lost the job.'

Cheryl had taken a job on the American show in a massive hail of publicity. There had been all sorts of huge TV ads in America heralding the panel of judges: Simon Cowell, Paula Abdul, ex-Def Jam chairman L. A. Reid and Cheryl. And now she was being booted off the show because they didn't like the way she spoke? Cheryl was a pretty big star: if she could lose her job just like that, then so could I. After all, I hadn't even signed my contract yet.

Within hours of the announcement that Cheryl was leaving *The X Factor USA*, the hot topic of showbiz gossip was about whether or not Cheryl Cole was returning to Britain to take back her job on the UK judging panel. Yep, my fabulous new job. Was this ever going to end? I resigned myself to the fact that it was Cheryl's job originally and that if she decided to come back and claim it, then there wasn't very much I could do about it. Even so, I felt like I'd been handed a huge opportunity and now it seemed like it might be taken away from me. Once again, everything went very quiet and we had no contact from anyone at *The X Factor*. Even when we did hear something, it was along the lines of: 'There's still a lot of love for Tulisa in *The X Factor* camp, but we just don't know what's going on at the moment.'

It was bloody torture, and it just seemed to go on and on. There were all sorts of 'secret location' meetings going on behind the scenes between Jonathan Shalit and the heads of ITV, and at one point Jonathan was trying to deal with it all while he was in Tokyo, I was in London and the director of television for ITV, Peter Fincham, was in LA. It was a nightmare.

The funny thing was that by the time it was finally and absolutely confirmed that I did have the job and that Cheryl would not be returning, I'd had all the excitement knocked out of me. I was just like: 'OK, whatever! Let's just get on with it, shall we?'

The amazing high soon returned though, and as the Love. Live. Life tour came to an end, I felt like I had a lifeline. I knew that this was going to be a whole new turning point for me, a massive one. At the same time, I felt horrible for Fazer. He was devastated and desperate for N-Dubz not to break up, even though at the time we all thought that it would probably be a temporary split. Fazer had no desire to be a solo artist. He knew that the band was only being torn apart because Dappy and I could no longer work together, and all he could think about was what Uncle B would have thought. It was a very painful time for Fazer.

'I don't know what I can do,' I said to him. 'Dappy wants this. He wants to go solo, and there's nothing I can do to stop him, even if I wanted to.'

'You could try to get along with him,' Fazer said. 'This is all because you don't get along with him and he can't deal with it.'

'Well, I can't deal with it either,' I said.

Dappy and I were just as stubborn as one another, and Fazer knew it.

We never made an official announcement that N-Dubz were splitting up, but after one final gig on 18 September 2011 – the day Dappy released his first solo single, 'No Regrets' – N-Dubz was as good as over.

Chapter Twenty-Two

I'd watched *The X Factor* in 2010, just after Fazer and I had first moved into our new place in Finchley. I was sitting there with Gareth one Saturday night, watching one of the live shows, when I came to a conclusion.

'I could do that job,' I said to him. 'I reckon I'd be good at that.'

Being a judge on the show was just the kind of thing I could envisage myself doing. I actually thought about it quite a bit after that night. I would read stuff about Cheryl Cole in magazines and watch her every week on the show, and I'd think to myself, 'Yeah! I'd love a job like that.'

'I can't imagine anyone retiring from the panel in the next few years, though,' I said to Gareth. 'I'll probably never get the chance.'

Yet here I was, preparing to be an *X Factor* judge. And how did I feel? Well, I was crapping myself. Yes, I had the job, but now I had to keep it. It was in my contract that I could get the sack on the first day if the show's producers thought that it wasn't working out, and I wasn't sure I was going to fit in. I mean, up until then, I was just known for being in N-Dubz and, as a band, we were considered controversial and thought of as rebels. I imagined that the kind of people who didn't like N-Dubz would be the exact audience who watched *The X Factor*. Shit! How was I going to make people like me? I'm edgy, aren't I? I'm outspoken. I've got a bit of a big gob. What if people didn't take to me? Cheryl seemed so graceful and ladylike up there on the screen, and I knew that there were a fair few people who thought I was just a chav.

The thing is, when I'm doing my thing in a band, I'm not trying to please everyone. I'm just playing to the people who are interested – our fans. If other people don't like what I'm doing, then they don't have to listen – I'm not asking them to. With something like *The X Factor*, though, I'm asking people who wouldn't usually be my fanbase to like me and accept me. As a TV judge, I was putting myself out there to be judged in turn. It contradicted everything that I represented, and that grated on me.

I first met my fellow judges Louis Walsh and Kelly Rowland the evening before the first day of auditions. I'd already met Gary Barlow, because I'd written a song called 'No One Knows Your Name' with him for the N-Dubz album *Against All Odds*. I'd stayed up in Guildford, where he had his studio, and we'd had a curry together.

Anyway, Kelly seemed pretty cool, and I clicked with Louis straight away. I find it easy to get on with people on the whole. Even if a person isn't someone I can see myself becoming good friends with, I'm pretty good at getting along with them, as long as they're cool with me. Louis had a slightly dark and very cheeky sense of humour that I identified with. The two of us had a banter right from the off, and we made one another laugh. In fact, we got on like a house on fire, and I was very drawn to his happy nature. People say that you are the company you keep, and I like to surround myself with happy, positive people whenever I can. It often helps me steer clear of the sadness or depression that I'm prone to. Anyway, the night before the first auditions, Louis and I ended up getting pissed and laughing and joking in his hotel room till four in the morning. We were mates from that moment on.

When it came to the first day of filming – the first day of auditions, in Birmingham – I wish I could say that all my worst fears simply evaporated, but instead they were confirmed. The show's producers had just told me that they wanted me to relax and be myself, but that was easier said than done.

As I said, I was terrified, and when I walked onto the set to take my place next to Gary – in Cheryl Cole's old seat – I could hear quite a few people in the audience booing me, just as I'd feared. 'They hate me,' I thought. 'They bloody hate me.' I felt like it was a very definite 50/50 response.

As the auditions progressed, I could feel that me sitting next to Gary wasn't working out. It felt like Kelly and Gary had a lot more to say to one another, and I felt out on a limb away from Louis. All afternoon I kept looking down the other end of the panel, to make eye contact with him. The producers obviously saw it too, and after a while I was asked to swap seats with Kelly. I was much happier next to Louis straight away, and I suddenly felt a bit more comfortable. Still, I wasn't out of the woods yet.

I think that because I felt that I might be unpopular with some of the audience, I was trying my best to be likeable, and that's not always the best bet when you're on a judging panel. Nice doesn't always make the best telly, does it? Still, there I was, trying to sugar-coat everything that was naturally 'me': my accent, how nice I was to the people who were auditioning. Even when I did make a comment that was less than positive about one of the contestants, I'd smile and say 'Sorry!' at the end of it. I was trying to be honest with my critique, but at the same time I was playing much too nice. Then, during a break in the filming, producer Beth came over to talk to me privately.

'Tulisa, you're not being yourself, we can all see it,' she said. 'This is not why we hired you. If we'd wanted "nice-as-pie", we'd have got somebody else to do the job.'

'I know, I know,' I said. 'I'm nervous and I'm feeling a bit of pressure from the audience – I know what I'm doing wrong.'

'Just be yourself,' Beth said. 'That's all we want at the end of the day.'

Within seconds of walking back onto the set, I snapped out of it, and suddenly I was full of all my usual confidence and bravado. I decided it was best not to focus on whether the audience liked me or not, just that I had been hired because of who I was. From then on, I wasn't scared to dish out criticism if it was needed. I spoke up and spoke my mind without worrying what the other judges might think. It all felt so much more comfortable.

Beth and Sid were suddenly smiling.

'There she is,' they said. 'THERE she is!'

I thoroughly enjoyed the rest of the auditioning process, and there were a few contestants who really jumped out at me over the next few weeks. I got really excited about Janet Devlin from Ireland, for instance, who eventually went through to the live show. My favourite audition, however, was Jade Richards from Scotland. She sang Adele's 'Someone Like You', and it was fantastic. I told her that while she was singing, I felt like I could see her whole life story, just through listening to the feeling in her voice, and that I'd never in my life heard somebody sing so much like they meant it. Unfortunately, Jade didn't get further than Kelly's 'judge's house' round, but I've heard she might be auditioning again in 2012. I hope so.

There was one woman who auditioned called Michelle Barrett who really reminded me of my mum. She was a thirty-one-year-old Irish mother of four who'd never got

Backstage at T4 on the Beach after such a good performance, with Gareth, Adam and my hairdresser Jason

The X Factor 2011 was one of the most incredible experiences of my life and I couldn't have been prouder of my little muffins, Little Mix

Filming my first solo video in the US was incredibly
exciting. I have some brilliant memories of partying
out there with my mates and they are all the sweeter
since the single went to number one

Recording the alternative video for 'Live it Up' at The Roundhouse in Camden

With the girls and Gareth in Ibiza

the chance to pursue a singing career, and as she sang Whitney Houston's 'All the Man that I Need' I thought about my mum's beautiful voice and wasted talent and I just burst into tears.

'It was brilliant,' I told Michelle. 'Just like you, my mum had a beautiful voice and she didn't do anything with it. I listen to her singing in the kitchen and she's so amazing. I wish she could get up there and do something like this.'

I suddenly felt so emotional. I was thinking about my mum and all that we'd been through, and where I was right at that moment – sitting on the judging panel of the biggest show on TV. I just couldn't stop crying, and by then Michelle was in tears too. Of course, we all put her through to boot camp.

When the first audition aired on the 20 August 2011, I was on a tour bus because N-Dubz were playing at a festival gig. I couldn't bear to watch it, though, so I just kept checking my Twitter feed to gauge the public's reaction. The first thing I noticed was that my Twitter followers had gone up by about 50,000, which surprised me somewhat. Then I started reading all the positive comments about my appearance on the show, and there were lots of them. The general sentiment had gone from people cussing me out, Tweeting stuff like, 'OMG! How did you get that job, you're shit?' to 'OMG! I was really wrong about Tulisa – she's really good on the panel.'

Over the next few days, I got many more supportive messages and Tweets. I won't lie: I was shocked. As much as I'm a pretty confident person, I just wasn't used to that kind of praise from the public, and I'm not all that good at taking compliments anyway.

'Why are people being so nice about me?' I said to Gareth. 'What did I do right?'

I didn't know what had happened, but I thanked God that it had, and suddenly I began to feel a lot more secure about the whole thing.

The category that I was ultimately given to mentor was the groups, and I was overjoyed. After my experience of being in N-Dubz, I knew I could do a great job with them and I wanted to make it my mission to mentor the first and only group to have ever won the competition. In fact, I'd been so determined to mentor the groups that I wrote a long and heartfelt email to Beth Hart, telling her exactly why I should have that category. I didn't know if I was even allowed to do that sort of thing – trying to sway the producers' decision – but I thought I might as well have my say. But on the day when the decision was due to be announced, I arrived at the studio only to discover that Beth hadn't even received the bloody email I'd sent. I had to re-send it while I was in the same building as she was. I couldn't say everything I wanted to say to her face to face, so I had no choice.

It was basically a begging letter. I told her how I would bring out the best in the groups, and that they would help me shine as a new judge. I told her that if she gave me the groups, she would see just how passionate I was. I've no idea if it made any difference to the final decision but I was delighted when I was told the groups were mine.

———

The judges' houses stage in the competition is when each judge takes the remaining contestants in their group to a glamorous location and chooses the lucky few who will go on to perform in the live finals. My judge's house was in Mykonos – well, I guess a Greek party island was the perfect choice for me – and the villa we filmed in was absolutely gorgeous. I didn't actually get to stay in that particular villa while I was there, but I had one very close by that was just as glamorous.

Now, I don't want to blow my own trumpet, but my judge's house section was easily the best. Apart from all the drama surrounding my final choices, the entire crew said that it was the most fun they'd ever had on a judge's house shoot. The best in *X Factor* history. I had Jessie J as my guest judge, and although I didn't really know her that well, I was a big fan and was very keen to have her as my right-hand woman. Jessie is great and, since working together on *The X Factor*, we've stayed friends. Of course, we don't see one another all the time, because we're both so busy, but she'll often drop me a text or a message to say hi. In fact, whenever I've had a hard time in the press about one thing or another, Jessie will text me and say, 'How are you holding up?' And I'll do the same for her. She's a cool chick!

After the two of us had seen all the acts, I was faced with a dilemma. I had two groups that were really good, The Keys and The Risk, but I just wasn't sure either group was a winner. In the end, I decided to take the one member of The Keys who I thought really shone, Charlie Healy, and join him up with three members of The Risk, to make one 'super-group'. This meant disappointing the other members of The Keys and The Risk, who I felt just weren't strong enough. It had never been done before at that stage in the competition, and the producers were a bit worried about what might happen.

'We don't want you to end up in the shit,' they warned me. 'There might be an audience backlash with you breaking up groups.'

In the end, they told me it was my decision, and

although I knew it was going to be controversial, it was clearly the best thing to do. After all, I wouldn't have chosen either of the groups to go through as they were. This way, four of the lads at least had a shot.

It's hard enough having to tell some of the contestants that they haven't made it to the live shows, but to split up and re-form two boy bands and then break the rejected boys' hearts was really tough. I knew that neither band had a chance of winning *The X Factor* as they were, though, so I went ahead and did it, despite the producers' warning. It was the boys' decision in the end anyway, and they took it. It really shook things up, and after that, I think everyone realised that I wasn't there to look pretty and keep my mouth shut.

At the end of a hard day's filming in Mykonos, it was time to party. Fazer had come along with me, which was lovely, because we were staying at the most gorgeous villa, just above the judge's house villa. Of course, that evening everybody ended up at ours, drinking, and going completely nuts. I came to be known as the party judge as the series went on, as there was always a post-show gathering in my dressing room after each live show. Well, this was the start of it, and everyone ended up getting totally bladdered and jumping into my pool with all their clothes on: the crew, *The Xtra Factor* team, even the producers. We were raving till four in the morning.

At the end of my trip to Mykonos, I was excited to have finally selected my team for *The X Factor* live finals: 2 Shoes, Rhythmix (later re-christened Little Mix), Nu Vibe and the brand-new, reconstructed version of The Risk. But as the first live show approached, I was starting to get terribly nervous all over again. This was going to be a whole new ballgame.

Chapter Twenty-Three

From the minute Dappy had announced that he was leaving the band to go solo, I started making plans for a solo recording career too. Despite the fact that I had my hands full with *The X Factor*, music was still my first love, and just because there was no more N-Dubz, that didn't mean I was ready to turn my back on singing. The truth was, Dappy's departure had freaked me out quite a bit, and I suddenly found myself worrying about where my income might come from in the future. So I made a list.

'I want to get into the studio, record some brilliant songs, release three singles and then I'm dropping an album.'

That was the plan I announced to my management, and I had no intention of hanging around either.

'I also want to write a novel, and maybe it's time to tell my story so far in a book too.'

I'd also been thinking about having a fragrance, and the possibility of doing a bit more acting. I saw this as my chance to try to achieve all the things I'd ever wanted to achieve, and I was willing to work hard for them.

As far as musical direction was concerned, being away from N-Dubz also meant that I was going to be able to try out some new styles of music that I loved but hadn't been able to explore within the band. I'm an Ibiza baby, so I was dying to write and record some amazing club tracks, for instance, but I didn't want my album to be all one musical genre. As long as it was a great song, in a style that I was into, then I was up for giving it a go.

I'd already recorded one solo track that I was over the moon with. The song, called 'Young', was written and produced by Fazer and Pete Ibsen, now a production duo called STL, and Ali Tennant. The song sounded like a huge pop/club anthem, and I was very happy with how it came out. In fact, I was immediately convinced that it was going to be my first single, even though I had a lot more recording to do before I had an entire album. Once I had 'Young' in the bag, though, I was ready to get going with the rest of the album, straight after the Christmas and New Year break, once *The X Factor* was all done and dusted.

———————

As the first *X Factor* live show approached, I was very, very nervous. Even though I'd found my feet during the auditions and had thoroughly enjoyed the judges' houses section of the series, I felt like I was going to be scrutinised and judged all over again once I was sitting on the panel every week, critiquing other people. It was like I was starting over from scratch.

For a start, there had always been such an emphasis on what the female judges on the show were wearing and how they were styled each week. When Dannii Minogue and Cheryl Cole had been judges on the show, the battle of the hair and frocks seemed to make the Sunday papers almost every week. Of course, I wanted to look great up there on screen, but to be honest, I've never been that fussed about fashion. I know what I like, and that's about it. So I just got a really good stylist, Gemma Sheppard, and I let her do her thing. She combined her ideas about what she thought I looked good in with what was fashionable, but she also kept in mind the kind of dresses that I really liked. After all, it was all well and good getting glammed up for a TV show, but I had no intention of dressing up in anything that I wouldn't have been happy wearing off camera. It was still me, but a dressed-up me.

That first night, when I stood behind the screen, waiting for it to slide open for the big judges reveal moment, I was petrified.

'Oh my God! What the hell am I doing?'

I was standing between Kelly and Louis, convinced that once I got out there, my mind was going to freeze because I was so nervous, and I was petrified that I was going to stutter when I spoke and make an idiot of myself in front of the nation. Doing live TV is very high pressured. After each act has finished – when you have twenty or thirty seconds of live TV to fill with your critique – you need to be focused and make sure that what you're saying is clear and coherent. You can't just chat a load of rubbish; you have to pay attention the whole time and be focused. The audience are hanging on your every word, and so are the contestants. You've got to be on it, because although you do get some direction from the producers before the show and during the breaks, once the cameras are rolling and the show goes live, you're pretty much on your own.

Once I'd finally sat down at the judges' desk and the show got going, I felt a lot better. As Dermot O'Leary came to me for my opening comments, a cheer went up in the room as he said my name, and I smiled. I calmed down. Dermot's a really lovely bloke, but he always comes across like he feels sorry for me and worries about me, which is quite funny and sweet.

'Are you all right, T?' he'll say.

'Sure, I'm good.'

'No, but are you really all right?'

Then he'll give me a really big, heartfelt squeeze, as if I really need a cuddle. It's almost as if he knows that shit goes down with me and he wants to make sure I'm coping. I love Dermot for that.

By the end of the first live show, I was ready to give myself a little pat on the back. I got through it, and I told myself that I was actually pretty good. I could do this thing! Still, I said a prayer every week before the live show started. And once I'd got over that initial fear, I realised something else – that I was in it to win it!

———————

As happy as I was working on the show and appearing on TV each weekend, *The X Factor* schedule was pretty packed and I was out of the house and away from Fazer quite a lot of the time. Although he liked the fact that I was on *The X Factor*, Fazer didn't come with me to the live shows very often, and as the weeks went by, I began to feel like something was very wrong. He started going out more while I was working and was coming home later and later, with me not having a clue where he was most of the time. We started arguing a lot.

My problem was that if I'm living with someone, I expect my partner to at least let me know what's going on with his life. You know, keep me informed. Fazer had never fully grasped that concept – this I knew – but now it was getting beyond ridiculous. So I would get home after the Saturday night show, for instance, sometimes after midnight, and call Fazer, who was usually out somewhere.

HONEST

'What time will you be back?' I'd ask.

'In about an hour,' he'd say.

'Cool!'

But not so cool four hours later, when he still wasn't back. It was a regular thing, even during the week, when I wasn't working late.

Sometimes I wouldn't have a clue where he was – his phone would go straight to voice mail and he'd take hours just to reply to a text. It went on and on. It's not very nice, when you're in a couple, to feel like the other person doesn't want to be around you, or even talk to you, and, as usual, I wasn't going to take it lying down. So every day I'd tackle him about it, and every day I was arguing with him and dealing with the same old issues. It wasn't rocket science, as far as I was concerned.

'Why can't you just pick up the phone and let me know where you are? And why would you say that you're coming home in an hour when you know you're gonna be four or five hours?'

We were clearly having major communication problems, and Fazer's answer was to ignore the situation. It got to the stage where he would tell me he'd be back at a certain time and I'd just add another four on top. Then I'd go out somewhere, because I was fed up with being on my own in an empty house, and when I came home he still wouldn't be back. We were becoming like strangers living in the same house, but what annoyed me the most was the childish way he was behaving. It was like he just didn't give a shit that he was upsetting me and damaging our relationship – it was really hurtful. Even when we reached breaking point on more than one occasion, the seriousness of the situation didn't seem to sink in.

'I can't handle this,' I told him one night in desperation. 'If this happens once more, I'm just going to leave.'

The very next night, it was the same story, with Fazer going AWOL for hours on end. Of course, I went mad at him.

'You've seen the stress this causes, you've seen the arguments it's causing. Why would you keep on doing it? I just want you to tell me what's going on. It's not too much to ask – just let me know!'

The trouble was that Fazer was as stubborn as I was, and instead of us both trying to move towards a solution, we both started to pull in opposite directions.

After that, I'm sorry to say, it got worse: flirty text messages from girls, lies about where he'd been. We actually broke up twice during *The X Factor* live shows, and at one stage we didn't even speak for a couple of weeks, it was that bad. We were both still living in the same house, but were sleeping apart and not communicating. I still wanted to make it work, though. I wasn't ready to give up on Fazer, so we got back together again.

I was supposed to be concentrating on being a TV judge, but there was so much other stuff going on behind the scenes, it was a bloody nightmare half the time. Still, I suppose it's the story of my life. I don't like to think of myself as a drama queen, but as I said right at the beginning of this book, I do seem to attract drama. For me, the good and the bad always seem to go hand in hand. I sometimes wonder if it will always be like that.

One night in particular really took the biscuit, when we'd planned to spend some time together.

'Where are you, babe?' I asked Fazer over the phone.

'I'm at the studio.'

HONEST

'OK, when are you going to be back?'

'I'll be home in an hour's time.'

It wasn't really any surprise when that didn't happen, but two or three hours later, when he still wasn't picking up his phone, I was furious all over again. At first, his phone just rang and rang, but after a while it was clear that he'd just switched it off, as it went straight to voice mail. I had such a weird mixture of emotions that night, sitting in bed. I was angry because he'd lied again, upset because I thought we were going to spend some time together, and also worried and panicky that something bad might have happened to him. I looked at the clock and it was 4.30 a.m., and Fazer had said that he was going to be home by 11 p.m. – I felt pretty hideous then.

I'm a proper detective – hardcore. I've had to be, with some of the guys I've dated. I went onto Twitter and typed 'Fazer' into the general search engine. I knew that if he was out and about and anybody had seen him, they might well Tweet about it. Lo and behold, I find a picture of Fazer with his arm around some blonde bird in a nightclub, with her kissing him on the cheek.

'Just met Fazer!' her Tweet exclaimed.

'Yeah? That's nice for you, love,' I thought. While I'm sitting at home in bed on my own at four thirty in the morning, after calling his phone non-stop for four hours. Still, at least I now knew exactly where he was. I was ENRAGED.

When Fazer strolled in at six thirty in the morning, of course, I went mental.

'Where the FUCK have you been?'

Instead of apologising for blowing off what was supposed to be our time together and ignoring my calls, he said, 'So what? I've been out. What?'

Of course, I knew the blonde in the club was probably just a fan, but the whole incident was too much. After that, I didn't even want to speak to him, and I started sleeping on the sofa. Sometimes I would just stay at Gareth's and let Fazer get on with it. It was getting harder and harder to see a way back for us.

What was worse was that I didn't really have the time to sit down and think about what was happening. Being on *The X Factor* is a full-time job, and I had to give it my full attention. Whatever was going on in my personal life, and however difficult things got, I still had to turn on a smile every Saturday night when the show went live.

Chapter Twenty-Four

During the live shows, I got fairly close to the acts I was mentoring. I gave them all my mobile phone number and I tried to be as supportive and as available as I could all the way through. It got to the point where Louis had a go at me for getting so involved.

'Stop getting so close and working so hard with your acts,' he laughed. 'You're making the rest of us look bad.'

I had such a brilliant colleague in Gareth too. He went absolutely everywhere with me, and my acts knew him as well as they did me. Gareth was almost like a second judge and mentor and was involved with everything, including helping me with the song choices. He was a rock for me throughout the series.

I still wanted to win, but by week six of the live shows, I had just one act left: my girl band, Little Mix. The groups are always a tough category to mentor because, up until that year, no group had ever won the competition. Still, I was going to help change all that. I was convinced it was meant to be.

On week three of the live shows, there was a massive hoo-ha on the judging panel while the show was being broadcast live, and I found myself smack bang in the middle of a controversy over so-called 'bullying' among the contestants.

During the week leading up to Saturday's show, I'd heard a number of the female contestants, not all from my category, complaining about one of Kelly's contestants, Misha B. Misha was a very talented singer, but I'd heard that she could be a bit mean when she wanted to, and she was starting to upset people. This went on for a few days, when I was hearing various stories that didn't sit right with me, and I became concerned about the effect it was having on some of the girls.

At the Friday afternoon rehearsal, all four Little Mix girls came to me, with one of them in floods of tears because of something Misha had said. I don't really want to divulge exactly what it was, because it would reflect badly on Misha, but let's just say I was livid. Any sort of meanness and bullying always drags up memories of my past. I'd spent so long suffering at the hands of mean chicks, and it eventually led me down a path of self-destructive behaviour and depression. Just the thought of someone being bullied or 'got at' in any way on my watch infuriated me, and now I was looking at a young girl who I cared about in tears. If it had been a one-off incident, I probably would have let it go, but that wasn't the case. Louis was getting much the same story from some of his team. I was riled, but I felt that Misha was a nice girl at heart, not to mention very talented. I thought maybe she'd just let her competitiveness get the better of her. Whatever the case, I decided to act.

After Misha had delivered her performance of Prince's 'Purple Rain' on the Saturday live show, Louis suggested in his critique that she might be a bit 'overconfident'. There were a few boos from the audience, of course, but then I had my say. I wasn't hostile or nasty; I just wanted to let her know that it wasn't cool to be over competitive and mean behind the scenes. And I was very careful not to use the word 'bully'.

HONEST

'There's no doubt about it, Misha, when it comes to talent, you are way up there, you are definitely a star of the show, but backstage, I think you can be quite competitive. And although you probably don't realise that you do it, you being quite feisty can come across as mean to the other contestants.'

I said that I didn't want to put her down, because she was amazing, but suggested she channelled her feistiness into her performance and left the other contestants alone. Straight away, Gary said that we shouldn't be talking about what went on backstage, and then Kelly chimed in with much the same thought. Then, suddenly, Kelly went slightly nuts with Louis, telling him that his acts needed some of the confidence that Misha had . . . and then all hell broke loose. Louis yelled down the judges' table that one of his contestants had complained to him about Misha's bullying, and Kelly started waving her hand and shouting, 'Oh! We're not gonna go there!'

I tried to explain that being on *The X Factor* was about having the whole package and if someone's bad behaviour was affecting other contestants in the show, then that wasn't on. By this time, however, Kelly and Louis were screaming at one another and the whole thing descended into a shouting match, with Misha and Dermot just standing on the stage in shock.

I wished that Louis hadn't used the word 'bully' about Misha, because that just took the incident to a whole other level, but it was too late. I was suddenly getting all sorts of online criticism about not supporting someone who was an urban music act like myself. Some people even thought that Louis and I were ganging up on – or bullying – her. The only reason I'd confronted her onstage, rather than off, was because I'd thought it would stop her nonsense once and for all. She obviously wasn't taking any notice of the team of people who were looking after the contestants backstage. I thought that, coming from me, it would really hit home, but now it had suddenly become a big issue, and I got a lot of stick for it. Still, people who know me will realise that Misha's comments to the Little Mix girls must have been pretty bad to push me to say those things on live telly, and I could have easily told everyone what they were, but I didn't, for her sake.

The thing that really annoyed me was Kelly's 'what happens backstage, stays backstage' stance. That's a load of bollocks, as far as I'm concerned. On *The X Factor* the contestants' lives are laid out for everyone to see, as a backdrop to their performances. The TV audience get an insight into their back-story and their personalities, so if they've had a tough life or lost someone close to them, that becomes part of their profile as a finalist. It makes the audience root for them more if they feel they know them. Every Sunday, in fact, the papers were full of stories about the personal lives of the contestants.

Also, we always get to hear from a judge when something has gone wrong for their contestant and they want to milk a bit of sympathy that week.

'My act has been very sick today. She's been throwing up, but here she is bravely tackling something by Lady Gaga.'

But if your act is being a bitch, we can't talk about it? I'm sorry, I don't agree. If we get to hear all the sob stories, why shouldn't we get to hear when someone is behaving badly towards other contestants?

'What happens backstage, stays backstage.' No, it doesn't, this is *The X Factor*! It's the reason people love to watch it.

That's when things went tits-up with Kelly and me. After the show that night, she stormed off backstage and wouldn't speak to me. It was a bit ridiculous really. Kelly knew what was going on with Misha, and she should have done something about it herself. In fact, the only reason she took her 'what goes on backstage . . .' stance in the first place is because she couldn't just say, 'That's not true.' She knew it was. Gary, on the other hand, had no problem with me at all. He knows what the show is all about and he's been in the music business for years. He wasn't going to suddenly start having a row with a twenty-three-year-old girl who was just doing her job as a fellow judge.

The following week, Kelly didn't turn up for work, and we were told that she'd gone back to LA and was now too ill with a throat infection to fly back. I don't know whether she really had a throat infection or not, but actually, I didn't really care either way. If Kelly wanted a feud, she was going to have to have it on her own. I wasn't in the slightest bit interested in fighting with her. In the end, Alexandra Burke, who'd won *The X Factor* in 2008, had to step in as an emergency judge for the live shows. The *Daily Mail* reported that 'Kelly flew to the US following a bust-up with Tulisa' and she was quoted as saying, 'Tulisa and I have no relationship. The show has become a living hell.'

When she came back to work, I had to put up with stormy looks and Kelly flouncing past me in the studio corridor. I wouldn't have minded, but it was Louis who she'd had the slanging match with and who had called Misha a bully, not me. Eventually, after about a week, she came to speak to me.

'I don't know why you did that,' she said. 'You should have come to me and not gone public with it.'

'Well, firstly, you knew what was going on and you didn't stop it,' I said. 'And secondly, this is a competition and, at the end of the day, I want the person who wins to deserve it. If there is any contestant standing up there acting like butter wouldn't melt and then is a bitch behind the scenes, I think people should know about it. Plus, this is *The X Factor*, and these things happen all the time.'

I didn't really care whether Kelly wanted to be my best friend or not, as long as I wasn't constantly feeling negative energy from her. I didn't want to feel so tense every week, with her sitting next to me seething. As the series went on, things got a bit better between us, but our relationship never fully recovered. We were amicable with one another after a while, but that was about it.

The funny thing is I'd acted in a moment of anger with Misha, which is probably what Misha had been doing behind the scenes. Looking back, I think that the two of us are more alike than people might think – both products of our environment. When I was younger I took my stresses and frustrations out on other people without stopping to think about the upset I might be causing. I can see now that Misha might have been doing the very same thing. I wish I'd taken her aside and shared my experience with her straight away, because I only learned from my mistakes once they were pointed out to me. A week after the drama, I invited Misha into my dressing room to explain to her why I was so angry, and I gave her the chance to explain her actions too. I'd like to think that we came away with a better understanding of one another.

Apart from that little drama, the rest of the series went pretty smoothly. As it turned out, Misha B stayed in the competition right up to the semi-finals – so she did really well anyway. In the end, though, it all came down to two acts on the night of the final show at Wembley Arena: Gary Barlow's young soul singer, Marcus Collins, and my four-piece girl band, Little Mix.

I wanted to win. I wanted to win so badly that I felt like my heart was right up in my mouth that night. Standing on the stage seconds before Dermot O'Leary made the announcement, I was staring towards the back of the room, looking at nothing – or what would have seemed like nothing to everyone else in the arena. I could see my Uncle B there, clear as day, smiling at me. And right there next to him, I was visualising Mother Mary, whom I always prayed to at moments like this. It was as if they were both spurring me on, telling me I could do it.

'You were meant to win this, T. You can win this. But it doesn't matter if you don't. That's OK too. You tried your best and that's what matters.'

Throughout the series, before every live show, I'd have funny little chats with God about it. Casual chats, you know, like he was my mate and we were just having a general conversation.

'Look, God, these kids that I'm mentoring really deserve to win this, but at the end of the day, if there's someone else in this competition that you think deserves it more, then that person should have it – I get that. But if I *am* meant to win in my first year as a judge, then please give the kids I'm looking after the strength to do the best they can do and be the best they can be when they're on stage. And if you reckon they deserve it as much as I do, then let them have it – let them win.'

At the crucial moment, Dermot wished both acts good luck.

'I can now reveal that the winner of *The X Factor* 2011 is . . .'

I was petrified, and I firmly gripped the hands of two of the Little Mix girls, Jade and Perrie, who stood either side of me.

'Little Mix!'

A deafening cheer went up in the arena, and I just put both my hands on my head and screamed. Then I grabbed band member Jesy, who was sobbing, and I hugged her and cried along with her. I was absolutely over the moon. As the girls started to gather around Dermot O'Leary, amidst the mayhem I could still see Uncle B. Only now he was punching the air and screaming.

'Yes, T, yes. You did it!'

It was an insane and wonderful moment – for the four girls that made up Little Mix, and for me too. We'd all wanted it so badly the whole way through. After all, I'd come from being the underdog on the judging panel, with half the country not even knowing who I was, and half the people that did know hating me. Now here I was, the winning judge. It was almost too much to take in.

Speaking from a purely practical level, I could not have been in a worse frock to win *The X Factor*. It was a purple-blue fishtail dress, and I was corseted down to my legs and teetering on six-inch heels underneath it. I could barely walk, let alone jump up and down with excitement! I ended up just sort of waddling backwards and forwards on the spot, screaming along with the girls, and then hobbling across the stage to hug Gary Barlow. I desperately wanted to leap up in the air and go mental, but I felt like a plank of wood. It didn't really matter in the slightest, though. It was still our moment, and it was a brilliant one – truly one of the highlights of my life. I'd absolutely loved the experience of working on *The X Factor*, and after it was all over, I dearly hoped that I'd done a good enough job to be asked back the following year.

A few months after the series finished, I was in a nightclub in Los Angeles when I spotted Kelly talking with a friend, so I went over to say hello. *The X Factor* was all done and dusted for that year: surely she wouldn't still be miffed about the whole Misha incident?

'Hey, you all right, Kelly?' I smiled. 'How you doing?'

'Oh, hey, boo-boo, how are you?' she said, and then she held up a perfectly manicured finger. 'Just give me one second.'

Then she turned away and continued chatting with her friend, but she never turned back, or even acknowledged me once for the entire rest of the evening.

That was the last I saw of Kelly Rowland.

As for Little Mix, well, they seem to be going from strength to strength. Their first single is due out soon, and I recently performed on the same bill as the girls at T4 on the Beach. I've seen them a few times since *The X Factor* finished, but so far I've only been able to sit down with them properly for one dinner, so we do need a good catch-up. They're going to be huge – I just know it!

Chapter Twenty-Five

Once I'd finished my judging duties, I felt like it was time for a holiday. Fazer and I had planned a trip to the Maldives, but things had been so up and down between us, I wasn't sure if it was the best idea in the world to even go. In the end, we made the decision that we should. It would surely be a good opportunity for us to spend some time alone together. Maybe it would help smooth out some of our problems. Fat chance!

On the day that we were due to leave for the Maldives, I heard through a vague acquaintance that some girl had been bragging that Fazer had taken her back to his house – our house. The girl had been pretty clear about where the house was and what it was like, so it seemed feasible. I couldn't believe I had to go through this again. You have to understand how hard it was for me, loving someone as much as I loved Fazer, but never being able to relax and trust him. It was torture most of the time, but I wanted us to work, and I didn't want to give up on our relationship unless I knew there was no point in going on. If I finally and positively discovered that he'd been unfaithful, I knew it would be time to throw in the towel – but I had to know for sure.

'You're crazy, you're delusional, you'll never be able to love anyone.'

Fazer rolled out all the usual responses, of course.

'You're fucked up from your past experiences, and you're letting that dictate our relationship.'

Yeah? Well, maybe I was distrusting of men because of past experiences, but sadly it was usually for a good reason.

'Don't use that bullshit on me,' I told him. 'It won't stick.'

So I start checking up on this girl, detective-style, just to find out the truth. I wanted to know who she was, what she looked like, where I could find her and, of course, what she had to say for herself. I was like some sort of ghetto Miss Marple, scouring Facebook, trying to hunt the bird down and calling up friends to see if they knew her. I didn't even really know the girl who'd originally passed on the information, but there I was on the phone to her, trying to get this mystery girl's number. Eventually, I managed to speak to a friend of the girl, who told me that the story was probably bullshit and that her friend was obsessed with Fazer and had most likely made it up. I then had to make a decision. Do I leave it and go on holiday, forget the whole thing? Or do I just give up and break up with Fazer?

This was all only a week after I'd finished *The X Factor*, one of the highlights of my career. The public were seeing me as some glamorous TV star, but in reality, there I was, being dragged back down to earth and having to deal with the same old crap that I'd been dealing with for years. I don't know why I attract drama wherever I go and whatever I'm doing. I don't feel like I'm a person who looks for constant grief and upheaval, but somehow that's what I end up with – God only knows why.

Anyway, I eventually went on holiday feeling like I was being driven mad with paranoia and jealousy. I didn't really know how much more of it I could take, but at the same time, I really couldn't face cancelling the three-week holiday I'd been so looking forward to. I'd earned it!

HONEST

When I look back on it now, some of the things that happened during that period were so ridiculous it was funny. Only a few weeks earlier, one of Fazer's other female 'friends' had been sending flirty text messages to him. One of them ended up as a full-blown text conversation, with her reminiscing about their past encounters and basically telling Fazer that she wanted to shag him. Little did she know that it was actually ME that she was 'sexting', not Fazer. I'd sneakily messaged her from Fazer's phone, pretending to be him and telling her that I had a new mobile phone number. Then I texted her *my* mobile number, so from then on, all of her flirty texts were coming straight to me. I know, devious! I was texting stuff like: 'Ah, come on, babe, you know I've got a girlfriend.' Then she'd text back: 'Well, that never stopped you before, did it?' You can imagine how pissed off I was. Suddenly, in the middle of it all, I sent the girl one final message: 'Fucking nabbed, mate. This is not Fazer you're talking to, it's his girlfriend, you dopey twat!'

I can laugh about it now, but at the time, it was mayhem, with me calling her and screaming all sorts down the phone, and Fazer, as ever, trying to play the innocent. It was never-ending.

When Fazer and I left for the Maldives, I knew that things weren't right and probably never would be. Then, when I finally had some time to really think hard about it, I realised that as much as I'd been fighting to hold onto my relationship with Fazer, I was tired of it – tired of the drama and fed up with arguing. It had drained me to the point of submission, and I eventually came to the conclusion that I wanted out. The irony was that once I'd reached that conclusion, we actually got on quite well while we were on holiday – but Fazer could tell that something had changed in me. He knew something was wrong. I didn't want to have sex with him or get too close to him, and we were more like mates than lovers. There was nothing I could do about it. I barely had anything left in me to give.

When we arrived back in London, I moved in with Gareth temporarily, telling Fazer I needed a bit of space away for a while. I don't know, maybe I thought I might miss him and want to give us one last chance. Within days of me moving out, however, there were press stories about him and Sir Philip Green's daughter, Chloe, out on the town together.

Now, I'd had a bit of a run-in with the *Made in Chelsea* girl a couple of months before, when she was asked to leave a private table at Whisky Mist nightclub. I'd been sitting with some friends at our reserved table, and at the time I had no idea who this person was, muscling in on our evening. She certainly didn't bother to say hello or introduce herself. Anyway, Chloe had a little public rant about me chucking her off my table, and that was that. We were never going to be the best of friends.

Now Fazer, who knew all of this, was out on the town with her, and I wasn't happy. We hadn't even bloody broken up properly, and yet here I was, faced with all these stories in the papers. When one of my mates called me after spotting Fazer and Chloe coming out of a club together one night, I asked my friend to follow them. Yep, Ghetto Miss Marple was on the case one final time! Sure enough, later that night, my friend sent me a picture of them going into Chloe's building together, which I then sent straight on to Fazer.

'BINGO!' I said. 'Got ya!'

Fazer's comeback was something about having been at

a party at Chloe's place the night before and him going back to pick up his phone charger. Maybe this was completely true, and I have no evidence to prove otherwise, but because of the long-running drama between us, and all my paranoia, I just couldn't take the stress anymore. I told him we were finished. I told him I was leaving him for good.

The next thing I knew, Fazer was banging on Gareth's door at three o'clock in the morning, screaming the place down and going mental.

'You're a psychopath,' he was shouting outside the door. 'I ain't done nothing! You have to believe me.'

I still didn't believe him, but I didn't have any evidence so I gave him one more lifeline just the same – I'm fair like that.

'OK then,' I said. 'If you'll take a lie detector test and you're telling the truth, then I'll give you a chance. Otherwise, we're finished. I can't trust you anymore. There have been too many scenarios like this for me to put up with it any longer. It's a lie detector test, or I'm gone!'

It might sound crazy and a bit extreme, but I had to follow my instincts.

Just as I suspected, he wouldn't do the test. He made every excuse under the sun over the next week not to do it.

'Well then, we're finished,' I told him.

And I meant it. I could no longer live like this so it was time for this chapter in my life to come to an end.

After I'd finally left our house and collected most of my things, I felt a sense of relief, but I was also sad that it had ended the way it had. A couple of months later, while I was over in LA, recording my solo album, there were all sorts of magazine stories coming out of the woodwork about different girls Fazer had supposedly been seeing while we were still together. Even though I know better than anyone that you shouldn't always believe everything you read in the press, I couldn't help but be upset by all the rumours and Chinese whispers. Still, when I got back from America, Fazer seemed to be convinced that we were going to get back together, so I spent one last evening at the house with him to make sure he knew once and for all that there was no going back.

Some of my friends thought I was nuts, and they told me so.

'You're paranoid, T. Fazer loves you too much, he would never do anything like that to you,' was all I kept hearing.

Although I knew that was true, it had gone beyond the point of no return by then. There has to be a point when self-respect takes over, and this was it. No more chances. I don't do second chances anymore.

Chapter Twenty-Six

In the summer of 2011 I sat down to watch a TV programme that I'd really been looking forward to. *The Runaway* was an adaptation of Martina Cole's novel, and being a massive Martina fan, it was must-see TV as far as I was concerned. I really love Martina's books – in fact, when people ask me who my idol is, I always say it's her. I'm a little obsessed, if you want the truth. After I'd watched the first episode of the drama, a friend of mine, who's also a big Martina fan, called me up to discuss the show in detail.

'Don't you think the male lead, the guy playing Eamonn, is fit?' she said. 'He's gorgeous!'

'Not really my type. I didn't really take much notice.'

Three episodes in, I got it.

'Wow, he is bloody fit, isn't he?'

Now, I'm pretty picky when it comes to guys, and I very rarely spot somebody on TV or in a movie who I'm attracted to, but the more I watched this guy, Jack O'Connell, the more intrigued I became. I thought I might like to meet him, and I knew if I set my mind to it, I could probably do it. I was bound to know someone who knew either him or his agent or his management or something. But why? What would be the point? I was still with Fazer back then, and I wasn't going to do the dirty on him. I put the idea of meeting Jack out of my mind, and then, because I was busy with *The X Factor*, I missed the last few episodes of the series anyway.

By the time I eventually caught up with the rest of *The Runaway*, towards the end of the year, I'd been going through a very rough patch with Fazer. It was one of our numerous mini break-ups before the final big one. Once again, Jack intrigued me as I watched the show, but I didn't know anything about him really. I hadn't seen him in the TV show *Skins*, which he was well known for, or anything else for that matter. But the more I watched him, the more I wanted to know about him. His whole character and demeanour seemed so attractive to me. I remember half-jokingly bragging to Gareth at the time, as I sat there glued to the screen.

'You see him there?' I said. 'One day I'm gonna have him.'

Gareth roared with laughter.

'You're mental, you are. You do this sort of thing all the time.'

'No, I'm telling you, he's going to be my man.'

I was saying it in jest, I suppose, but the way things had been going with Fazer, I secretly hoped my silly brag might come true. It certainly didn't seem beyond the realms of possibility, let's put it that way. Once again, though, as things sort of got back on track with Fazer for a while, I put thoughts of Jack O'Connell aside. He was just my TV crush and nothing more. That was allowed.

Just before Christmas and the end of *The X Factor*, I was starting to think about the video for my first solo single, 'Young'. The plan was to shoot the video in Ibiza and the storyline required a leading man to play opposite me. Hmm . . . who better than Jack O'Connell? He's hot. He's an actor. He's the guy I wanted for my romantic lead, so I got straight on the case. Coincidentally, Gareth knew one of the other cast members of *Skins*, the TV show that

HONEST

Jack had starred in a year or so before, and my friend Ny was a mate of the musician Plan B, who'd acted alongside Jack in the movie *Harry Brown*.

I was going to make this my mission, and when I make something my mission, I won't stop . . . Anyway, I put the word out that I wanted to meet Jack. My relationship with Fazer was obviously in its final stages and I guess I sensed that the end was near and was keeping my options open. After all, I felt that's what Fazer was doing. It's not like I would have cheated on him, even though things were pretty terrible between us leading up to Christmas, what with him staying out all night plus all the lies and suspicion. Still, something in my subconscious was telling me that I should meet Jack, so I decided to go with my gut.

On the night of Gareth's birthday, he had invited his mate from the *Skins* cast, Luke Pasqualino, to celebrate with us at a nightclub. Luke had heard that I'd been trying to wangle a meeting with Jack and so he kindly brought him along for an introduction – at last!

As Jack descended the stairs of the club, I remember thinking how very different he looked to the character he'd portrayed on *The Runaway*: still very attractive, just very different. It turned out that he wasn't even a cockney, but a down-to-earth Derby lad. As soon as I spotted him, I walked boldly up to him, grabbed his hand and shook it firmly, smiling.

'Jack O'Connell, nice to finally meet you,' I said confidently.

His eyes very definitely lit up!

We sat down and talked for most of the evening, with me chattering away about how much I loved Martina Cole, and how good I thought he was in *The Runaway* as

Eamonn. He wasn't a disappointment in the flesh either: Jack was a very good-looking boy. Still, there was no flirting. I told myself that it was all very well fancying somebody off the telly, but now he was there in front of me, I had to keep in mind that I was in a relationship, however broken it might be. In fact, Jack asked me if I had a fella and I mentioned Fazer right off, always referring to him as 'my boyfriend' so that there was no grey area. I guess Jack must have had an idea that I found him attractive and I got the impression that the feeling was mutual, but I made it clear that it was strictly business between us. Still, the two of us ended up getting along like a house on fire. He was a bit of a cheeky one – just like me!

Later, a big group of us decided to head back to Gareth's place after the club, and Jack came along. I noticed, as we got up to leave, however, that he was absolutely rat-arsed. By the time we got back to Gareth's, Jack was a little bit green, and while the rest of us were chilling out and having a drink, he made a beeline for the bathroom and proceeded to spew his guts up. He was in there for ages being as sick as a dog – it wasn't pretty. The upshot was that I spent the rest of the evening taking care of him because he was so off his face. It wasn't quite what I'd had in mind for my first meeting with my TV crush, but there it was.

We exchanged numbers before I packed Jack off to where he was staying that night, and I was very happy because he'd agreed to be in my video. He told me I was 'proper sound' for looking after him when he was ill, and I thought I'd made a very nice new friend, if nothing else. We agreed to stay in touch, but it was nothing more than a few friendly calls and text messages, with Jack saying

how much he was looking forward to shooting the video.
Then, just before I went to the Maldives with Fazer, I was
having a chat with Jack and I ended up telling him how
miserable I was. I was driving myself nuts with all the
rumours flying round about Fazer, particularly the
revelation that he'd brought a girl back to our house while
I wasn't there. As it turned out, Jack was a really good
sounding post, and a great listener.

'What are you going to do about it?' he asked me.
'You'll have to make a decision about this holiday.'

'I'm going to go for it and try to make it work,' I said. Of
course, by the time I got to the Maldives, I kind of knew
that wasn't going to happen, so on New Year's Eve, when I
got a text from Jack, it made me smile.

All the text said was 'Happy New Year, hope you're
having a good one. Jack.'

Unfortunately, Fazer had been standing right behind me
in our hotel room when I opened the message, and he was
far from happy.

'Who the fuck's that?' he shouted.

I was as honest as I could be with him. I'd already told
him about meeting Jack at Gareth's birthday, and that I
wanted him for the leading man in my video.

'He's the actor I told you about,' I said. 'We're just
mates.'

It was the truth, but I felt guilty nonetheless. As much
as I would never have gone behind Fazer's back, I was
attracted to Jack. That was the reason I'd gone out of my
way to meet him in the first place. And the worse things
had got with Fazer and me, the more I'd thought about
Jack.

About a week after Fazer and I finally split, I spoke to
Jack, and we were at last able to be a bit more honest

about our feelings for one another. We both acknowledged that there was an attraction between us, but Jack told me over the phone that he was worried.

'I don't like the fact that you've just broken up with someone,' he told me. 'I don't know if you're going to get back together with him and I don't like the thought of stepping on another man's toes.'

Jack didn't have a steady girlfriend, but he was definitely getting some female attention from somewhere, I was sure of it. He was only twenty-one and still a bit of a free spirit in that department. My guess was that he had a couple of girls on the go. A few days later he came down to London from his home in Derby for an audition and we decided to meet up. He turned up at Gareth's with a bottle of wine and a cocky smile.

'All right, T, how you doin'?'

I'd already primed Gareth to hang around for a while, just to keep the vibe relaxed, with all three of us hanging out together. I'd also told Gareth that if I wanted to be alone with Jack, I'd give him the nod, and he'd promised to make himself scarce.

Once we'd had a couple of drinks, I cooked us all a spaghetti carbonara and Jack and I settled back into the same relaxed banter that we'd had the night we met. Jack admitted that before he met me, he had a completely different idea about the kind of person I might be. On paper, I wouldn't have been his type at all, in fact. For a start, he didn't like modern pop music or pop stars very much – he was much more into The Beatles and The Rolling Stones. He also disliked shows like *The X Factor*, and he hated the whole idea of celebrity culture. He imagined I might be one of those stereotypical media girls who said 'like' or 'babe' after every other word. He certainly wasn't expecting someone who was down to earth and straight-talking.

As it got too late to head back to Derby, Jack ended up staying over at Gareth's. And although he shared my bed, we didn't even kiss, let alone anything else. I'd explained a bit about my past to him, about how I'd let myself fall for guys far too easily when I was younger. That was something I didn't want to do any longer. 'I'm not that kind of girl anymore,' I said. And he was totally cool with it.

It was obvious to both of us that there was something going on between us, and on our second date, again at Gareth's flat, the atmosphere was much the same: nice and relaxed. This time, however, Jack moved in close to me while we were talking and we had our first kiss. It was pretty mind-blowing, I have to say: deep and passionate. Jack pulled slowly back after he'd kissed me.

'Wow, that was a bit intense,' he smiled.

He wasn't kidding! I certainly hadn't experienced that level of intensity from a first kiss before either. Then Jack surprised me again.

'Look, T, I'm not sure what to do about all this. I was at the pub on Saturday night flirting with some girls, but because we've got this new thing going on, I felt guilty. But I don't even know what this is yet.'

After the relationship I'd just come out of with Fazer, I found his honesty quite shocking – and, I have to say, refreshing.

'D'you know what? That actually makes me feel good,' I said. 'I'm glad you told me that.'

Jack's honesty drew me to him even more. Even after kissing me like that, there was no bullshit, no 'I'll love you forever, now let's go to bed' or any of that stuff. Instead, he told me that as much as he was into me, he hadn't been expecting someone to blow his mind like I had. He hadn't been looking for a serious commitment either, and he still wasn't sure he wanted one – in fact, the thought of it freaked him out.

When we met up for a third time, still in the safety of Gareth's flat and away from the eyes of the paparazzi, it was just before I was leaving for a month in America, to record some solo material. I knew that if we were going to take the plunge and sleep together, it could well be that night, but I still wasn't sure. It would have been so easy to just fall into bed with Jack – I liked him so much – but I couldn't face the idea of giving myself to him if that was all there was to it. I knew that he was scared of commitment; so was I after the relationship I'd just come out of. But I also didn't want to fall any harder for Jack than I already had, not if we weren't going to take it any further than just sex. Gone were the days when I'd jump into bed with a man, not knowing where it was going to lead, or just for the hope of something more.

I suggested that we both took time to think about what we wanted from one another while I was in America. Then, when I came back, if we both agreed there might be a future for us, we could take things to the next level. What would have been the point of diving in head first one minute and then disappearing to America for a month filled with uncertainty? If Jack really liked me as much as he said he did, then he'd still be there when I got home, wouldn't he?

Chapter Twenty-Seven

I was so excited about going to Los Angeles and then Miami in February 2012 to record tracks for my first solo album, especially as Gareth and Ny were both coming along with me. I knew we were going to get up to some mischief and have some fun when we had a bit of downtime. I was working alongside my old friend from Island/Def Jam records, Max Gousse, who was co-ordinating the recording sessions out there for me. I'd stayed friendly with Max even after N-Dubz had left the label, and, in turn, he'd always been supportive of me and confident in his vision of me as a solo artist in America.

When I arrived in Miami everything just seemed so fun and glamorous – except, that is, our accommodation, which I thought was a bit pokey, with Ny and me sharing a bed in the same room as Gareth. Eventually, though, we moved to a penthouse room at the Shore Club Hotel, Miami Beach. This place was stunning, and I loved everything about it. It was proper rock-star!

While I was there, I met Mark Wright of *The Only Way is Essex* fame, and we hung out together for a couple of evenings. Mark is a really cool bloke, and we actually spent quite a lot of time putting the world to rights together, sitting on the terrace of his room with a glass of wine. We also talked about my tough time with Fazer and his on/off relationship with his ex-girlfriend, Lauren, and I found him really charming and pretty chilled out. He's a very cute guy too, but not really my type.

Still there was a bit of daft flirting, but it really was just innocent fun. Of course, the papers in the UK were straight on it, proclaiming that we'd slept together. NOT TRUE! Why is it that I can't be friendly, or even have a bit of a flirt, with a guy without everyone presuming I banged him? I guess it's because I'm so loud and out there – a bit of a party girl. Some people think: 'Oh yeah, she must like a bit of the other as well then!' It's hilarious. Yes, I may love hanging out with guys, and sometimes I've been known to have the odd sleepover with some of my male pals (my friends laughingly call me 'the snuggle slut'), but that doesn't mean I'm going to be indulging in any nookie! I've even got a tattoo on my bikini line that says 'Lucky You'. It's true. Ask Mark Wright if he bloody well got to see that. He did not!

In all seriousness, sex is a very big thing to me, and because I've been hurt so much in the past my self-respect is very important. My ego is also quite fragile, and when I have sex with a guy I feel like I'm giving them a big part of myself. If that guy doesn't love or respect me then I don't feel like I'm getting anything out of it. I feel empty afterwards. That's why I only enjoy sex within a relationship, and I have a lot of self-control in that department.

The plan, while I was in Miami, was to meet a few different producers and songwriters and get some amazing tracks together, but one suggestion in particular from Max Gousse really grabbed my attention.

'I think you should meet The-Dream,' he said when we met at his office.

Wow! I knew all about The-Dream. His real name was Terius Nash and he'd written and produced some worldwide mega-hits, such as Rihanna's 'Umbrella' and

Beyoncé's 'Single Ladies'. The guy was a giant in urban music, and if an artist had him on side, they had their hits sorted. He could help break an artist around the world. Of course I wanted to work with him.

'There's a problem, though,' Max continued. 'The-Dream is a tough nut to crack. He works with huge worldwide superstars, not just anyone. He doesn't really work with British artists; he's just not that interested. I think if you met him, though, you might be able to make him fall in love with you. I think if you were just naturally "you", he would really like you.'

'Oh Max, what are you trying to do to me?' I groaned. It didn't sound in the slightest bit like an easy task.

'What do you think?' he said. 'I could take you to his house to meet him.'

'OK, cool!'

I didn't really need to think about it: this was much too big an opportunity to pass up. Working with The-Dream *would* be a bloody dream, scary or not.

Although Max had warned me that Dream was a bit of a cool customer, I wasn't at all prepared for someone quite as cool as he turned out to be. We arrived at his beautiful house overlooking the ocean on South Beach, and Max, Rich from my management and I sat by the swimming pool at the back of the house. It was like something off the MTV *Cribs* TV show – stunning in every way. Eventually Dream, an imposing black dude in his mid-thirties, came out to meet us, but he didn't say much. In fact, he barely said a word. Instead, he looked me up and down, carefully, and then eventually sat down with us.

'Whaddup?' he said.

'You all right?' I smiled.

'This is not going to be easy,' I thought, and I was right.

For the first fifteen minutes, I had to make all the conversation, while Dream just glared at me as if he might be about to kill me. This wasn't a man for the timid souls, I can tell you. I wasn't deterred, however, telling myself, 'T, you can handle it!'

'So,' I said breezily, 'have you ever worked with any British artists before?'

'I was supposed to,' he muttered.

'Oh yeah? What happened?'

'They weren't good enough.'

'Right. So why haven't you considered working with some other UK artists?'

'Because I haven't met any that are good enough.'

It was quite an intimidating thing to say to a young British pop artist who was there looking to record with him, but I managed to stay composed.

'Well you ain't fucking met me yet, have you?

And with that, he giggled.

'I like that,' he said.

Now, I like to think of myself as a chameleon. It's one of the things I pride myself on, being able to adapt to any given social situation. You could stick me at a dinner table with President Obama and I reckon I'd be able to find something to chat with him about. You could also sit me down with a kid from the ghetto slums of God-knows-where and I would be able to get along with them too. The-Dream had indeed been a hard nut to crack, but suddenly I saw a way in. He obviously reacted well to people who were as tough as he was, so I was going to have to pull out the Female Boss.

'Well, I'm the fucking shit!' I told him, thinking tons of swearing might be effective and show Dream that I wasn't scared of him.

HONEST

'I'm about to fuck shit up and take over the fucking world! I'm gonna smash up the music scene in the UK, and then I'm gonna smash it in America as well. So I suggest you get on board!'

It was very funny, and although I couldn't see Max, I was sure he was grinning from ear to ear. Max has a lot of time for me, and he believes in me too, and I knew that he'd primed Dream that I was likely to be feisty. It's what Max expected of me, and why he'd taken me to meet Dream in the first place.

Despite my bravado, though, Dream was still not that chatty, and suddenly, in the middle of a serious discussion about music, he made an announcement.

'I want a peanut butter milkshake!'

Then he went on and on about this damn milkshake, which was from a certain café and was apparently really good.

'Well, if you want the fucking milkshake so badly, let's go and get it,' I suddenly snapped.

'OK, cool,' Dream said. 'Do you wanna ride with me?'

The next thing I knew, I was hurtling through the streets of Miami in a red Ferrari 458 Italia, heading for Johnny Rockets on Ocean Drive. We ended up having burgers and cocktails with some of his friends, plus Ny, Gareth, Rich and Max. And eventually, while I munched my way through a huge burger and sipped on my Long Island Iced Tea, the two of us began bantering and laughing and playing mental ping-pong like we were old pals. Once we got talking, I realised how funny and very intelligent Dream was, and in turn, he made no secret of the fact that he appreciated a woman who had something to say for herself. That was refreshing to me, I must say. I've met plenty of guys who would much prefer the female of the species to be seen but not heard. It was nice to meet someone so high-powered who respected a bit of intelligence in a woman.

We partied away for a couple of hours in the restaurant, and I felt a bit drunk. As the day wore on, though, Max and Rich were eager to ferry me off to a recording session that had been scheduled with another producer that day, but Dream had other ideas.

'Max, she ain't goin' to no session. She's chillin' with me the rest of the day.'

'Oh, I don't know about that,' Max said anxiously.

I could see that Ny and Gareth were both looking a bit nervous too. They thought that Dream had set his sights on me.

'Is he on you?' Ny said to me, but I wasn't really worried.

'Guys, it's fine,' I said, merrily. 'You know me, I can handle it.'

When I got back into Dream's Ferrari, he made an announcement.

'I'm kidnapping you,' he smiled. 'Let's go to New Orleans.'

'Listen, I can do kung fu,' I said. 'You're not kidnapping me, and if you don't drive me to the studio now, I'm gonna bust your bloody arse!'

It was all in absolute jest, but it was clear that Dream's cold, hard exterior had now completely melted and he'd become a warm, funny guy and new friend all in one afternoon. Our repartee and verbal jousting was so funny and natural, I don't think I've ever mentally clicked with someone like that so fast before.

Meanwhile, on that same trip, we recorded the video for my first single, 'Young'. And after all the trouble I'd gone to trying to track down Jack to play my leading man, it wasn't to be after all. Originally, the video was supposed to feature me and Jack, Gareth, Ny and a bunch of other friends going wild in Ibiza, peppered with a few alcohol-fuelled hot, kinky love scenes – a typical Ibiza clubbing holiday, as far as I was concerned. Unfortunately, because of the scheduled timing of the single release, it wasn't really the right season for Ibiza, so we had to shoot it in Miami. Jack couldn't get a visa to work in America in time, and therefore couldn't do it.

Anyway, at the last minute, I had to re-work the video treatment slightly and we found another actor to step in. The message in the video was simple. It was four young friends getting wild and having fun, cruising round Miami in a classic convertible, hanging out on the beach, busting into a hotel room and pillow-fighting, gatecrashing a posh art gallery party and partying on a hotel terrace. At the end of the video, all four of us are just crashed out together on the hotel bed. To be honest, it isn't a million miles away from what really happens when Gareth, Ny and I hang out together! And although the whole thing was very simple, it worked brilliantly with the party vibe of the track, and of course the lyrics: 'We live on the edge of life. We don't even compromise. We rush because we're out of time. We're young!'

After that first meeting, The-Dream and I were almost inseparable. I heard from Max that Dream had told Def Jam that he liked everything about me and wanted to work with me – I was so happy.

'I see the vision, she's gonna be big,' he told Max. 'I want to be involved.'

This meant a lot coming from someone I admired as much as I did him. It made me all the more enthusiastic for the next trip to Miami, when we could actually start working on some tracks together. As it was, I was working with some other cool producers on my present trip, but at the end of the sessions, I would always go and chill with Dream – I adored him. We went out for dinners and to Disney World – he's a big kid at heart. He got to know and read me like a book, and I was able to get away with so much more than some of the other people who hung out with him, who seemed to tiptoe nervously around him. I'd pull him up on various misdemeanours, like if he swore too loudly in public and there were kids nearby.

'Oi, you! Language!' I'd scold.

And, in turn, he would put me straight when he thought I was talking crap.

One night, The-Dream had a very interesting proposition for me.

'Do you wanna go to a strip club?'

'Er . . . OK!'

Why not? It wasn't like I hadn't been to one before. My friend and ex-boyfriend Adam Bailey manages a strip club. Gareth and Ny were coming along too, so I knew we'd have a laugh, whatever happened. However, when we all rocked up at the swanky King of Diamonds lap-dancing club, I was amazed when we sat down and Dream slapped about twenty thousand dollars on the table in front of us. Then he handed me a couple of grand and smiled.

'Let's get a dance,' he said.

I have to say, I felt a bit awkward at first. I didn't like the idea of a guy suddenly handing me all that cash.

'I've got my money, thank you,' I told him. 'I'm not really comfortable with a guy spending cash on me like this.'

HONEST

'Shut up and get yourself a dance,' he laughed.

After we'd had a few cocktails and a few shots of Patrón, which is a premium tequila, I decided I was ready for action, so Dream called over two girls. Before I knew it, the two of us were both getting lap-dances from these two gorgeous women, and I start showing off with all this cash and acting exactly like a seasoned punter. Everyone else around the table just watched in astonishment – it was hilarious. I'd had quite a bit to drink by then, so you could say all of my inhibitions had disappeared by that point. So while I'm sitting there, with this girl bent over me with her boob in my face, I start 'making it rain' with cash over her backside – showering her with money. By this time everyone round the table and half the rest of the club were just staring over at me, writhing around with thousands of dollars, getting a private dance. It must have been quite a sight, when I think about it. I was dressed up in a pretty dress, looking quite demure and innocent, and there I was, laughing and whooping, making it rain dollars and slapping a stripper's booty! People must have wondered, 'Who is this crazy white English chick?'

'You gangster!' Dream shouted at me. 'You gangster!'

Of course, the press were all over it, and it made the papers in Britain the next day. In fact, whenever I was out with Dream, we got papped, so lots of people started to think we were dating. Gareth and I were Tweeting from the strip club too, so there really was no chance we were going to be able to keep it under the radar. Some of the papers made it out to be really seedy, but it wasn't. I got a dance off a girl. So what? There's no point in calling myself the Female Boss if I'm not living up to it, is there? I've never said I was an angel, and it's not like I took the dancer back to my hotel and had a lesbian orgy, although it wouldn't have been anybody else's business if I had! I didn't care, anyway. It was so much fun that night. 'Some funny-assed shit' as Dream would say. The Female Boss was out in full force that night!

I'd made such a great new friend in The-Dream on that Miami trip, and since then, I've been back to Atlanta to work with him in the studio. He's worked on four tracks on my album now, and one of them might even end up being a single. What's cool about our relationship is that although we love one another as friends, we both knew that romance was not on the cards from the outset. We even jokingly discussed what it might be like if we were dating, but decided very early on we were much too similar and it would never work. We agreed that we'd just stay the best of friends – and we certainly have.

Chapter Twenty-Eight

On the way back from America, I got held up slightly at Miami airport, when check-in staff discovered that something weird was going on with my luggage.

'Ma'am, your suitcase is vibrating,' the check-in lady exclaimed as she picked up my case to put it on the belt.

'Shit!'

I felt the quivering case and I knew what it was straight away. It was a sex toy. My sex toy! Gareth clocked it straight away too, and we both burst into fits of laughter: we were cracking up. I had to open the bloody case and take the batteries out of the damn thing because I couldn't get it to stop buzzing.

Of course, the papers made a big deal out of it. 'OOH! Tulisa's got a sex toy!' At the time I was a bit embarrassed about it so I said it belonged to a friend, but actually, yes, Tulisa has got a sex toy, and so have millions of other women. As I've said, I'm not into casual sex anymore, so when I'm not in a relationship, it comes in very handy, thank you!

Once I was back in London, I had to decide whether I wanted to try to move things forward with Jack or not. Before I'd left for Miami, he'd told me that he would much rather be a good friend to me than a cheating lover.

'I don't want to get to the stage where I'm being dishonest with you,' he said. 'I can't do that to you. You've been lied to enough and I don't want to do that. But at the same time, I'm not sure I'm ready to give you what you want.'

His honesty had actually astounded me. This was a new breed of man, as far as I was concerned, and it only made me want him more at the time. Still, I knew he was right. What was the point in starting something serious if I was going to get my heart broken down the line? All the time I was in Miami, I'd questioned the whole idea of being with Jack – it had been much easier to consider things logically from afar. Yes, I'd certainly pursued him and made it my mission to make him mine. But I started to think, 'Is this *really* what I want? After everything I've been through with Fazer, do I *really* need to fall into another complicated situation, putting in all that hard work for something that might end in tears? Shouldn't I just take the easy option and get out now? Find someone that's 100 per cent sure that they want to be with me and *only* me?'

Once I'd returned from America, however, Jack called and asked me to meet up with him straight away, and it was clear when we met that the feelings we'd had pre-Miami were still there on both sides.

'I can't keep away, T,' he told me. 'I say all this stuff about not wanting to get serious with you, but I still feel like I want to be around you all the time. I don't know what to do here. I can't keep my distance, but I can't commit either.'

I suggested that we just carried on 'dating' in the way that we were. We hadn't had sex yet, so I didn't feel disrespected. I thought we should just see how things panned out.

A few weeks later, however, in a night of drunken passion, I went against my morals and slept with him. But now what? Were we finally going to be a couple? I took a practical approach.

'Look, it's happened, we've had sex. Let's not put the relationship stamp on it. Let's just go with the flow. No pressure. If it's not right for me in a month's time, because you'd prefer to be a free agent, then so be it. Let's just enjoy what's happening now.'

That same weekend, Jack invited me to go to Derby for his sister's birthday party, and of course I had to meet his entire family on the first day that I got there, which was quite nerve-wracking, I have to say. They all assumed that because Jack had brought me home to meet them, I was his full-on, official girlfriend, but that wasn't the case. Still, I ended up staying in Derby for about a week, and I had a great time.

By that time, there had been a couple of paparazzi shots of Jack and I out and about, and Fazer wasn't especially happy about it.

'So you were seeing him all along then?' he said, when we spoke on the phone. 'I knew when you got that text in the Maldives.'

He wanted to make me out to be the bad guy, flip everything so it was my fault that we'd split up. In the end, I managed to convince him that wasn't the case. I think he knew I was telling the truth. Fazer has known me since we were kids. He knew I wasn't a cheater: he'd seen it a hundred times over the years. Whenever a dude would hit on me or ask me out while I was in a couple, I'd always say the same thing: 'Not while I'm with someone.'

It was because of this that Fazer never had trust issues with me, not like I did with him. He tried to pretend that he was angry with me for seeing Jack, but deep down he knew that Jack wasn't the reason our relationship had ended.

Soon after I came back from my week in Derby, it was Jack's turn to fly to America, as he was due to start filming in LA. And although we still weren't officially a couple, Jack's many texts and calls while he was away told me that he was missing me. He actually confided in me later that while he was there, instead of making the most of being a single boy in Los Angeles, he had thought about me all the time. He found that despite being supposedly footloose and fancy-free, he didn't want to sow his wild oats with other girls after all. It was good to know that, because I was thinking about him too. I was happy that he missed me, and in truth I couldn't wait for him to get back to London. Maybe this thing was going to work out after all.

But as usual with me, nothing is ever that simple. Quite suddenly, my whole life was turned on its head, and that little rug of happiness I'd been standing on for the last few months was completely ripped out from under me.

Chapter Twenty-Nine

On Saturday 17 March 2012, three months after the wonderful highs of *The X Factor*, my world crashed down around me in a big way. I was in the car with Gareth when I got a message on my BlackBerry, and because I was driving, I handed Gareth my phone to see who it was from and what it was all about. The look of horror on Gareth's face immediately told me it wasn't something good.

'It's out, T,' he said. 'It's out!'

And my heart sank.

This particular drama had started way back in the previous August, when I got a telephone call from Simon Jones, my publicist. I was in bed and was still half-asleep at the time, but the words I heard coming down the phone shook me violently out of my cosy slumber, and I sat bolt upright.

'WHAT?'

Simon nervously repeated the words, and by this time I was wide awake, so there was no chance that I might be dreaming.

'The *Sun* says they have seen a sex tape of you.'

I was suddenly thrown into complete and utter panic.

'What tape? How? When? Where?'

I was all over the place. Who would do such a thing? Simon had no idea, and the newspaper wouldn't tell him where it had come from. All they told him was that a journalist had been to meet a man who claimed to have footage of me performing a sexual act on a guy. The footage was on a phone, and the journalist had now seen it. It looked like me, but they weren't entirely sure it was, and they were hoping that Simon would either confirm or deny it, as they were running the story the next day!

'Simon, there's no way that can be me,' I said, horrified. 'I'd never allow myself to be filmed having sex.'

Someone was having a laugh, surely? I'd never made a bloody sex-tape. My mind was suddenly going nineteen to the dozen, and I began to imagine all sorts of things: a hidden camera in a hotel room, perhaps, or a proper professional camera that had filmed me without my knowledge?

'Look, I'll get back on to the *Sun* and I'll see you later,' Simon said.

And that was that. The start of a complete nightmare.

That afternoon I had a cover shoot for *You* magazine, which wasn't exactly the best timing in the world. Simon told me that the *Sun* was now definitely going to run the story, because they were now convinced it was me, and on top of that, it looked like I knew I was being filmed, that it wasn't a hidden camera at all.

'Well then, it can't be me,' I said angrily, 'because that's not something I've done. It's not possible. It has to be a fake.'

I was pretty terrified about a story like that running in the papers, though, and during the shoot, I suddenly ran into the make-up room and burst into tears. Of course, this wasn't a great look for the *You* magazine cover, and my make-up had to be completely re-done. When it was finished, I started crying once more, and the make-up was ruined all over again. It was a vile situation.

HONEST

During the photo shoot, I went out into the corridor with Simon and called all my ex-boyfriends, just to find out if any of them had something they needed to tell me, but none of them admitted to knowing anything about any tape. I particularly remember calling Justin, because he was the one I was most worried about. We were always filming one another around the house when we were together, although, as far as I was concerned, we'd never taped anything that intimate. I asked him if he had ever filmed us together, if he had lost his phone at any time, if there was any way that this was something to do with him, but he was absolutely adamant that he had nothing to do with it. Simon had already told me that the guy's face wasn't visible in the footage, just the girl's, so I had to take his word for it. I was now even more convinced that this was all a load of fake crap, and I suddenly felt a little better.

Simon got straight back on the phone to the *Sun*, who refused to let us see the footage, which seemed to confirm my suspicions that it was, in fact, a phoney. Meanwhile, my lawyer, Jonathan Coad, contacted them, stating that I had never allowed myself to be filmed in that way, and if by some chance it was me, then it had been filmed without my consent and was therefore illegal. The next day the *Sun* ran an article saying that there was a fake Tulisa sex tape doing the rounds. It turned out that they weren't even in possession of any footage anyway, that they'd only briefly seen it on the guy's phone. I breathed a large sigh of relief – for a while at least.

After that, I didn't hear anything more about this alleged sex tape for some time, so I hoped and prayed that that was the end of it. A couple of months later, however, I got a call from Adam Bailey, who told me that the word on the street was that Justin did, in fact, have provocative footage of me, taken on a phone camera, and that he believed Justin was trying to sell it. This was still difficult for me to believe, but the mere mention of it sent my heart into free-fall all over again.

'How do you know it's me?' I asked Adam.

'Trust me,' Adam said. 'Someone I know has seen it, and it's definitely you.'

Shit. What had I done? And when? And why would Justin do something like that when we had once been a couple? He'd been so adamant over the phone when the original rumour had started.

'I don't know what you're talking about,' he'd told me casually. 'It's nothing to do with me, it must be a fake.'

After the 'fake tape' story came out in the newspaper, Justin had sent me a text saying, 'See! I told ya!' but I was never completely convinced.

After Adam's new and very scary revelation, I called Justin again, but this time his manner was anything but casual – in fact, it was extremely defensive. He denied any knowledge of the tape again, and so, trying to give him the benefit of the doubt, I considered the possibility that maybe someone else was trying to leak footage of us, that maybe he didn't know about it. Maybe he was a victim too.

'Well, if it wasn't you, let's try to figure out who it might have been,' I said.

I was desperate and asking for help, but as the conversation continued, he became more and more strange and defensive, eventually telling me his battery had died and hanging up the phone. I could tell he was lying through his teeth, but what could I do? I couldn't even think what the tape might be, let alone prove it was

Justin trying to distribute it. It was a very confusing time, and incredibly upsetting too. Justin obviously didn't want to talk to me about it, so I had to leave it alone, hoping that whatever it was would just go away. I sent Justin one last text on the matter: 'If this tape does exist, then I know it's you!'

Simon Jones tried to put my mind at rest again. 'Look, as far as we're concerned, this tape doesn't exist,' he said. 'If the *Sun* had footage and evidence that it was you, they would have run it.'

He was convinced it was just the rumour mill going into overdrive, but by now I was seriously concerned, especially after talking to Justin.

Not long after that, another friend called me, informing me that they too knew somebody who had seen the tape and that Justin was now trying to decide whether to sell the tape or simply extort money from me directly to stop its distribution. I was absolutely horrified. It felt as though there was a massive axe swinging above my head, and I had no idea if or when it was going to fall. It was both frustrating and terrifying all at the same time. My heart was telling me that it couldn't be true, that this tape couldn't really exist, but as time went on, my mind was telling me otherwise.

I was distraught. What was worse was that I had to try to concentrate on work: on my job as a judge on *The X Factor*. I had to smile and be smart and funny on the outside, but underneath I was petrified of being made to look like some kind of slapper in front of the nation. I would try to put the whole thing out of my mind as much as possible, but it would always creep back – it was pretty much all-consuming.

The situation, and my stress over it, was also affecting

Fazer, who was enraged by the whole thing and furious with Justin. We were still a couple then and he hated seeing me upset. Fazer was always very supportive of me, but unfortunately there was nothing he could do. The fact remained that we had no evidence against Justin, and that so far nothing had actually happened – it was all just ugly speculation.

As time went on, I had a few more thoughts about what the contents of the tape might be. I recalled having a terrible hangover after a drunken night with Justin. I remembered him bursting into the bathroom and filming me because he thought it was funny, and then me yelling at him to stop it and to get out. I then remembered him filming the night before, and that the next morning I'd told him to delete whatever it was he'd filmed. It rang a bell. So what had he filmed when I was drunk the night before?

Eventually, when we heard that Justin planned to sell the tape to an internet site, I contacted him again, this time with a warning.

'If you do this, your career will be over,' I warned. 'Think very carefully about what you're planning to do.'

I'd tried to support Justin in his career while we were together, helping him get a singles deal with All Around the World Records, among other things. I'd been very encouraging of him as an artist. But if it turned out that he had leaked the tape, then I certainly wasn't going to keep quiet about *his* identity. And surely he couldn't think that any record company would ever go near him again once everyone knew who he was? He'd just be forever known as the guy that released the sex-tape! People who try to launch their careers on the back of publicity stunts like that never have credible music careers. You can't come out of the *Big Brother* house, for instance, and expect to be the next hot music act. I was hoping that my warning text might make him reconsider his actions.

Yet again, though, Justin's denial about the tape was absolute, and I just had to sit back and wait it out. By this time, I'd suffered for months. I was becoming moody and tearful on a regular basis. It was miserable, and I knew that I had to cover myself by warning the producers at *The X Factor* what may be about to happen. I was dreading it, but I knew it had to be done, and my management agreed.

One night, while I was at the studio before recording the show, I tearfully told *X Factor* producer Beth Hart everything. Beth was someone that I respected and trusted, and we'd become quite good mates, so I knew I could confide in her. I was desperate, and I thought I'd better let someone on the show know, in case it was suddenly front-page news. I was also worried how it might affect my position on *The X Factor* judging panel.

'If the tape gets released, will I lose my job?' I asked Beth. 'What will it do to my career? Will I get sacked from the show?'

'I don't know,' she answered.

It wasn't particularly reassuring, I can tell you! Meanwhile, I got a call from another ex-girlfriend of Justin's, reiterating the same old news – Justin was planning to sell the tape to an internet site. She wanted to get my take on the situation, and it was pretty obvious that she was snaking me on Justin's behalf, trying to find out what I might do if he leaked the material. Eventually, Jonathan Coad had letters delivered to Justin's house, warning him that if he was trying to sell footage of me shot without my consent, that would be unlawful and he would be sued or possibly even prosecuted. Once again, Justin categorically denied he was doing any such thing.

Ultimately, all this crap tarnished my whole time at *The X Factor*, and though I loved being on the show, I was constantly afraid that I was going to be made to look like a terrible person on a national scale and then get fired. It wasn't like I let it affect my performance or my confidence on screen, but it did mean that all the time I wasn't on camera I felt very low and anxious.

On one occasion, I received a tip-off about the tape's imminent release minutes before I went live on air. I remember having to really snap it on and pretend everything was hunky-dory as the cameras rolled. All I really wanted to do, though, was run to the bathroom and hide, or get pissed, smoke cigarettes and cry. Having to sit there on live television, pretending everything was fine when it wasn't, was tough, but what choice did I have? As Simon Jones kept saying, we had to deal in facts, and the fact was that there was no evidence of a tape.

It was torture! Weeks went by and still nothing happened. No tape, no revelation. *The X Factor* final came and went, but still nothing. I began to think that maybe Justin had had a change of heart. I was wrong.

Chapter Thirty

When Gareth delivered the news to me in the car that night in March 2012, that the tape was finally out there, I went completely numb and pulled over to the side of the road, breathless. Gareth told me that he'd actually seen a screen grab of the tape on the message, so I knew that it really couldn't get much worse. It had been uploaded to an anonymous website called nottulisa.com. The site was charging six dollars for people to download it, and there was nothing I could do to stop it. It was very late on a Saturday night and I knew my lawyer would be asleep, plus we had no idea who was responsible for the website or where it had come from. I suppose I was in shock, but I didn't cry, and my next reaction was odd, to say the least.

'Fuck it!' I declared. 'I've lived with this hanging over me for months. There's nothing I can do about it, so I'm just going to have to get on with it. I'm gonna invite some of my mates over to the flat and have a bit of a drink.'

What followed was a drunken night of full-on denial, partying with my mates at the flat like nothing had happened. It was a proper rave-up!

The next day, however, it hit me like a train. I couldn't stop crying, and I felt unbearably low and empty. It was like my whole world was ending, and I was tortured by thoughts of what everyone might think of me: my parents, my grandparents, my friends, my fans. It wasn't so much shame at what I'd done – it wasn't like I'd committed a crime – but I felt terribly embarrassed and also scared of what would happen next. Surely I'd lose my job on *The X Factor*?

I just had no idea what the outcome might be during those first few days of the tape going public. I was devastated and I was angry with Justin. I hated him for what he'd done, and I didn't really know why he'd done it. I knew it wasn't just for the money. I thought it was more likely that he was still bitter and angry at me for breaking up with him. It's strange, because I'd always known he had a dark side to him, that there was something disgusting lurking in there, but I never imagined he would do something so vile.

By this time, my lawyers were trying to get the website taken down, but the damage had already been done and there were stills of the footage all over the internet. Gareth, meanwhile, was checking the online reaction, finding out what the fans and general public were saying on Twitter. I didn't dare go near it, because I was terrified of what I might see or read. It was amazing that something I'd done years before, while I was blind drunk, was now coming back to haunt me in such a terrible way, but it was now a headline everywhere. Absolutely everyone was talking about me, spouting their opinions, calling me names, having a good old laugh. I felt like everyone thought I was some sort of slut.

'Isn't this illegal?' I asked my lawyers in desperation. 'How can someone do this to me without being punished?'

The problem was, there was still no concrete evidence against Justin. My lawyers knew it was him on the tape, but that didn't prove that he was the one circulating it, or that he'd been paid for it. It was my word against his.

HONEST

Mercifully, the lawyers managed to stop the website from displaying or selling it with an emergency privacy injunction, which happened very quickly. Still, some of the screen grabs and snide comments were out there, and there was nothing either my lawyers or I could do to make those go away. 'Tulisa sex tape' was the phrase splashed over every paper and social networking site, and there was absolutely nothing I could do to stop it.

For the next few days, I wouldn't leave the flat. I would speak to Gareth and my lawyers, but no one else. Dappy and Fazer both called and messaged me, but I didn't want to talk to anyone. Fazer was clearly very worried about me, so I answered him only by text. He said that he wanted to be there for me and make sure I was all right, no matter what was going on between us. He was trying to be supportive, and I really appreciated that, even though I now had feelings for someone else.

The thought of speaking to my family – to my mum and dad – filled me with absolute dread, so I let Gareth do all the talking. In fact, in the end, I just handed Gareth my phone, so I didn't have to deal with any of the calls and texts that were coming through. He took over everything, while I retreated to the bathroom to curl up in a ball on the floor. I actually slept there for days, just like when I'd been upset when I was a kid. I think if I'd had a pair of scissors to hand in some of those lower moments, I might have gone back to some other old habits too. That was how bad it got. By this time, all my friends were desperately worried about me, and with good reason, but nobody knew what to say or how to help me. It was great having their support, though, especially as I didn't feel like I could talk to my family about it. I still haven't done that.

After hearing about some of the crazy speculation

surrounding the tape on Twitter and other public forums, I suddenly felt like I needed to have my say. I pulled myself together as much as I could and made a decision to speak publically about what had happened and how and why this awful tape was out there. I didn't want to go to the papers looking sad and remorseful, or do some exposé TV interview, but I couldn't sit there suffering in silence anymore – it was killing me. I decided to post a YouTube video on Twitter: just me talking from home, telling my side of the story honestly and calmly. Simon Jones thought there were pros and cons to this plan, and my management was dead against it, suggesting that I might be making an even bigger deal out of it, but I didn't agree. I needed to let my fans know what this footage was really all about. Eventually, I just turned my phone off and got on with it.

First, I went back to my old flat and gathered some pictures of Justin and me as a couple. Then I asked one of my friends to come round with her laptop and simply press 'record'. I wanted people to know who the person circulating this material was. Why should he have anonymity while I was being hung out to dry in front of the nation? I wanted people, especially my fans, to understand that the footage wasn't filmed during some seedy hook-up, but was in fact a betrayal by a so-called man of his ex-girlfriend. So I put a little bit of make-up on, tied my hair back, and once the camera was recording, in the dim light of our flat, I took a deep breath and started talking.

'Hi, everyone, the reason for this video is to set the record straight on a certain tape that has been circulating online that consists of footage of me and an ex-boyfriend having an intimate moment . . .'

HONEST

During the five-minute clip, I said pretty much everything I wanted to say. I pointed out that I was never one to sit back and keep quiet, and also that I'd done nothing wrong. I then held up two photos of Justin – aka Ultra – explaining that he was once my boyfriend, that we'd been in love, and that I'd trusted him completely.

'When you share an intimate moment with someone you love and you care about and trust, you never imagine for one minute that it's going to be shared with the rest of the UK or people around the world. As you can imagine, I'm devastated, heartbroken and I've been in bits for the past few days.' I said that Justin was sitting in silence, pretending that it wasn't him on the tape, but I wasn't going to let myself be violated or taken advantage of by anyone.

The next day I woke up on the bathroom floor once again, after sleeping for about one or two hours, tops. It was now five days after the release of the tape, and even after putting out the YouTube video, I still felt terrible. I tried to get myself together, but I was just in bits from having no sleep – I had terrible heart palpitations, and feelings of despair and panic completely overwhelmed me. I was sobbing my heart out when Gareth came into the bathroom and found me on the floor, shaking. His face said it all: I was a mess, with tears and make-up dripping down my face – it couldn't go on.

'T, we need to call the doctor,' Gareth said.

'I know, I know, I need help.'

What I really wanted was to call the doctor and shout, 'Give me some fucking Valium.' I simply couldn't control what was going on with my mind or my body. I wanted some peace, some calm, for everything to go away and for everyone to stop calling and texting and talking about me.

During that morning, I'd been getting texts and calls from Jack, who was now over in Los Angeles, ready to start shooting a movie, but the last thing I wanted to do was speak to him in the state I was in – plus I was a bit angry with him anyway. I'd pre-warned him about the footage some time back, and we'd been messaging one another every day since it had come out. Jack had been really supportive about the whole thing, even though we weren't officially together, but on the day I'd put the YouTube video out, he'd messaged to ask me if I was OK, and I'd texted back in a state of considerable distress. 'No, I'm not. I'm not good at all. Terrible. Everything is fucking shit!' I think that was the general gist of the message! Anyway, did he text me back after that? No, he bloody well did not, and twelve hours later I'd still had no response. I wasn't in the mood to deal with anyone who was only pretending to care, so, with my mind all over the place and in a fragile state, I deleted him from my contacts.

So, that morning, when I saw that he was calling me over and over again, I simply didn't pick up. Gareth, meanwhile, called the doctor, who told us to come straight in and meet her, so she could check me over and maybe even admit me to hospital if she thought I needed it.

'I don't want to do that,' I told Gareth. 'I'm going to call my Aunt Moira instead, and see if I can go and stay with her for a few days.'

Gareth agreed that I needed some sort of maternal love right now, and I knew I couldn't face my mum, so one of her sisters would be the next best thing. Once it was all agreed, I sat there on the bathroom floor, feeling like I was about to snap. 'This is it,' I thought. 'I'm done. I can't take anymore.' I actually admitted defeat to myself, and that's something I try never to do. I suddenly thought about the calls I'd had from Jack, so I checked my phone for messages. There was a text from him asking if I was OK. I sent a text back: 'Where are you?' He replied: 'I'm in London.' He was still having a few hiccups with his working visa and had had to come back to the UK to sort it out. The reason he hadn't messaged me the day before was that he was on a flight back from LA and wanted to surprise me. I felt a bit silly, of course, but I also felt like it was fate, and so I called Jack straight away.

'I was worried about you and wondered if you wanted to meet up,' he said.

'I'm supposed to be going to my aunt's, but I'd rather come and meet you,' I told him. 'And I'm really sorry about deleting you!'

Jack just laughed, and we met up the next day. Silly me for not picking up the phone. As soon as I saw him, everything started to feel better, easier, and for the next three weeks, he never left my side. It was the distraction I needed, and as time went on, I started to feel stronger. Jack really cheered me up. We talked, we hung out, we even laughed – he was brilliant. I realised then that I had to pull myself together, that I had to snap out of the depression I'd allowed myself to tumble so deeply into. I wasn't going to throw my life and career away over one setback, however terrible it seemed at the time. No, I was better than that. I couldn't even think about Justin anymore, he was irrelevant, insignificant. From now on, I would just let my legal team deal with him.

For me, it was all about dealing with what was happening in the moment and sorting my head out, so I got my Female Boss mode on and decided to just push through it. I suppose that's something I had to be proud of myself for. After all, I wasn't ashamed, because I'd done nothing wrong – aside from trust the wrong guy – and the YouTube response was two fingers up to him! I knew that Justin would be devastated now it was all out in the open that he'd acted like such a low-life, just like I'd been devastated when he released the footage. I'd been accused of lying to the press, of releasing the tape myself for publicity; the whole thing had been so terribly embarrassing and hurtful. Now at least people knew the truth.

During the next few days, my lawyers got a court ruling to say that the footage was an infringement of my personal rights and therefore illegal. They also got the judge who had granted the emergency injunction preventing anyone from distributing it to continue the order on a longer term basis. Meanwhile, Justin turned up at the hearing completely unannounced and defiantly told the court that he had had nothing to do with the footage or the website. He also hypocritically told the judge via his barrister that he thought that the video should never have been made public, and that he had been brought up to behave better than to have had any part in it at all.

After I'd put the video clip up on YouTube, I noticed that the tide was turning. People suddenly stopped slagging me off, or making salacious jokes about me; they seemed to be saying, 'Oh! OK, so that's what happened.'

Let's face it, I'm not the first person to get drunk and fool around in front of a camera, and I won't be the last. We all do things that we would never want anyone else to witness during intimate moments, and if I were guilty of anything, it would be naivety in trusting a person like

HONEST

Justin. I suddenly started seeing many messages of support from friends and fans and even the national press! There was one column in the *Observer*, written by Eva Wiseman, calling me 'feminism's new hero'. She wrote:

> **There's no shame in happy sex, Tulisa asserts. The shame should lie with the person who uses it as currency against his partner's wishes, who uses a record of it as a weapon. She's not in the wrong for having sex, for enjoying sex, or for being filmed – her (until now anonymous) ex should be ashamed for betraying her, embarrassing her and attempting to damage her career.**

She also wrote that she'd whooped and cheered when she watched my YouTube response to the tape. In the end, even my management had to agree that I'd made the right decision in having my say, despite advising me against it. Always trust your gut instincts, I say. It's a little rule I always try to live by.

It's funny some of the things you worry about when something as traumatic as this happens. One of the things that had really bothered me about this footage was that people were criticising my performance! Mad, I know, but true. Of course, there was no way I was going to go online and watch the bloody thing myself, I couldn't face it, so I got some of my mates to describe exactly what was happening on the video. What they described really brought back memories of how Justin and I were together in our happier times. We used to talk in silly baby voices and call one another 'muffin', and it was all very affectionate and comical.

From what I'd heard about the footage, it was just a young couple mucking about with a camera phone and it was all a bit drunken, lighthearted and daft, which is probably why I couldn't remember it. It was blatantly obvious to anyone that knew me that I was completely taking the piss with it. Yet here it was, being described as a 'sex-tape', for Christ's sake! So yes, I was horrified that people watching somehow thought that this was Tulisa showing off her finest technique. If I'd wanted to release a bloody sex-tape, it would have been a proper one! I mean, it's bad enough that half the world has to see me with a dick in my mouth (which, let's face it, is something millions of people have done and should remain a personal moment), but now people thought that I couldn't even give a proper blowjob! That made the whole thing even worse. I even jokingly said to Adam, 'For God's sake, go and do an interview and tell everyone I know how to give nosh!' I don't know why I cared really. But at least I can now look back at that bit of the horrible situation and laugh.

After a month or so, of course, all the fuss died down, like those things do. My single had been released and was heading up the iTunes charts, and I was looking ahead to my new career as a solo artist. I remember that, in the midst of all the drama surrounding the tape, I had a weird premonition one day.

'I'll tell you what,' I said to Gareth, 'something seriously good is going to happen after all this shit, I know it is.'

I've always had to go through a really bad time to get to a really good one – it's always been the way with me. It makes me understand the good for what it is, and it helps to keep me grounded. So, with this in mind, I figured that I must be due a bumper crop of fabulous sooner or later!

Sure enough, less than two months after I was curled up on my bathroom floor crying my heart out, my first ever solo single, 'Young', was at the top of the charts. It had always been my dream to have a number one record and finally it had actually happened. This was coupled with the brilliant news that I'd been voted number one on *FHM*'s Sexiest Women in the World list. I was over the moon! And on top of that, I'd found this amazing person in Jack, who had been so fantastic and caring throughout the whole terrible ordeal. It all seemed to appear in one great little bundle, and I felt very lucky.

It was only then that I spared a thought for Justin Edwards. 'I bet you're not laughing now. I bet you're reeling, because you tried to break me, to ruin me, but I've come back even stronger and more successful than before. No, you won't be laughing now.'

I was sure there was a reason why all this stuff had happened when it did. It seems to me that so many things in my life are a fight. I'm either fighting to prove my worth, or fighting to be heard, or fighting to pull myself out of bad situations. The whole 'sex tape' thing proved to me more than ever that I had to know myself and to trust my instincts about what was best for me. It is so important to me to show people who I really am and to be myself. I know not everyone is going to love that person, but then that's the case with anyone in the public eye.

After it was all over, there was nothing particularly inspirational that I felt that I could say to other women who were in a similar position, but I hoped that my attitude and actions would speak for themselves. I'd stayed as strong as I could and I'd stood my ground. I'd kept my job on *The X Factor*, and I'd still managed to achieve this fantastic new success of finally having a number one record. Don't get me wrong, if I could turn back time and change things so that it never happened, I would, but I was now in the midst of one of the most amazing times of my life. And although, as always, I'd had to go through all that bad shit to really appreciate it, I was now really ready to appreciate it, I'll tell you!

Chapter Thirty-One

By the time all that good stuff was starting to happen, Jack and I had officially started dating, and I have to say, we had a brilliant time together, even though, as it turned out, our relationship only lasted a couple of months. I knew right from the start that Jack was a caring and honest guy, and I guess that's why I went after him in the first place. He was a good friend, a good lover, but although the timing was very good in some respects, because we were there for each other in the dark times, it was also very bad in terms of where we were at in life and what we still had to do. It's strange, because once we were officially together, things moved pretty fast, and we both felt like it was perfect between us for a while. We even dropped the 'L' bomb, which is a pretty big thing for me, and even more so for Jack in my opinion. The trouble was that the relationship did get quite intense very quickly, to the point where there wasn't really anywhere else for it to go, and I think, in the end, we could both see that.

One of the problems was the fact that Jack had to go to Bulgaria to work on a movie, and although I went to visit him out there, we were apart for weeks at a time. That definitely changed things. It was like ripping two people that were on their honeymoon apart, and Jack found that very difficult. It was OK for me – I was at home most of the time, surrounded by my mates – but he was out there on his own, and I know it got to him. Still, I constantly told him he was panicking and stressing too much about everything.

When I visited him in Bulgaria for a second time, I could sense that things weren't right between us. The atmosphere was quite strained, and I felt like the magic had been sucked out of our relationship. We'd been on such a high before he left, and suddenly it didn't feel as good between us anymore. There was no mystery left. The excitement of the chase and the courtship was over, and what was left didn't seem all that exciting. I guess, if it had been left to me, I would have let things run their course, but after a couple of silly little rows, we sat down for a talk, and Jack started to say what we were both thinking. I didn't even let him finish. I knew where he was going with it, and although it hurt my heart, in my mind I totally agreed. We both cared deeply for one another, but as for being a full-time couple – well, it wasn't working for either of us.

Of course, it was sad, but at the same time I felt like I handled things very differently than I had in the past. There was no screaming and yelling, just sensible discussion. Jack seemed quite stressed, but I did my best to reassure him that it was going to be OK.

'This will be good for both of us,' I told him. 'We're both going to walk away from this taking our experiences and using them in our next relationships.'

I was quite proud of myself for being so mature about the whole thing, especially given the drama of some of my past relationships. When I think about it now, I probably would have tried to hold on to my relationship with Jack if we hadn't had our talk, but at the same time, I'm a realist. If something is never going to change or get better, you have to do your best to move on. One thing I can walk away with is that he taught me to trust again, and I will always be grateful to him for that. And I hope I helped him to grow in some ways – not that he needed to, but I think I added to his knowledge.

That night I stayed with him at the hotel before catching my flight the next day and we cuddled one another, talking most of the night. The next day I flew home, and that was that.

We haven't spoken very much since then, but I know in time that will change. I do miss Jack's friendship, and I miss being in a relationship. But then again, I've never liked being single much, have I?

I have one last story about Jack, and it's a funny one. During most of my sexual experiences, I was always concentrating more on getting a man to love me rather than relaxing and enjoying what was happening. Sadly, I never really liked sex back then; it was just the means to an end. In fact, I only really began to enjoy it in my early twenties. Since then I've started to explore and appreciate that side of my life a bit more, but only with proper boyfriends of course.

In May 2012 I first visited Jack in Bulgaria, and at that time we hadn't seen one another for almost two weeks. While we were at dinner, I made a confident announcement.

'Tonight I'm going to rock your world!'

And I did! The two of us had an incredible night together. I was finally a woman who enjoyed the physical side of romance and it was a proper 'Oh my God' moment for both of us. But hang on a minute . . . all of a sudden the entire room was moving – no, shuddering – with a terrible rumbling sound. The room was suddenly swinging from side to side. The furniture, the curtains, the bed – everything! Jack suddenly jumped up.

'Oh my fucking God!'

It took a second to process what was happening, but as Jack grabbed me off the bed, I shouted, 'Calm down, it's an earthquake, it's a bloody earthquake!'

For the next few seconds, the two of us ran hysterically around the room like headless chickens, stark naked, trying to decide where we should shelter while the room shook violently.

'Get under the bed,' I yelled.

But the divan bed went right down to the floor and there was no gap, so that was out. Jack was in the middle of the room, panicking and desperately looking for anything that we could hide under, and at the same time he was trying to reach out for me so he could pull me to safety.

'Bloody hell, T,' he said. 'When you said you were gonna rock my world, I didn't think you meant it literally!'

Then, suddenly, it stopped. Jack grabbed some clothes and I threw a robe on, and we tore down the stairs of the hotel and out into the street. It was quite a scary few moments, but God how we laughed about it later.

I don't really know what's next for me on the romance front. I've learned that, at the end of the day, all you can do is take things one step at a time in any relationship and try to respect yourself and the other person. I know I've made a lot of bad calls in the past, but I also know now that I've learned from my mistakes. Surely that's the important thing?

At the moment, I'm single and, although at times I feel lonely, I'm enjoying the ride. I'm working hard, enjoying my success and I'm having a great time hanging out and partying with my friends. In fact, as soon as I split with Jack, I headed out to New York to visit Dream, and inevitably there was some media speculation about the two of us dating. It wasn't true, though, we just hung out together and had fun, and that was all there was to it. I adore the man, and I admire his intelligence and appreciate his mind, but there hasn't been so much as a kiss between us – we're great mates and that's that! For the time being, I'm just relishing the life of a successful single girl.

Chapter Thirty-Two

The song that became my number one single, 'Young', wasn't even earmarked for me originally, that's the weird thing. Fazer and his team were working it up with another artist in mind; I don't want to say who it was. I nicked it, though. As soon as I'd heard it in the studio, I was certain.

'I have to have this song,' I told the guys. 'I'm having it! Give it to me!'

They hadn't even finished the song yet, but I felt like it represented everything that I'm about, plus it sounded like a smash. I did have a few doubts about putting out a debut single that I hadn't co-written myself, but the lyrics were crafted in such a way that I could have written it anyway – I related to it that much.

'Yep, that's fine. Give me that record – I'll take it. Thank you!'

When the song finally hit number one, it really was a dream moment. I was overwhelmed and so relieved and happy that all the 'sex tape' press coverage hadn't ruined it all. I'd already achieved so much with N-Dubz, and we'd enjoyed a huge amount of chart successes, but the one thing we never had was a number one single. This was something really special for me, and of course I threw a massive party – it had to be done! It's not every day that your childhood dreams come true, is it?

My career as a solo artist has got off to an amazing

start, and I couldn't really ask for more. Just recently, I've been performing 'Young' at some fantastic gigs: T4 on the Beach, G.A.Y. nightclub in London and the Wireless Festival in Hyde Park, and the reaction from the crowds has been fantastic. I'm so looking forward to releasing my album and showing off the new songs I've written, and then I can't wait to get started on my novel. I know I've got a lot of hard work ahead of me, but that's cool – I'm ready for it.

Meanwhile, I'm climbing back onto *The X Factor* roller coaster too. We've already finished the 2012 auditions, and we have found some fantastic talent this year. And, after a few guest appearances and much speculation, the new judge on the show is Nicole Scherzinger, who used to be in The Pussycat Dolls and was a judge on the American version of *The X Factor* last year. I think she's going to be great! This series, I'm going to dive in with a renewed confidence and an even more positive attitude. I've already been much more feisty and honest during the auditions, and I've decided that I'm not going to do anymore sugar-coating. If people don't like me for me, then there's not much I can do to change that. I can only be myself at the end of the day. Honest!

There's been another big development while I've been filming for *The X Factor* too. Jonathan Coad, the lawyer who got the injunctions for me and was now representing me in my damages case against Justin Edwards, has uncovered some amazing new evidence. This evidence proves beyond any doubt that not only did Justin attempt to sell the tape before he distributed it through the website, but also that he had help from several people, including a big name in the entertainment industry. I guess I wasn't surprised about that, because I knew Justin wasn't bright enough to have masterminded it all on his own. To start with, he signed a contract with an ex-porn actor called Marino Franchi, agreeing to give Franchi 25 per cent of any money they made from the footage once he'd helped Justin get it online.

Next, Franchi contacted a media company called Devlin Media, whose director, Jim Deans, agreed to help them get a website set up to distribute the video. They were all convinced that they were going to make a seven-figure sum because I was 'a big name', and it was all carefully plotted, with contracts and financial agreements between all the parties involved.

Most shocking of all was the fact that the person doing all the negotiating on Justin's behalf was a well-respected music industry manager called Chris Herbert, via his company, Safe Management. Chris was the man who put together The Spice Girls and has been a well-known music business manager for years. It seems that he is now Justin's manager – which is a bit of a step down from The Spice Girls! There were payment methods and bank accounts set up, ready for all these millions to pour into. They were expecting at least a million downloads at $5.99 a pop! Meanwhile, not one of these men stopped to think about how this would devastate me or affect my career and my family. Jonathan Coad showed me copies of some of the emails between Deans and Franchi, and they made me sick. They planned to tell my management that I'd either have to sign an agreement and take a cut of Justin's money, or 'If not, she will need to sue Justin and get fuck all!'

On the night of the footage going live, there were emails between them talking about 'throwing the switch' and going 'over the top, hold onto our arses!' While my life was about to fall apart, these guys were all rubbing their hands together. Can you think of anything more horrible?

They were calling one another 'mate' and clearly thinking it was all so fabulous that they were going to get rich by publically humiliating a young woman whose only crime was to trust someone like Justin Edwards.

Unfortunately for them, after their big launch on Saturday 17 March they had made the grand sum of thirty-five dollars before the site was taken down, which is bloody hilarious as far as I'm concerned. My legal team now had all this evidence and much more, and consequently all of these men have been made defendants in the case alongside Justin. I found it hard to believe that there are people in this world who could have such fun plotting something that could ruin somebody's life and career. It really disgusted me, but while it all came out, bit by bit, I tried not to think about it too much because it was just too upsetting. I would not let these people get me down.

While all this new evidence was coming to light, Justin appeared in *Loaded* magazine, giving them an interview in a ten-page spread entitled, 'It Wasn't Me'. In the interview (aside from promoting his single) he repeatedly claimed that although, 'it is his cock in the video' he didn't film it or distribute it and had never owned a copy. He also said that I had been victimising him and dragging his good name through the mud. He was also splashed across the magazine cover with a cucumber in his mouth, clearly taking the piss out of the whole thing. After seeing our evidence, though, *Loaded* magazine were furious with Justin.

On 9 July 2012 at a hearing in the High Court, Justin finally admitted that he was responsible for releasing the sex-tape. At last I was able to prove what I always knew to be true: that Justin Edwards is a bitter, evil liar who had not only tried to ruin me, but continually denied doing it – even suggesting that I was the one who was lying. He apologised for doing it and agreed never to speak about our relationship publically again.

Three days later, the day before my twenty-fourth birthday, I went to court to formally settle the legal action against him. My lawyer Jonathan Coad read a statement, co-signed by Justin, in which Justin finally apologised to me for what he had done to me. And standing beside my publicist, Simon, and my manager, Jonathan, I made a statement to the media who were gathered outside the courtroom.

'I am relieved that this is finally over. It has been a very testing few months, and this was not a case I ever wanted to go through.

'Justin Edwards' actions were to spite me, make money and ruin my career. He has succeeded in none of these things.

'I stand here today a stronger, wiser young woman who has taken this experience and learned from it. I am disgusted by Justin and saddened by the people that believed I released the footage myself.

'Today the truth has prevailed. After months of lying to the public and lying in court, Justin has finally admitted to being guilty and I hope justice is served.

'I would now like to draw a line under this and put it in the past. I also would like to thank from the bottom of my heart, the fans that stood by me. I'm especially grateful for all the support I have received from the public, my friends, family and team.

'With that support and my determination I have won this battle. Justin messed with the wrong woman.'

I could finally draw a line under the whole terrible mess and it was such a fantastic relief. It would now be up to Jonathan Coad and the rest of my legal team to go after the men who'd had a hand in helping Justin distribute the tape; trying to make money out of my misery. I'm suing them for damages.

This includes Chris Herbert, the music business manager who looked after Justin's interests in the negotiations over getting the footage online and who, by a mad coincidence, had just landed a music-consulting job on *The X Factor*. This meant that there was a good chance I'd actually have to deal with him face to face on a weekly basis while working on the show. Once his involvement in the case was made public, though, Herbert was fired from the job before he'd even started it. Karma can be a bitch!

Once I left the court that day I picked up my suitcase and then I took a private jet – zooming off to Ibiza with some of my best friends, including Gareth. We intended to celebrate big-time, and why not? This amazing result had been the best birthday present I could have wished for.

So, what about all the other important stuff in my life? Well, I wish I had more time to spend with my mum and chill out with her properly. My work schedule, as always, is pretty ridiculous right now, so more often than not, I end up catching up on the phone with both her and my dad these days. Having a proper relationship with her is still not easy, as much as I love her. Her illness can cause cloudiness in her thoughts and forgetfulness too – that's just the way it is, and I've learned to live with it. I've never had the typical parent–daughter relationship with either of my parents really. My dad is more like a funny, wild brother than he is a dad half the time. And unfortunately, I've never really been able to go to Mum for the motherly advice that most girls rely on, but I know it's not her fault. My plan now is to take a decent amount of time off work as soon as I can and then take Mum somewhere fabulous on holiday, so we can spend some proper time together.

HONEST

I'm still angry with Fazer for a lot of the things he put me through while we were together, and also how he dealt with the break-up, but during the whole 'sex tape' nightmare he had wanted to be there for me, and he tried to be as supportive as he could. I know that eventually we will build our friendship back up, but I also know it's going to take some time. I've started to make headway, though. I recently saw his cousin and told him to ask Fazer to get in touch with me. I'd like to get together with him for a drink, and have a go at patching things up. Fazer has been too much a part of my life to lose him as a friend forever.

As for Dappy . . . well, we've made up already! There was a horrible period at the start of 2012 where he was mouthing off on Twitter, saying that he missed me and that I was neglecting him and that I never bothered to phone him. I felt like he was trying to make me look bad in front of the fans, the N-Dubletts, so I had to have my say too – you know me! I said publically that Dappy knew where I was and had my phone number, whereas *he* had a new phone number. I'd also told my dad to ask him to call me, but Dappy still hadn't called. Eventually, though, we did speak on the phone and promised to spend some time together, and then recently we bumped into one another while I was playing a gig in Ibiza and he was there shooting a video. It was really good to see him, and he was obviously happy to see me too. We actually sat down together and had a nice chilled-out conversation for the first time in ages. His girlfriend, Kaye, was there too, and she told me that the kids were missing their Auntie T, and that Dappy needed me. She wanted me to be a part of the family again, and that made me happy.

As it happens, my nan and granddad have just moved from Greece to the UK, so I'm going to plan a huge family party to get everyone together, including Dappy. Now that the pressure of working together has lifted, I realise that I miss my cousin. We're joined together as family, and we always will be. And as much as I've hated Dappy at times, I also love him more than almost anyone else in my life. It sounds mad, after all we've been through, but at the end of the day, we have a bond unlike any other. I have his name tattooed on the back of my neck and Dappy has my name tattooed down his arm – that's how deep it goes between us. There's no getting away from it.

My real hope is that someday soon N-Dubz will reunite. Dappy and I talked about the possibility of that happening when I saw him in Ibiza, and we are both definitely up for it. While I'm incredibly excited about releasing my new album and starting on a new series of *The X Factor*, one thing I've realised since I started on the road as a solo artist is that I miss my band. I really miss them – in fact, I hate performing without them – and I feel it every day. For such a long time, N-Dubz was my family when I had no real family at home. Dappy, Fazer, Uncle B and me in that studio in Dollis Hill, all working towards the same goal, was everything to me. I learned so much during that time, and all the stuff we did together back then shaped my whole life, making me the person I am today. Uncle B was often more of a father to me than my own dad, if I'm honest, and Dappy was always like the big brother I never had. I owe a hell of a lot to N-Dubz.

I reckon that in a future N-Dubz there would be a lot less fighting too, which has got to be a bloody bonus. There'd be less of a battle to establish ourselves as individuals within the group, because we've all done that now. We all know who we are now – I certainly do! And yes, I know I might be looking at the past through rose-tinted glasses, but it's still a nice thought. And it might happen. After all, there's still plenty of time – I'm still young.

Picture Credits

All pictures © Tulisa Contostavlos, except for Section 2:
p1, p4–7 © Rex Features; Section 3: p2–3 © Thames/
Rex Features; p4 (top left), p5 © Andres Hernandez;
p6–7 © Carsten Windhorst/Nice&Polite.

$\mathcal{I}ndex$

Aaliyah 41
Abbot, Russ 4
Abdul, Paula 195
Against All Odds 153, 200
Against All Odds tour 154–5, 157, 160
albums and songs
   Against All Odds 153, 200
   'Bad Man Riddim' 64
   'Every Day of My Life' 96–7, 107
   'Feva Las Vegas' 128
   'I Need You' 153
   'I Swear' 108, 109, 112, 128, 129, 131, 133
   Love. Live. Life. 183–4, 188
   'No One Knows Your Name' 200
   'No Regrets' (Dappy's solo single) 197
   'Ouch!' 130, 131–2, 189
   'Papa Can You Hear Me?' 130, 132, 189
   'Playing with Fire' 153, 184
   Uncle B 132–3, 152
   'We Dance On' 184
   'You Better Not Waste My Time' 108, 127, 128–9, 132–3, 189
   'Young' (Tulisa's solo single) 208, 232, 270, 279, 280
All Around the World 132, 157, 258

Backstreet Boys 32
'Bad Man Riddim' 64
Bailey, Adam (Van Damage) 98–9, 100–4, 111, 135, 136–40, 255–6
   engaged to Tulisa 139
   GBH court case 139–43

relationship with Tulisa 98–9, 100, 103–4, 111, 135–9, 141–2, 143–4
SLK crew 98, 99
split with Tulisa 142
strip club manager 246
Tulisa moves in with 144, 171
Bailey, Joe 138
Barlow, Colin 108, 109, 128–9
Barlow, Gary 200, 201, 217, 219, 222
Barrett, Michelle 202–3
Beese, Darcus 95
Being N-Dubz documentary 165, 166–7, 170, 185, 187
Beyoncé 183, 241
Big Brother 258–9
Big Narstie 116, 120
Black Eyed Peas 183
Boyz II Men 117
Buena, Mutya 125
Bugsy Malone 31, 32–3, 41
Bulgaria 273–6
bullying
   anti-bullying campaign 149
   at school 23–7, 54–5, 58, 64
   X Factor controversy 215–20
Burke, Alexandra 219
Burt, George 96, 109, 131
Byrne, Anne (mother) 3–4, 6–10, 11, 13–17, 18–19, 20–1, 28–9, 37, 51, 61–2, 66
   divorce 18–21
   mental illness 6–11, 13–15, 20, 32, 67, 88, 109–10, 111, 167–9, 284
   My Mum and Me documentary 167–9

overprotectiveness 11, 28–9, 66
singer 3–4, 6
Byrne, Brian (uncle) 3
Byrne, Louise (aunt) 3–4, 7, 14, 20,
34, 36
Byrne, Michael (uncle) 3
Byrne, Moira (aunt) 3–4
Byrne, Paula (aunt) 3–4
Byrne, Tom (grandfather) 3

Cadman, Matt 132
Carey, Mariah 117
Carlos (first boyfriend) 51, 59, 61
Castillo, Rich 126–7, 184, 241, 243
Channel U 96, 97, 98, 108, 109, 121
Chris Moyles Show 148
clashes 42, 63
club tracks 207, 208
Coad, Jonathan 255, 259, 280, 281,
283
Cole, Cheryl 191, 195–6, 199, 200, 208
Cole, Martina 231, 233
Collins, Marcus 221
Contostavlos, Byron (Uncle B) 5, 9,
19, 41, 43, 44, 45, 57, 128, 286
death of 118–23
in Mungo Jerry 16
manages Lickle Rinsers and
N-Dubz 63, 95, 96, 107, 108,
109, 112–13, 122, 126
recording studio 4, 42
song tribute 130
tough love 64–5, 110–11
Uncle B album 132–3, 152
Uncle B tour 147–8, 150–2
Contostavlos, Dino/Dappy (cousin)
19, 28, 36, 41–2, 43, 47, 53, 54,
62–3, 72, 73, 105, 106
and Adam Bailey's court case
139–41
bad press 149, 150
Being N-Dubz documentary 165,
166–7, 170, 176, 185
bunks off school with Tulisa 34–6
childhood closeness to Tulisa
5–6, 29–30, 34–5

conflict with Def Jam 183, 187
conflict with Tulisa 147, 148, 150,
165, 166, 186, 189–90, 197
Dubplate Drama 115, 116
and father's death 118–22, 126, 147
'No Regrets' solo single 197
reconciles with Tulisa 285–6
resents Tulisa's relationship with
Fazer 186, 190
solo career 190, 197
sparring matches with Tulisa 63
takes up MC-ing and rapping 42
threatens radio show listener
148–9
Tulisa at school with 37–9
see also Lickle Rinsers; N-Dubz
Contostavlos, Maria (aunt) 4, 19
Contostavlos, Plato (father) 5, 8,
9–10, 15–17, 18, 31, 36, 53, 57, 62,
70, 88, 284
divorce 19–21
early life 4
girlfriend 19, 20
in Mungo Jerry 16
meets and marries Anne 7
parental discipline 36, 57, 88
partying and drug use 7, 9
recording studio 4, 15, 42
short temper 7, 9
Tulisa moves in with 11
unable to cope with Anne's
illness 7, 8, 9, 14
Contostavlos, Spiros (cousin) 5, 19,
120
Contostavlos, Tulisa
acting career 115–16, 117, 145–7
and Adam Bailey see Bailey,
Adam
alcohol, early experience of
48–50, 51, 72, 73
anxiety habits 66–8
bathroom as sanctuary 11–12, 18,
66, 263, 265
bullied 23–7, 54–5, 58, 64
childhood fear of being
abandoned 10, 11

and Dappy *see* Contostavlos, Dino/Dappy

defence witness in court case 140, 142–3

discipline, attitude towards 92

drama in personal life 1, 65, 150–1, 212, 226

drugs 72–3, 74, 100, 102

Dubplate Drama 115–16, 117, 145–7

early life 4–21

engaged to Adam Bailey 139

face-picking 66–8, 69, 168

family background 3–4

and Fazer *see* Rawson, Richard (Fazer)

fear of being alone 10–11, 157

Female Boss 157, 193, 242–3, 247, 248, 267

FHM Sexiest Woman in the World 270

first boyfriend 51

first recording session 15 16

first sings with Dappy and Fazer 44

gang fights 56–8, 59

geeky period 28, 30, 38

girl gang member 81–3, 88–92, 98

Greek holidays 17, 105–6

Greek influences 5

home burgled 171

home ownership 169, 170–1, 187

homebody 182, 187

image changes 30–1, 33, 38–9

in school performance of *Bugsy Malone* 31, 32–3

and Jack O'Connell *see* O'Connell, Jack

and Justin Edwards *see* Edwards, Justin

loner 8, 30, 33, 34

longing for love 70, 73–4, 78, 79

loses virginity 39, 75

loves long car journeys 116–17

macho persona 154, 155

makes career plan 207

male attention 30–1, 33, 58, 73–4

mistrust of men 79, 179, 225–6, 229

mood swings and depression 59, 61, 65, 66, 110–11, 167–9, 170, 200, 267

and mother's mental illness 6–11, 13–15, 20, 32, 67, 88, 109–10, 111, 284

music company secretary 107

My Mum and Me documentary 67, 167–9

name 5

panic attacks 100–3

and parents' divorce 18–21

passport doctoring 83–4

physically abusive relationship 77–9

rebelliousness 86–7

religious beliefs 17, 65, 221

schooldays 23–8, 30–40, 47–50, 53–9, 84–8

self-confidence, growing 31, 83, 99–100, 135–6

self-harming 68–70

sex, attitude to 50, 51, 74, 76, 238, 240, 275

sex tape *see* sex tape

sex toy in luggage 249

signature perfume 193

and Simon Cowell 192–4, 195

solo recording career 207–8, 239, 245, 270, 279–80

spiked drink incident 93–4

suicidal behaviour 79

taught to fight 63

'The Bitch' nickname 193

and The-Dream 240–4, 245–7, 248, 276–7

Twitter followers 203

and Uncle B's death 118–23

work ethic 106–7

X Factor judge *see X Factor*

see also Lickle Rinsers; N-Dubz

Contostavlos, Zoe (aunt) 5, 19, 34, 35, 120, 121

Cowell, Simon 191, 192–4, 195

Daniel (boyfriend) 76–9, 86
Dappy *see* Contostavlos, Dino/
    Dappy
Deacon, Adam 115, 116, 118, 145
Deans, Jim 281
Def Jam 181, 182–4, 187–8, 245
Dennis, Les 4
dermatillomania 66–8, 69, 168
Devlin, Janet 202
Devlin Media 281
Dino (cousin) *see* Contostavlos,
    Dino/Dappy
discipline, Tulisa's attitude to 92
Dizzee Rascal 83
DJ Ultra *see* Edwards, Justin
drugs 35, 40, 51, 72–3, 74, 100, 102,
    149
Dubplate Drama 115–16, 117, 145–7

Edwards, Justin (DJ Ultra)
    attitude to women 156, 157
    career help from Tulisa 156–7, 258
    relationship with Tulisa 137, 143,
        144, 155–8, 160
    see also sex tape
Emmet Spiceland 3
'Every Day of My Life' 96–7, 107

face-picking 66–8, 69, 168
fan base 129, 130–1, 151, 170–1, 186,
    285
'Feva Las Vegas' 128
FHM Sexiest Women in the World
    list 270
Fincham, Peter 196
Flirta D 99
Franchi, Marino 281
Fruity Loops software 42

G.A.Y. nightclub 280
girl gang 81–3, 88–92, 98
Glastonbury 171–2
Go For It (TV show) 4, 7
Gousse, Max 181, 182, 184, 187, 188,
    239, 240, 241, 243, 244
Green, Chloe 228–9

Grey, Naomi (Ny) 97, 233, 239, 243,
    244, 245
GuilFest 171

Hammersmith Apollo 154
Harnett, Ricci 145, 146, 147
Hart, Beth 192, 201–2, 204, 259
Haverstock comprehensive 37–8,
    39–40, 51, 53–5, 58
Healy, Charlie 205
Herbert, Chris 281, 284
Hyams, Luke 116, 117, 145
'Hype Hype' 99
hypnotism 68

'I Need You' 153
'I Swear' 108, 109, 112, 128, 129, 131,
    133
Ibiza 166–7, 284, 285
Ibsen, Pete 208
Island Records 95
Isle of Wight festival 171

Jackson, Michael 15
Javina (school friend) 47, 48, 49, 54,
    55, 56, 59, 69, 72, 73
Jeep 3–4, 6
Jessie J 205
Joanne (school friend) 28–9
Joe (school bully) 25–7
Johnson, Wil 127
Jones, Simon 163, 253, 254, 255,
    257, 260, 264
Jono (boyfriend) 74–5

The Keys 205–6
Kidulthood 59
King of Diamonds lap-dancing club
    246–7
KISS 100 FM 109
Kouame, Jean Baptiste 183

La Sainte Union school 33–4, 37
Lady Envy 99
Led Zeppelin 107
Lewis, Leona 130

Lickle Rinsers 45, 51, 63–4, 95–6
    Channel U video 96–7, 98
    first studio recording 42–4
    Metropolitan Police
        Crimestoppers tour 64
    N-Dubz name change 97
    name 45
    NW1 name change 96, 97
    see also N-Dubz
Lickle Rinsers Crew 108
The Little Mermaid 15
Little Mix 206, 215, 216, 218, 221, 222,
    223
live TV, pressures of 209
Loaded 282
Los Angeles 181–2, 187, 229, 239
Love. Live. Life. 103–4, 188
Love. Live. Life. tour 189–90, 196–7

MAD Music Awards 166
Maitland Park Estate 40, 56
Maldives 225, 227–8, 235
Manchester Evening News Arena
    189
Mazer 118, 119, 120
Mercedes (school friend) 47, 59, 81–2
Metropolitan Police Crimestoppers
    tour 64
Miami 12, 239–48
Michael, George 130
MIND media award 169
Minogue, Dannii 208
Minogue, Kylie 130
Misha B. 216–18, 220
MOBO (Music of Black Origin)
    awards 125–6, 127–8, 152, 184
Mr Hudson 153, 184
Mrs. Doubtfire 103
Mungo Jerry 16
My Mum and Me documentary 67,
    167–9
Mykonos 204–5, 206
Myspace 108

N-Dubletts see fan base
N-Dubz

All Around the World deal 132
bad press 149–50
Being N-Dubz (documentary)
    165, 166–7, 170, 185, 187
Channel U videos 108, 109
Def Jam album deal 182–4
dropped from anti-bullying
    campaign 149
fan base 129, 130–1, 151, 170–1, 186,
    285
first major single release 129
Glastonbury 171–2
growing fame 108–9, 112
GuilFest 171
in-fighting 122, 147, 148, 150–1, 153,
    160, 165, 167, 190
Isle of Wight festival 171
leave Def Jam 188
leave Polydor 131
management team 126–7, 138
MOBO Best Newcomer award
    125–6, 127–8
MOBO Best Single award 184
MOBO Best UK Act and Best
    Album awards 152
name 97
origins of 42–5
Polydor development deal 108–9
reunion possibility 286
splits up 190, 197
T4 on the Beach 171
trademark phrase 127, 170
US market, break into 181–5,
    187–8
see also albums and songs; tours
Nash, Terius see The-Dream
News of the World 162
'No One Knows Your Name' 200
Nu Vibe 206
Nuttall, Cris 132
NW1 96, 97

O2 Arena 125, 189
O'Connell, Jack 231, 232–8, 245,
    249–52, 266, 267, 271, 273–6
O'Leary, Dermot 209–10, 221–2

The Only Way is Essex 239
'Ouch!' 130, 131–2, 189

panic attacks 100–3
'Papa Can You Hear Me?' 130, 132, 189
parental discipline 92
    Tulisa's father 36, 57, 88
Pasqualino, Luke 233
passport doctoring 83–4
Plan B 233
'Playing with Fire' 153, 184
Polydor Records 108, 109, 128–31, 132
practical joking 29–30

Quintin Kynaston school 84–8

Rawson, Richard (Fazer) 44, 62–3, 71–2, 148, 149, 150, 263
    Being N-Dubz documentary 165, 166–7, 170, 176, 185
    buys apartment with Tulisa 187
    and Byron's death 118, 119, 120, 121
    meets Tulisa 35
    and N-Dubz break-up 190, 197
    relationship with Tulisa 72, 73, 75, 105, 160–4, 165, 171–3, 175–9, 184, 185–7, 206, 210–14, 225–30, 232, 233, 235, 251–2, 258, 284–5
    sparring matches with Tulisa 63
    STL production 208, 279
    supportive during sex tape ordeal 263, 285
    takes up MC-ing and rapping 42
    Tulisa denies relationship on Twitter 163
    Tulisa moves in with 175
    see also Lickle Rinsers; N-Dubz
reality TV 187
Reid, L.A. 181, 182, 187–8, 195
Remi, Salaam 183
Rhythmix *see* Little Mix
Richards, Jade 202

Rihanna 182, 240
Rising Stars (TV show) 4
The Risk 205–6
ROAR Global 126–7, 138
The Rosary primary school 27, 33
Rowland, Kelly 200, 201, 217, 218, 219–20, 223
The Runaway 231, 232, 233–4

Safe Management 281
Sanctuary 107
Scherzinger, Nicole 280
schizoaffective disorder 6
    see also Byrne, Anne, mental illness
school discipline 92
self-harming 68–70
sex tape 253–70, 271, 280–4
    legal action 268, 280–4
    Tulisa's YouTube response 264–5, 268, 269
Shalit, Jonathan 127, 167, 181, 191, 192, 196
Shepherds Bush Empire 151, 181
Sheppard, Gemma 208–9
Shield, Miss (teacher) 87–8
Shystie 118
Sidaway, Mark (Sid) 192, 202
Skins 232–3
SLK 97, 98, 99
So Solid Crew 96
Solo 116, 120
Spice Girls 281
STL 208
street reputation 62
Stryder, Tinchy 125
Sugababes 125
Sun 253, 254, 255, 257
Sylvia Young Theatre School 31–2

T4 on the Beach 171, 223, 280
Tarbuck, Jimmy 4
Tennant, Ali 208
The-Dream 240–4, 245–7, 248, 276–7
tours

Againts All Odds 154-5, 157, 160
Love. Live. Life. tour 189-90
Uncle B tour 147-8, 150-2
Tulisa *see* Contostavlos, Tulisa
2 Shoes 206

Uncle B *see* Contostavlos, Byron
Uncle B album 132-3, 152
Uncle B tour 147-8, 150-2
Unger-Hamilton, Ferdy 132
urban music, negative press around
95-6
urban slang 183

Van Damage *see* Bailey, Adam
Varey, Gareth 11, 158-60, 166, 169-70,
175, 189, 195, 199, 215, 232, 233,
236, 239, 243, 244, 245, 247, 249,
253, 261, 263, 265, 266, 284
violence
abusive relationships 77-9
at clubs and concerts 96
at school 53
street violence 59, 90-1

Walsh, Louis 200-1, 215, 216, 217, 219
'We Dance On' 184
West, Kanye 182
'What Is This World Coming To' 44

Whisky Mist 228
The Who 107
Wiley 83
Wireless Festival 280
Wiseman, Eva 268-9
Wootton, Dan 162-3
Wright, Mark 239-40

X Factor 191-6, 199-207, 208-10, 214,
215-23, 257, 259, 260, 271, 280,
284
bullying controversy 215-20
conflict with Kelly Rowland 218,
219-20, 223
female fashion 208-9, 222
finals 221-2
group mentoring 204-6, 215, 221
judges' house stage 204-6
Tulisa fears losing job 259, 260,
262
Tulisa's nervousness about
199-200, 201, 202, 208, 209
X Factor USA 188, 195, 280

'You Better Not Waste My Time'
108, 127, 128-9, 132-3, 189
You magazine 254
'Young' 208, 232, 245, 270, 279,
280